H.I.H. THE LATE GRAND DUKE CYRIL OF RUSSIA

My Life in Russia's Service — Then and Now by H.I.H. the Grand Duke Cyril

Published by Selwyn & Blount, London

1939

First eight chapters edited by H.S.H. Prince Leonid Lieven, B.A.(Oxon)., Barrister at Law of the Middle Temple

A ROYALTY DIGEST REPRINT IN 1995

Printed at Thomson Press (India) Limited

Note

The memoirs of the late Grand Duke Kirill of Russia have been published under the name of Grand Duke Cyril, by which he was better known in this country. He himself, however, always used the first form.

Contents

I.	Childhood	Page	11
II.	Youth	,,	33
III.	Eastward Bound	,,	69
IV.	Return to Russia	,,	98
V.	Service at Sea	,,	118
VI.	War and Marriage	,,	152
VII.	Exile and Return	,,	183
VIII.	War and Revolution	,,	196

My Father (an Epilogue), by H.I.H. the Grand Duke Vladimir   Page 214

Appendix   Page 245
Manifestoes of the late Grand Duke Cyril of Russia, the Head of the Imperial Dynasty

Index   Page 281

Illustrations

H.I.H. the late Grand Duke Cyril of Russia
                              Frontispiece

H.I.H. the late Grand Duke Vladimir of Russia
                            Facing page 28

T.I.H. the Grand Duke and Duchess Vladimir of Russia   Facing page 29

The Grand Duchess Vladimir   ,,   29

The Author   ,,   64

The late King George V with his Cousin, the late Emperor Nicholas II   Facing page 65

The late Emperor Nicholas II   ,,   104

The Author   ,,   105

The Author and his Wife   ,,   142

The late Emperor Nicholas II and the Czarevitch   Facing page 143

The Author's Wife, the late Grand Duchess Victoria   Facing page 178

The Grand Duchesses Maria and Kira   ,,   179

Prince Louis Ferdinand of Prussia and the Grand
Duchess Kira of Russia   Facing page 208
Breakfast at Ker Argonid   ,,   209
H.I.H. the Grand Duke Vladimir of Russia
                                   Facing page 250
The Author at work in his Study at Saint-Briac
                                   Facing page 251

I
Childhood

I WAS born at Tsarkoe Selo[1] on 13 October[2] 1876. My father, Grand Duke Vladimir, was the third son of Alexander II.[3] My mother was the only daughter of the first marriage between Grand Duke Frederick Francis II of Mecklenburg-Schwerin and of Princess Maria Reuss. The line of the Grand Dukes of Mecklenburg-Schwerin is of Slavonic origin and dates from the time when parts of Northern Germany were Slavonic speaking, as some place names still indicate. That is the reason why my mother sometimes used to tell my father that she was more of a Slav then he!

I do not remember my maternal grandparents, my grandmother having died before I was born and my grandfather when I was quite small.

I was older than my brothers, Boris and Andrey, and my sister Helen,[4] as my eldest brother Alexander died a year after my birth.

[1] One of the residences of Russian Emperors and of members of the Imperial Family near St. Petersburg. Famous for its exquisite architecture and splendid parks.
[2] 30 September, old style.
[3] Alexander II reigned 1855–1881. He married Princess Marie of Hesse-Darmstadt. He was the eldest son of Nicholas I and of Princess Alexandra of Prussia.
[4] Wife of late Prince Nicholas of Greece. Her children are Marina, Duchess of Kent, Princess Olga of Yugoslavia, and Countess Elisabeth Toerring.

The house where I was born at Tsarskoe was a bright and very jolly country place built in the late eighteenth-century style of Catherine the Great. It stood in a large garden which had a pond in it. We called it 'the lake' as it appeared so very large to us then, and it was my first introduction to water upon which I was to pass so much of my life. On this lake we used to be taken to sail when quite small, and later we rowed on it.

The earliest recollection of my life are the rides in the great park of Tsarskoe on a black pony called 'Ugoloek,'[1] which carried us in a double saddle. I still remember the warm smell of its coat.

The four of us were brought up together and were constant companions throughout our childhood. We lived very closely and intimately and were the best of friends.

My father was a man of strict conservative nineteenth-century principles. None the less, he had exceedingly broad-minded views. His knowledge and memory were fantastic, and surprised those men of learning with whom he came into contact both in Russia and abroad. History was his speciality, and I remember his reading history books dealing with the eighteenth and nineteenth centuries to my mother in the evenings while she sat knitting.

He had made a special study of the Court journals which dealt with the daily and hourly records of Russian Emperors and Empresses since, I think, the Empress Elisabeth, but certainly since the Empress Catherine the Great. They were accessible only to members of the Imperial Family, and were not only fascinating reading but of the greatest historical interest.

My father stands out in my memory as an exceedingly kind man, one respected by all for the nobility of his character as well as for his culture and profound erudition. Although gruff in manner and apt to intimidate those who

[1] Little burning lump of coal.

came into contact with him for the first time, yet behind this natural gruffness lay a golden heart.

Later on, he became my dearest friend, and during the decisive moments of life I always turned to him for advice.

All Grandpapa's[1] sons were men of parts; the most remarkable of them, in my view, was Uncle Serge,[2] who had the loftiest principles coupled with a character of the rarest nobility. Such he will always remain in my memory.

The friends of our childhood were very carefully chosen, as were the houses which we visited, of which there were not many.

The earliest educational influence to come to us was our English nurse, Miss Millicent Crofts, whom we called Milly. She is still alive, and lives, I believe, in Wiltshire. Milly's near relative was Kitty Strutton, who had been nurse to Father and my uncles Sasha,[3] Serge, and Paul.[4]

When after a long service Miss Strutton retired, she was given a house of her own at Tsarskoe, and when she died, my uncles, including Uncle Sasha and Father, followed her coffin on foot.

This was a singular honour which was rarely bestowed by Russian Emperors, and then only on the highest dignitaries.

Milly was with us from our earliest days, and it was through her that the first language we talked was English. I remember her singing nursery rhymes to us; later she introduced us to the works of English literature, the first of which were *Barnaby Rudge* and *Oliver Twist*.

[1] Alexander II.
[2] Grand Duke Sergey Alexandrovitch, Governor of Moscow, assassinated in 1905. His wife was Grand Duchess Elizabeth, Princess of Hesse, sister of the late Empress Alexandra.
[3] Alexander III reigned 1881–1894.
[4] Grand Duke Paul Alexandrovitch, married Princess Alexandra of Greece. Their children are: Grand Duke Dimitry and Grand Duchess Marie.

When we left our nursery and were given tutors, Mrs. Savell was appointed Helen's governess.

My father was greatly attached to the country and liked to remain at Tsarskoe as long as he could after Christmas, although my parents entertained a great deal during the season in St. Petersburg. In early January we were taken to the Vladimir Palace in the capital, where we remained until late in April, when we returned to Tsarskoe. This was repeated every year.

The Vladimir Palace, father's town house, was a large and sombre place, built in Florentine style, standing on the Neva embankment, and although it was smaller than many other Imperial palaces, it appeared huge to us after Tsarskoe.

Of that period I remember two things: one was its gas-lit passages; interminable they seemed to us and cavernous! Gas at that time was something of a novelty, and even now I remember the interest which it aroused in us. The other memory I have is that of the Carcelle oil lamps, which were wound up like clocks by special lampmen.

It was in our nursery at the Vladimir Palace that I remember several visits from Grandpapa. This must have been two years before his murder.

One occasion especially stands out clearly in my memory of early childhood days in connection with him. He had given us what might best be described as a wooden 'hill'—a kind of slanting platform from which we used to slide down on a carpet one after the other, like little icebergs sliding down into the sea. Grandpapa on these occasions would stand at the window watching and enjoying our performance with Nurse Milly next to him encouraging us.

I remember, too, the dolls he gave us. They were little stuffed soldiers, dressed in the various uniforms of the Guards.—We were Grandpapa's special favourites.

Of Grandmama,[1] I have only one recollection when we were quite small children. She was ailing at the time and we were taken to the famous bedroom in the Winter Palace to kiss her.

Grandpapa was most accessible. He took the keenest interest in everything that went on in his vast empire, and I have heard it said that he could often be seen going for walks in the streets of his capital in the early mornings, accompanied only by a large Newfoundland dog of which we were very frightened.

After his murder on 13 March 1881,[2] members of the Imperial Family were at first closely guarded, but the precautions taken were soon slackened.

It was not until after the revolution of 1905 that it became necessary to take serious measures to protect the life of a Russian monarch. The most exhaustive precautions were then taken to assure the safety of the late Emperor.

Grandpapa's murder was the first sad tragedy of its kind. There had been palace revolutions, that is true, but as far as the people were concerned, their loyalty to their Emperors was exemplary. The life of their sovereigns was something sacred, and the very thought of an attempt on their lives scarcely suggested itself to them.

When Paul I[3] was murdered by those who were close to him and owed him their positions and honours, the Russian people, of whose cause he had always been a champion, considered him a martyr, and before the revolution there were pilgrimages to his tomb in the Cathedral of St. Peter and Paul. People went there to pray, popular belief invested him with almost a halo of sanctity, and miracles were expected. This was the old-fashioned attitude of Russians to their Emperors, until all this

[1] Empress Marie Alexandrovna, who before her marriage was Princess Marie of Hesse-Darmstadt, 1824–1880.
[2] 1 March, new style.
[3] Paul I, reigned 1796–1801.

disappeared with the so-called progress and enlightenment.

Mother often told us of the homely ways of Grandpapa, of the tea parties, for example, at which Grandmama presided at the head of the table. These were held in her private apartments and were attended by people of interest, men of letters, scientists, and by important members of Society. Alexey Tolstoi[1] was a frequent guest.

All talked freely on those occasions and there was a thoroughly cordial and homely spirit at these gatherings. It was Grandpapa's habit to visit private houses and balls of those people whom he respected and liked. He was the leader of Society, and all those who came in contact with this kindly and enlightened man were won over to him.

All these cordial relations and this homely spirit between Emperor and subjects and members of the Imperial Family were to disappear completely at a later period.

The only thing which I remember now of the time of his murder are the street lamps shrouded in black for his funeral. I recollect looking through the window of the Vladimir Palace and being impressed by this unusual sight.

It is typical of Grandpapa's character that what led to his death was his solicitude for a Cossack wounded by the first bomb of his assassin. Quite unconcerned for his own safety, he left his sledge to see whether he could help and to try and comfort the wounded man. This gave his murderer the second chance.

My childhood reminiscences would not be complete without some mention of my recollections of some remarkable figures who played important parts in Russian history. These were my great-uncles, uncles of father, Constantine,[2] Nicholas,[3] and Michael.[4] They were the

[1] Russian poet and man of letters, distant relative of Count Leo Tolstoi.
[2] Grand Duke Constantine Nikolaevitch, 1827–1892.
[3] Grand Duke Nicholas Nikolaevitch, the elder, 1831–1891.
[4] Grand Duke Michael Nikolaevitch, 1832–1909.

brothers of Grandpapa and sons of Nicholas I. They belonged to that generation and were heroic figures from another age. Quite exceptionally handsome, severe, and exalted men—magnificent types of manhood, they embodied what is best in man in the purity of their character and personal appearance.

Uncle Constantine had been the head of the Navy under Grandpapa. He had also been Viceroy of Poland, but in this capacity, which was a very delicate one, he had not been a success. He was a man of great learning, and, I have heard it said that he wrote his memoirs in Arabic!

He had strong liberal leanings, which made his position none too easy during the period of his activity. He lived at Pavlovsk, which had belonged to Empress Maria Feodorovna, the wife of Paul I. His palace has magnificent parks and woods where we used to ride and drive about at a later period. I remember Uncle Constantine driving up to our skating rink at Tsarskoe. He was paralysed, and we used to run up to his sledge craning our little necks to be kissed by him. I remember his hard fingers and that he smelt of cigars.

We were taken to his funeral service in the Cathedral of St. Peter and Paul, the burial place of the Dynasty, where, according to the rites of the Orthodox Church, his body lay in state in an open coffin for the mourners to pay the last respects to the departed. It was the first time that I was brought face to face with death.

I remember, too, our great-aunt, Grand Duchess Constantine—Aunt Sanny, we called her. She was a Princess of Sachsen-Altenburg.[1]

We were somewhat frightened of this old lady when we used to be sent to her from our nursery, and I remember distinctly her high-pitched voice, fine white hair, and that she always spoke German to us. I can still see her driving in an open carriage with a kind of awning over it,

[1] Grand Duchess Alexandra Iosifovna.

which could be opened and closed like an umbrella. I have never seen anything quite the same anywhere else, and think that she was the only person in the world who had such an ingenious cover to her carriage.

Uncle Michael, the other of my great-uncles whom I remember well, was the youngest brother of Grandpapa. He was married to Olga Feodorovna, a Princess of Baden. His only daughter, the Grand Duchess Anastasia, married Mother's brother, Grand Duke Frederick Francis III of Mecklenburg-Schwerin, whom I used to call Uncle Pitsu. Their children are the present Queen of Denmark, the present Grand Duke of Mecklenburg-Schwerin,[1] Cousin Fritzy and the Crown Princess Cecilia of Prussia, mother of Prince Louis Ferdinand of Prussia, who married my youngest daughter Kyra this year.[2]

Uncle Michael had been Viceroy in the Caucasus and in that capacity had brought about that territory's complete subjugation. He annexed the western portions of that country, and as a result of this campaign he was promoted Field-Marshal in the year 1878.

I remember him distinctly with his great black beard, and the splendid impression he made on us.

These men represented all that was best in a great age of which they were typical, over which the polish and the unsurpassed refinement and culture of the closing years of the eighteenth century had thrown the dying but still brilliant rays of its sunset. And yet these men and their father, Nicholas I, were in their private life very simple and almost ascetic. They slept on camp beds with leather cushions, as Nicholas I had done before them, covering himself with a military cloak. My father resembled his uncles in this and in other respects.

I will never forget the dignity of their bearing and the fine way in which they wore their uniforms. They were Olympians among men—memories of a past age belonging to history.

[1] Grand Duke Frederick Francis IV.　　[2] 1938.

Those Christmases which we did not spend at Tsarskoe, we passed with Uncle Sasha,[1] Aunt Minnie,[2] and our cousins at Gatchina. We went there quite often during the course of the year, but Christmas at Gatchina provided special occasions for family gatherings.

We admired our older cousins and envied them somewhat because they could do things for which we were yet too small.

Misha[3] was Uncle Sasha's special favourite, I too was particularly fond of him because he had a lovable character.

About a week before Christmas Mme Flotov, one of Aunt Minnie's ladies-in-waiting, used to come to us to inquire what we wanted for Christmas.

Among the things we chose were books, music, interesting clocks, and much else that delighted us. From my childhood up till now I have been very fond of music, and I remember that on one of these occasions I chose the works of Chopin and Tchaikovsky, but that, of course, was later.

The Christmas tree and the presents were always preceded by a religious service, then, following the traditions of our family, we used to gather in a dark room. Uncle Sasha would then go into the room where the Christmas tree stood to make sure that all was ready. Meanwhile our nerves were on edge with excitement with what awaited us beyond that door. Uncle Sasha would then ring a bell, the door would be flung open, and we would rush into the room of our expectation, preceded by the smallest. The splendid presents were spread upon tables round the Christmas tree.

We were very fond of Uncle Sasha, who was exceedingly kind to us, and many of the happiest hours of my childhood were spent at Gatchina, especially in winter and early spring.

[1] Emperor Alexander III.
[2] Empress Maria Feodorovna, wife of Alexander III.
[3] Grand Duke Michael, youngest son of Alexander III.

We were often invited there by Cousin Misha to spend week-ends, and in early spring we went rowing on the fine lakes in the park which were fed by cold springs. I remember how very clear the water was. Later we used to ride bicycles along the drives.

During the winter we played all sorts of games in the snow. We skated and tobogganed in the palace grounds down steep banks which, during winter, provided a splendid sliding surface. I remember how we used to slide down these banks in little tubs which were tied one to the other—a whole convoy of them. Down we went one side, along specially prepared runs dug from the snow, and up the other. The incline was steep and the descent was very fast. I used to sit on the knees of a sailor who led this procession.

These occasions provided enormous merriment. Uncle Sasha was often present and would look on, enjoying it all as much as we did.

The palace where he and Aunt Minnie lived had low-ceilinged rooms, and the contrast in their size and low ceilings specially impressed me, as did also the smell of clean wood. Here we gathered before Church when Uncle Sasha used to come in and say: "Minnie, il est temps." They were in the habit of speaking French together although she spoke fluent Russian.

Another clear recollection which I have of Uncle Sasha of that period is that of his enormous strength. We played a game of our own invention in the grounds of the Anichkov Palace. It consisted of hitting black rubber balls with sticks and then running after them. On such occasions, Uncle Sasha frequently came to join us, and I can see him to this day coming out in his grey *toujourka*.[1] From the skating rink, using a stout stick with a knob at its end, he made the balls pass clean over the roof of the palace, which was a high building. Only a man of quite

---

[1] Everyday military tunic from the French *toujours*, always.

exceptional strength could have done this. Then we would run after the ball to recover it.

From early May to early August we used to spend at Tsarskoe and at Krasnoe Selo.

Father was the Commander-in-Chief of the Imperial Guard and the St. Petersburg Command, which included the provinces not only within the immediate radius of the capital, but also Finland, Esthonia, Livonia, the province of Pskov, Novgorod, and Archangel. Stretching away as it did to the farthest North it covered a very extensive territory.

The Guard regiments were encamped at Krasnoe from late May into the second half of August, and there were drills and manœuvres which provided us with many thrills when we joined Father in camp. We lived in little wooden houses allotted to Father, and as we were frequently with the troops, we saw much of military life while we were still children. Mother was an accomplished horsewoman. I remember her galloping among the troops with us trying hard to follow on our little ponies. We looked after them ourselves and rode daily in those summer months. On our return from those rides, a groom would meet us with a plate of carrots and sugar. The ponies, which we drove four in hand, belonged to an Esthonian breed and were reared, I think, on the Baltic islands of Dago and Oesel. The hooves of our mounts and carriage horses were polished with a special mixture of tar to make them black and glossy.

Mother was very popular with the troops, and whenever a cavalry regiment passed her windows they would play those waltzes which they knew she liked. To this day I can hear those tunes.

Mother's and Aunt Minnie's names' days coincided on August 4,[1] and, on that occasion, we used to go to Peterhof for the fireworks and illuminations.

[1] July 22, old style.

At Peterhof, I had my first glimpse of the sea, the sea to which I later became apprenticed, which was to become my close companion throughout my life, and which is with me now.

The fireworks were set off from pontoons moored at the sea front in the close proximity of a little castle called 'Monplaisir.' We went there when it was dark, in a large brake, drawn by four horses each mounted by a fore-rider dressed in the picturesque liveries of French postillions.

The way to the sea front took us through the large park of Peterhof, to which the public had free access. It was a famous park of its kind with many fountains in it. On these occasions it was lit with many little coloured lamps and looked very attractive. Uncle Paul[1] sat in front controlling the brakes, and, as there was no coachman, he directed the fore-riders and was like the captain of a ship. I can still hear his huge voice. "To the left—to the right—stop," resounded through the great darkening park, as the brake followed the sombre avenues of trees.

We were generally sitting in front enjoying ourselves immensely. It was all very friendly and jolly—a thoroughly warm atmosphere. These are happy memories of youth which were later to disappear completely.

As children we had one valet each—all old soldiers of the Guard. Mother's servants were mostly drawn from the Naval Guards,[2] whilst her maids were Germans. I remember specially Frau Knark and her Hungarian page, Hodura.

[1] Married Princess Alexandra of Greece; his children are Grand Duchess Marie and Grand Duke Dimitry.

[2] 'Gwardeyskiy equipage' in Russian. There is no equivalent to this in the Royal Navy. They were not Marines, but contingents of sailors belonging to the Imperial Guards and allotted to special escort ships and the Imperial yachts. They were the pick of officers and men of the Russian Imperial Navy. At the time of the war the cruiser *Oleg*, the flotilla-leaders *Voiskovoi* and *Ukraina*, and the several yachts were manned by the Guards. They wore a distinctive uniform.

Frau Knark was a native of Mecklenburg and had those strange gifts which are found among some country folk in those parts of Europe which have been spared by urbanization, where ancient traditions of the 'folk' have succeeded in surviving. Whenever a member of our household had been scalded by boiling water or burnt Frau Knark was called, and by strange and quite inexplicable means in which entirely incomprehensible incantations were muttered by her, she invariably succeeded in curing the scalded skin or the burns and in mitigating the pain.

When we had emerged from our nursery days our first teacher, a Russian, Mlle Delevskaya, was chosen for us. She came daily, but did not live with us. She was an excellent teacher, a good woman, and very popular. It was she who taught us to read and write Russian. This was done in the old-fashioned way—on slates. We rather teased her, and at times she encouraged our flagging efforts by giving us sweets. This helped considerably in our first studies.

One day Father called Boris, Andrey, and me to him and said: "You are to have a supervisor for your studies; obey him as you obey me." I must have been about seven or eight then, and we were all very frightened at this announcement.

The supervisor chosen for us was General Alexander Daller, a retired and oldish artillery officer.

It fell to his duties to choose tutors for us. Of this he acquitted himself in a somewhat haphazard manner, and some of his choices were far from satisfactory. Among other things he had to supervise our conduct. Each of us had a special conduct book, a sort of log-book for our early navigation on the sea of life.

When Father and Mother were abroad, a thing which often happened due to Mother's rather delicate health, reports were sent to them by Daller.

Much later on in life when we were grown up, these

reports were read to us by Mother. They were most amusing and made us nearly burst with laughter.

One thing, among others, for which I will be always grateful to Daller, is that he taught me to work with my hands. He was a good carpenter, and I took a fancy to this work myself.

In spare hours he read Jules Vernes' novels to us, then quite new and greatly appreciated.

That period which lies between early childhood and youth, the period of boyhood, is a very important one. Therefore I wish to mention specially those who took a part in my education. They were, with some exceptions, chosen by Daller from the *milieu* of students and poor officers of the Guard.

First, there was Father Alexander Diernoff, our almoner, who remained with us all our lives, and who was instructor in religious subjects till about our eighteenth year. He was our spiritual guide. For him I have nothing but the greatest esteem. He was a man of the profoundest knowledge and of the most exhaustive culture—a well-trained cleric, who taught us Church history, the catechism, and much else belonging to the scope of his authority.

Very unfortunately my early training in mathematics was poor. This was the most important subject which concerned me personally, as I was later to join the Navy. I was not at this stage taught any higher mathematics, trigonometry, mechanics, or dynamics.

History was taught by Vsevolod Chernavin, an officer of the Imperial Family's own Rifle Regiment, a knowledgeable little man, an excellent teacher, handicapped unfortunately by the manner in which history used to be taught in my youth. More stress was laid on memorizing dates than on the events of importance and the men and women who are the actors in the world drama which history really is. This made this fascinating subject barren and repulsive in the extreme. He only taught Russian history, with a smattering of that of other nations, and no comparative history at all.

The history of other peoples was left to those who were our language masters.

Thus my liking for this important subject was spoilt. Vsevolod Chernavin was an excellent amateur actor, and in this connection I remember distinctly the first time we were taken to the opera. It was *Othello*. After that Helen's life was not worth living. We smothered her with pillows—a mock murder—and bullied her rather mercilessly in the way of children, meaning no harm at all. She defended herself splendidly, although there were three of us, all boys, against her. Not very fair play, as generally it is the little girls who bully their brothers. Here, however, she was in a conspicuous minority.

Chernavin's brother, Vyacheslav, who taught us geography, was christened by Helen—'the Kitten,' for he was a rotund little fellow with black whiskers.

French was taught by M. Fabien d'Orliac, who, I think, died recently. He had three little boys; two of them were twins, who came to play with us.

Mr. Browne was our English teacher. He was a thorough gentleman and very pleasant indeed. He had long white moustaches, and I remember that he was proud of the fact that his name ended with an 'E.' We went through the whole of English literature with him, starting with Walter Scott's novels and Shakespeare's plays.

Herr Ketzerau, a very typical Teuton, was our German master. He was not attached to the staff of our teachers, but visited us daily. He was an excellent instructor in physical training and fond of out-of-door exercises. From him I acquired a liking for sports—riding, swimming, skating, and golf. I was very fond of gymnastics and a good performer at this. All my life I have been a keen musician, and owe much to Herr Kündiger in that respect. Our first music instructor was most unsatisfactory, and we learnt no music at all with him. He was a German, a Hussar bandmaster, Bode by name.

Herr Kündiger, on the other hand, was excellent, and from him I acquired a fondness for the piano, which I have played all my life.

There was an amateur orchestra in which members of the Imperial Family performed. It had been founded by Uncle Sasha. Uncle Serge[1] played the flute and I the cornet. A Herr Fliege, who was the conductor of the Imperial orchestra, conducted these amateur performances, twice a week in the Grand Duke Michael's palace. One evening was set aside for string and the other for wind instruments.

In our childhood we suffered from skin trouble owing to the exceptionally hard water at Tsarskoe. The water was so bad that Father had some specially brought from St. Petersburg, where it was taken from the Neva. It was soft and excellent.

To cure us of this complaint we were sent on two occasions to Hapsal, in Esthonia, a delightful watering-place on the Baltic, famous for its curing mud-baths.

Our first visit there was accompanied by an adventure. We went to Hapsal by sea on an ancient paddle steamer, the *Olaf*, which, not content with its old age, succeeded in running aground in the skerries on a submerged rock, of which there were plenty.

In the end we were towed off by a big battleship, which added considerably to the comic aspect of this episode.

At Hapsal, we lived in a house provided by two very kind old maids, the Countesses Brevern de la Gardie, who sometimes came to visit us. We took a complete staff with us—our servants, cooks, coachmen, and horses.

Hapsal was an excellent place, and we bathed in the sea, went out for drives in the pinewoods, and danced with the girls of the 'Patriotic Institute'[2] who were on

[1] Grand Duke Sergey Alexandrovitch.
[2] A High School for girls, usually orphans.

holiday there. There were thirty of them to three of us. We frequently went to concerts, and had a good time.

Our medical attendant was Doctor Hunius, a dear old man, a German Balt, true to his type. He was a great connoisseur of apples and plums, of which he had a great stock in his orchard, and to which we were allowed free access.

In connection with Hapsal, I remember an incident which was as comical as it was dangerous. We had an enormous flagpole near the house in which we lived. An equally large flag had been made for it, which was hoisted by us every morning. One day we decided to hoist Helen instead of the flag. She was a willing party to this conspiracy. Accordingly we tied the flag-rope round her and began hoisting her up. A sailor had become suspicious of our proceedings, but could not see clearly what was going on, as the foot of the pole stood amongst some bushes which hid us from view. But when he saw a human parcel, in the shape of a small girl, proceeding slowly up the pole, he ran up to us and arrived just in time, as Helen was by then merrily swinging in the breeze about thirty-five feet up from the ground. Needless to say, the incident closed with a well-deserved dressing down.

During our second visit to Hapsal—also in the 'eighties—mother was very ill, and she very nearly died. We were not told anything about it at the time.

Suddenly, one night, we were rushed off to Peterhof, and in order to catch the train there we had first to go to Reval, the nearest station. This was a matter of about one hundred kilometres, or about sixty-two miles, and had to be covered during the night as the train was due to leave Reval early in the morning. Doctor Hunius provided us with a huge amount of apples, and off we went into the night in a carriage drawn by six horses mounted by outriders. We arrived in time to catch the train, to which an Imperial carriage had been added for us. At Peterhof, we met Aunt Marie, the Duchess of Edinburgh, my father's only sister. She was to become my future mother-in-law, and was, during that critical period, staying with my mother.

I remember that to keep us quiet she frequently took us for drives. Through her we got to know many places which we had not seen previously. She knew the place excellently. I remember that she would sometimes stop the Imperial carriage in which we drove to buy fruit from pedlars at the wayside. With us she was strict and allowed no fooling, but had an exceedingly kind heart.

Nearly every second or third autumn, when father was off duty after the camp at Krasnoe, we went to stay with Uncle Friedrich,[1] Aunt Anastasia,[1] and our cousins[1] at Schwerin. We loved these visits, and were on the friendliest terms with our relatives. The old Crown Princess of Prussia, the sister of William I, the Grand Duchess Alexandrine of Mecklenburg-Schwerin, we called her Grandmamma, lived in a little *schloss* at Schwerin. She was always charming to us, speaking the very perfect and exquisite French of the eighteenth century. They had all been brought up according to the best traditions. She was the daughter of King Frederick William III of Prussia and of his famous and beautiful wife, Queen Luise, a Princess of Mecklenburg-Strelitz. Frederick William IV of Prussia and Queen Luise had two other children, one of which was the Emperor William I and the other the Empress Alexandra Fedorovna, wife of the Emperor Nicholas I. On one occasion she gave us a dinner, and although we were small children and she was over eighty years of age and paralysed, she had herself rolled into our dining-room in her chair to be with us during this dinner. In spite of our youth, she had put on full evening dress with her decorations, and wore the Romanoff Family Order, and, according to the old traditions, she carried a fan in her hand. I will never forget this outstanding example of

[1] See *supra*.

H.I.H. THE LATE GRAND DUKE VLADIMIR OF RUSSIA
The Author's father.

 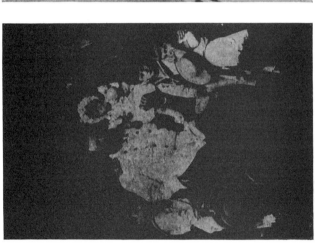

(*Left*) T.I.H. THE GRAND DUKE AND DUCHESS VLADIMIR OF RUSSIA
The Author is on the extreme left, with his sister Helen and brothers Boris and Andrey on the right.
(*Right*) THE GRAND DUCHESS VLADIMIR
The Author's mother.

old-world discipline and supreme refinement that belongs to another age.

Grandmamma's son was my maternal grandfather, the Grand Duke Frederick Francis II of Mecklenburg-Schwerin. I remember the very striking and beautiful family seat of the Grand Dukes of Mecklenburg-Schwerin. Surrounded as it is by a great lake it is one of Germany's famous historical castles and has, moreover, the reputation of being haunted. It was here that we used to stay during our frequent visits to our relations.

It is a magnificent and imposing edifice, and stands in the great lake of Schwerin. On one of these visits, I and my brother Boris were lodged in the two towers which flanked the great entrance gate to the courtyard of the castle, so that I occupied a room in one of the towers and he slept in the other. This occasion coincided with the death of Uncle Pitsu.[1]

The rooms in which we were lodged were cavernous and circular, and what struck us as odd and uncanny were the many doors which were always kept locked and led 'goodness knows' where. As we were children, and were afraid of sleeping alone in those gloomy rooms, it was decided that we should sleep together in one of those towers. Uncle Pitsu's body was at the time lying in state in the chapel of the castle.

One night, while Uncle's body was still in the chapel, we heard quite distinctly the clatter of the hooves of galloping horses entering the courtyard, and then, after a while, the sound of more horses and the rattling of a carriage as its iron-ringed wheels heavily bumped on the cobbles of the yard. Then there was silence, but only for a brief spell. Then we again heard the galloping horses and the sound of a carriage passing the towers through the gate. For the moment, and having no other explanation, we thought that this unusual din was caused by the changing

[1] Grand Duke Frederick Francis III of Mecklenburg-Schwerin.

of the guard which used to be posted at the gate of the castle.

Later we told our experience to Mother, from whom we heard that, according to an ancient tradition, there was a story current among the members of her family that whenever a Grand Duke of Mecklenburg-Schwerin passed away the carriage of death was supposed to come for the spirit of the departed Grand Duke to fetch him away from his castle, but neither she nor any of her family had seen or heard it.

This was only one of the many uncanny things that went on in this awe-inspiring place. There was, for example, the story of a dwarf of the sixteenth century, who, at one time, had been a Court jester, and who was supposed to be haunting certain rooms of the castle. One of the Grand Dukes had sought to appease that restless spirit by erecting a monument to him in the castle grounds. I know not whether this device succeeded in preventing the ghost from his nocturnal wanderings.

We used to go out rowing on that large lake with our tutor and a boatman, who, I remember, wore a peculiar blue livery. On one occasion we were surprised by a squall and ended very nearly in disaster. We were too small to row well, and one of us had to do the steering, of which he did not acquit himself well, so that the brunt of the work fell on the tutor and the boatman. We rowed for life and began to ship water. In the end, however, we reached land safely, but only just in time.

Father liked these visits particularly, as he was a keen shot, and for this the forests of Schwerin were ideal, especially for stags. Later I, too, shot there once or twice.

These visits to Schwerin are among my most pleasant recollections of that period.

I think that my earliest memory of a journey abroad was a visit to Switzerland. Mother's health required frequent visits abroad, and this particular one, I believe, was to Vevey. I recollect little of it now except that I was told that people stopped in the streets and remarked to my attendant: "What a pretty little boy." According to the fashion of that time I wore a little frock with ribbons.

Another very dim recollection is a visit to Biarritz. The only thing which I remember about it now is that I made little sand-pies in a tent.

About the same period in the early 'eighties I have my earliest recollections of Paris. We stayed at the Hôtel Continental, which, I believe, still exists. I remember distinctly the horse-drawn buses in the rue de Rivoli, the grey horses which drew them, the clatter of their hooves on the wooden pavements and the cracking of their drivers' whips, as well as the smell of fresh asphalt.

In the late 'eighties and in 1891, when I was about twelve or thirteen, we went to St. Sebastian in Spain. There we met Queen Christina of Spain, who was a Hapsburg by birth. I remember well her pretty gait and her elegant and truly queenly bearing. She was there with her children, Alfonso XIII and his sisters, Mercedes and Maria Theresia. The King was a rather naughty little boy, always running away from his nurse and scampering about all over the beach.

We bathed in the sea, my first introduction to the Atlantic Ocean, and Queen Christina offered us the use of her bathing machine. This had several rooms and stood on rails. It could be adjusted to the state of the tides by being pulled up and down by a steam winch from the land. She gave us some delicious, dark, sweet Spanish wine, Malaga, in little glasses.

Many well-known people came to St. Sebastian, and the Grand Duke Alexander Michaelovitch was one of them.

We often went for drives inland to visit places of interest like Tolosa and the famous monastery of Loyola.

Sometimes we went over factories. I remember two of them especially—one was a biscuit factory and the other manufactured the famous Basque berets in all the colours of the rainbow.

Queen Christina had a famous historical castle not far from St. Sebastian, where she lived simply in the entourage of a very amiable Spanish Court.

She was a remarkable woman, and we admired her very much.

Our visit to Spain was suddenly interrupted by the death of Aunt Alice,[1] Grand Duchess Paul, who died in giving birth to my cousin, the Grand Duke Dimitry, in the year 1891. Father and Mother had to leave hurriedly to return to Russia.

The last reminiscence of a journey abroad in my childhood was one to Finland, a Grand Duchy, and not, properly speaking, a part of the Russian Empire, but under the suzerainty of the Crown. We went to see the famous rapids of Imatra and Walinkosky, truly magnificent examples of the force and beauty of nature. There was good trout-fishing in that region on the property of General Astasheff. It was the custom there to weigh and measure every trout caught and to record the result on the stone quays of the Saima Canal.

During my childhood I had never been taken to visit the interior of Russia, bnt that was to come later.

[1] Princess Alexandra of Greece, wife of Grand Duke Paul, brother of Alexander III.

II

Youth

As I have already explained, my early instruction in mathematics had been, to say the least, unsatisfactory, and when, in the autumn of 1891, I started on the syllabus of the Naval College, I had to struggle hard to catch up with those of my own age who were to become my first shipmates.

At first I did not leave Tsarskoe for St. Petersburg, but received my lessons on the spot from instructors of the Naval College, who came specially to Tsarskoe for that purpose.

I found the work very laborious, as I had not the least knowledge of chemistry, mechanics, or trigonometry. All this was virgin soil to me. At the same time, I had to continue my other lessons in scripture, languages, drawing, and music.

All this hard work had one great advantage—it taught me from my early youth to organize my time, to divide the hours of the day, and set aside times for rest, and physical exercise, without which the mind is more apt to exhaust itself. During the whole of my life I have laid great stress on the necessity of keeping fit, being convinced of the benefits that arise from a well-trained and disciplined body. In this respect I may have been somewhat of an exception in Russia, where young men and women, overawed by the terrors of examinations and the consequences of failing in them, worked themselves to a state of complete exhaustion. Examinations were always considered a matter of family honour. A boy or girl who failed in them was a disgrace to the family, a person to be shunned for a time, a 'ne'er-do-well,' to be sure ; he would never get on in the world. Youth was dominated by the ominous shadow of examinations and the malignant spectre of failure.

That fear of failing, coupled with the enormous ground which had to be covered for any of the State examinations, a scope of knowledge which was far too crammed and altogether too general, resulted in those pale, nervous, hysterical, and physically unfit persons, who could be seen wandering about like shadows during examination time and after. Russia in no way benefited from this system, which to no mean degree contributed to some of the sad events of later years. It was this class of overworked, ill-trained, and discontented students who, during the best years of their youth, had been subjected to these nerve-racking terrors that formed the fertile soil for terrorism, nihilism, and all the other evils, which could only flourish on such unsound ground. Had there been less cramming of brains and more physical training—and there was a total absence of it—among the youth of Russia, the sad events that were in store for us might yet have been avoided. It was the so-called 'intelligentsia,' the intellectual proletariat, and not the workers and peasants, who were the real carriers of discontent and revolutionary ideas. It is a trite but a true saying: 'In corpore sano, mens sana.' This ought to have been the device of our educationists.

I, too, was later to go through the teeth of that grinding mill, and to experience it in all its terrors.

It was during this winter of 1891, while I was being initiated into the secrets of theoretical navigation, that I was first brought into contact with the elegant and charming trivialities of Society. This, also, was one of the necessary equipments for setting out upon the course of life.

For the first time I met girls of my own age during our dancing lessons, arranged for us by Mother, who chose our partners. Some of the boys and girls I met during those jolly occasions—the Cantakouzenes, Bibikoffs, Gortchakoffs, Bariatinskys, and many others—became my friends for life. In this connection I especially remember Boris and Misha Cantakouzene,[1] and their charming sister 'Dally,' who later became Countess Nieroth.

Then, all of a sudden, the curtain fell upon my childhood, upon that atmosphere of culture and refinement, which had formed the guarded environment in which I had grown up. Hitherto I had experienced nothing but the very best examples of polished manners, of kindness, justice, and exalted moral and ethical standards in a home that was typical of the very best traditions of a brilliant and cultured period.

All this ceased suddenly in the summer of 1892, when I stepped across the shadow line which separates childhood from youth, and for the first time started life outside the parental home. I had never been pampered at home, and, as I have already pointed out, had been brought up strictly, but the things that lay in store for me exceeded all my imagination. It was a rude awakening, to be sure, an awakening, moreover, in which I found myself completely alone, in absolute isolation, to tackle all the new problems as well as I could, but only with the resources which I carried with me. I had to rely on myself for the first time, and with this reliance on myself I had crossed the frontier between childhood and the world outside.

I was to go to sea.

Father, of course, realized how hard it would be for me to separate myself from home and to enter into this completely strange new world, and so to lessen the rigours of this experience he had my future fellow-shipmates, boys of my age and stage of instruction, brought to Tsarskoe,

---

[1] Prince Cantakouzene, Ct. Speranski.

so that we should get to know each other. We had tea together to get over our mutual shyness, and played all sorts of games in the park of our house. It was decided that my tutor, the Chevalier de Shaeck, and my old servant, Poliashenko, should accompany me on board my training-ship.

The separation from parents and home early in life is an experience which is quite natural to English boys, and is part of their usual public school education. Not so in Russia, however, where there were very few institutions for boarders. Boys lived at home while in their school years.

The Chevalier de Shaeck was an excellent individual, and more of a friend than a tutor. We shared in common our enthusiasm for hard physical exercise, and he was a past-master at gymnastics. He had been educated partly in Vienna, where he had graduated at the University, and in Geneva. To give him an official status on board he joined the officers' mess in the capacity of language instructor, but this was entirely a fiction, as no teaching of any accepted European or other language, except of a quite different kind, to which I will have occasion to refer later, was done at all.

My personal servant, old Poliashenko, was a native of 'Little Russia,' better known abroad as the Ukraine. He was entirely representative of the region of his origin, being a severe puritan in the orthodox sense of the word, and very religious. He had been with me from my earliest childhood, had carried me about in his arms, and was to accompany me to all the various training-ships in my early stages of naval apprenticeship. Poliashenko's wife had been one of our nursemaids. The couple were devoted to me, with that special kind of devotion to be found only with Russian retainers, who never stepped over the line of respect to become familiar, and yet treated their young master with something approaching parental solicitude. This was a relic of the feudal days—the feudal loyalty of the old patriarchal Society—which had come to an end in Russia in 1860; it had its parallel elsewhere, too, in the relations between squire and tenant. This spirit of fealty had drawn to a close with the industrial revolution, and with the retreat and surrender of the land to towns and factories. It bred a class of disinterested factory-owners, and a discontented proletariat, that in its wild and unscrupulous chase after wealth paved the way for the great disaster.

Poliashenko and his wife were invaluable to me as housekeepers in the years preceding my marriage, remaining with me until their deaths. They had been born serfs.

The great day had come. I was sent off to St. Petersburg with Shaeck and old Poliashenko, and was heartily glad of their company.

I assembled with my fellow-shipmates on the Neva quay, and with bundles, packages, and sea-boxes we were all hustled on board a small steamer, which soon cast off and began ploughing its way down the broad current of the Neva River, seaward bound to the Baltic naval base of Kronstadt.

When a midshipman goes to his 'first ship' in these modern times he comes into a world where the marvels of engineering and the ingenuities of science are blended into a floating town, where everything is cleverly devised to dovetail utility, defence, speed, and comfort into one great harmonious whole. Not so with me! When I started on my naval career, sail was still an almost indispensable part of a ship, although the period of transition to steam had already set in by that time.

I went to sea when the memories of the old, rough, salty days were still fresh in men's minds and when the sea and those who fared upon it were more intimately bound to each other in a bond of fellowship, and by the spirit of their craft, when men were more at its mercy, and their success or failure, victory or defeat, life and death, were both in the gift of the sea and of the winds.

To master the elements one thing was essential above all others, and that was sail, its management, and the ability to manœuvre in all the possible and seemingly impossible situations with which the cunning and the vicious nature of the sea could confront one. From the days of the Armada to Trafalgar victory and defeat had been decided in no small measure by the greater ability to make the most of sail, wind, and sea.

We were pestered with sail, we were crammed with every conceivable thing appertaining to that fearsome divinity, until in our sleep almost we could recite all that the riggings, the yards, the sails, fore, aft, and amidships, contained, even to the smallest details, until one got to hate the whole confounded thing. And of what use was it to us, who, when we became fully qualified ship's officers, never set foot on board a sailing craft of the kind again?

However, there it was, and the futility of it all became quite obvious to me later, because that Noah's Ark upon which I set foot that day, His Imperial Majesty's Ship *Moriak*,[1] nearly capsized the first time they tried to hoist a few sails on her. She was top-heavy, unmanageable, and entirely unseaworthy. To add to the absurdity of it all, she was brand-new, having just been commissioned, but who had designed her and why, forsooth, she had been built at all in this manner, have remained an unsolved mystery to this day. Properly speaking, she ought to have finished at the bottom of the sea, but possibly her end was more appropriate to her very nature. She became a restaurant on the Neva side—an institution of the place, a sight to be seen, and a landmark. A dead hulk with none of that glamour about her of having done great things in her time, and resting from her labours, like a war-scarred veteran. No, she just lay there, a monument to inefficiency, an embodiment of the conception of failure.

If those who were responsible for her existence had been

---

[1] Sailor.

moved to hurry the deaths of those who were to entrust their lives to her, I would have understood this maritime enigma, but as this was unlikely, I had to accept this conundrum as unsolvable.

What made things considerably worse was the fact that her captain was what may be best described as an old fogy, and her commander a ruffian.

He was a brute, a bully, and a pestilent fellow all in one, whose sole mission on earth, his *raison d'être*, so to speak, appeared to consist in manhandling the crew. His aim in life seemed to be nothing else than to ill-treat the crew like a devil specially appointed to lord it over us. Meanwhile, the captain, whose task it should have been to put a stop to these goings-on, contented himself with a perpetual state of *far niente*.

It appeared to me then that it was a special sort of fetish, a kind of indispensable ritual, that before anything could be done on that hulk of a frigate, a three-masted one, for such was her official status, there had to precede a storm of vehement abuse, without which no yard could be squared and no sail trimmed. This flow of dirt, for it was nothing but the uttermost filth, resounded from morning till night, accompanied by the savage outbursts of violence on the part of our commander. Those who are not acquainted with the Russian language have no conception of what Russian swearing is like. There is no comparison with it. It excels itself in unadulterated filth.

This is what came to my ears, and it was fortunate, indeed, that much of it was lost to me, I who had scarcely ever heard an angry word spoken.

But it was not lost on poor old Poliashenko, that kindly soul, who was most concerned for the welfare of his young Grand Duke, whom he had carried about as a babe.

"What sort of place is this, Your Imperial Highness, that we have got into," he would say in utter despair, shocked to the marrow that a member of the Imperial Family should be allowed to flourish in such a rough, uncongenial atmosphere, more like a river-side ale-house than an educational establishment afloat, for about the only thing the 'hulk' could do was to float.

She was the most uncomfortable and fantastic vessel I have ever had the misfortune to be in. The pungent smell of her new paint and tar is still fresh in my nostrils. She had neither proper lighting nor heating, and the only machinery on board were the steam pumps. Fortunately, due to my status, I escaped the clutches of the commander, also, I had a bunk of my own, whereas the rest of my shipmates, about forty of them, slept in the usual way, in hammocks.

Not being able to move under our own power, we were taken in tow to Tralsund among the skerries of the Bay of Finland, between Viborg and Kronstadt. There, during the summer of 1892, we lay at anchor until August.

Only one attempt was made to set sail. It had to be abandoned at once, because the 'hulk' heeled over to such a dangerous angle that disaster was imminent. Thereafter the Admiral forbade any further efforts of the kind.

The officers on board fell into two groups. The first were real sailing men, and they taught us seamanship and navigation, whilst the others were a strange collection of 'landlubbers' from the Naval College, in no way suited to be in charge of boys. These latter had to supervise our conduct, in which capacity they did not prove themselves at all efficient.

They were longshoremen, who had, at one time in the very distant past of their youth, sailed upon the seven seas, but had lost all touch with it, since they never, unless they had to, set foot upon a deck, and with the passage of time had forgotten all they had known.

Once they entered the Naval College and donned its special uniforms, they remained there for life, like permanent fixtures. Old retired gentlemen they were, an archaic collection of worthy old fogys, who spent all their time at Kronstadt, where they did—nothing whatever!

However, they were considered by the naval authorities good enough to be supervisors.

Fortunately, all this was changed completely later, when first-class officers were appointed to this very responsible task.

My shipmates on all the training-ships to which I was apprenticed were, with very few exceptions, the sons of naval men, and some of those I met there became my friends. Most of them perished during the Japanese War: and with special regret I think of my good friend Kube, my earliest shipmate from the *Moriak* days, and my dearest friend. Later he became my A.D.C. on the ill-fated *Petropavlovsk*. They have no grave but the sea.

There were about forty of us all told on the *Moriak*, and a happy, carefree lot we were, in spite of the atmosphere around us, which, incidentally, we soon got used to.

The crews of the Baltic Fleet, which, as one might have expected, should have been recruited from the Baltic and the White Sea coasts, with their excellent supply of material in men born and bred to the sea for centuries, were as a rule taken quite illogically, and for no earthly reason whatever, from the Central and Southern provinces of Russia. This fact is as incomprehensible as it is absurd. Our sailors were men who came straight from the plough, some of them had even never seen any water of navigable size, and that, indeed, when there was material of Viking stock available to us on our very threshold, and in close reach. To train these peasants took seven years, coupled with much State expense and an unnecessary waste of time. Even when they had been turned into the finished product they never looked upon the sea as their natural element. Yet it must be admitted that they proved themselves most adaptable and remarkably useful in their new environment. Later on the Navy had the further attraction for them in that they received elementary education there as ratings, and if they reached the higher ranks of able seamen and petty officers, they could, if they wished, have the benefits of intermediary education as well. In any case, those who were mechanics took with them, on leaving the fleets, a valuable knowledge of engineering, electricity, and much else.

We were divided in the usual watches, kept either on board or on the steam launches, and were given permission to choose our watch-mates from our friends.

The work was divided into practical seamanship, which included navigation, sailing-boat drill, training aloft, and signalling, and theoretical work below.

Up and down the rigging, along the yards, we clambered like a lot of little monkeys until we knew and had become perfectly familiar with every detail of the regions aloft, ropes, sails, and all else, a whole world of cumbersome detail, the particular functions of which had to be known by heart *ad nauseam*. Everything was concentrated on sail —which ruled supreme and unchallenged.

My shipmates were a rough lot, but good fellows. In our spare time we used to organize expeditions in the boats to the islands nearby, of which there were literally myriads among the skerries, most of them moss-covered granite rocks of small size; there we picnicked.

During one of these expeditions we had no fresh water, and tried to make our coffee with sea-water, which in those regions is not very salty. The result was shocking! We spewed the poisonous stuff out into the sea, whence we had drawn it.

Although the Gulf of Finland is not in itself dangerous for navigation, being well marked by buoys and lights, yet the skerries had to be surveyed once every year, and the channels marked afresh, due to the heavy ice which during the winter months shifted boulders into the channels through the force of its expansion.

One day I received an unexpected but very welcome visit from my early friend, philosopher, and guide, General Alexander Daller, accompanied by my brothers Boris and Andrey.

I was delighted to be able to show myself off to them by my knowledge of sails and rigging. I considered them with that patronizing air of contempt which is usual with sailors when dealing with landsmen on board their little realms. This visit was a very welcome diversion in the humdrum of my routine.

Towards the end of August there came a fearsome visitation, an infliction, in the shape of the Admiral Commanding the training-ships squadron, with the Naval College Board of Examiners. The Admiral was a fine old sailorman, very representative of the old days, a real old 'salt' to look at. He was straight and honest, and knew his job. In appearance he was a clumsy old fellow, very ugly indeed, and what struck me most about him were his boots with upturned toes, which looked as though they had been stuffed with walnuts.

The examination consisted mainly in testing our knowledge of sails and rigging, and the management of a ship under sail in various conditions of wind and weather. Considering that the only time we had put sail on her she nearly capsized, I think that I acquitted myself well of this examination. I passed successfully, and this was important in itself, as a failure in one's knowledge of sails was tantamount to being put on the black list as ' no good.'

This brought my days on the *Moriak* to a conclusion, and I was heartily glad to shake her dust off my feet.

I was not sorry, however, to have had this experience. It was a rude entry into the world, but I had faced it squarely, learnt the lessons, roughed it as well as any of the others, and had stood the test. It was invaluable to me as an experience of youth.

During the winter of 1892 and 1893 I continued my studies for the intermediate Naval College examination for which I was going to sit in the spring of 1895. An enormous field had to be covered by then, and the nearer the time drew to this first serious test of my knowledge, the more exacting my studies became.

Most of the winter of 1892 and the spring of 1893 I spent between Tsarskoe and St. Petersburg.

My instructors were men well qualified in their special subjects, and I remember especially Youri Michaelovich Shokalsky, an oceanographer of repute, who, I believe, was a Fellow of the Royal Geographical Society. At any rate he went frequently to London, where he was well known among the learned men of his day.

Although I had paid many visits abroad with my parents during my childhood, I had hitherto not been into the interior of Russia. St. Petersburg and the regions surrounding it were the New Russia, territories comparatively recently added to my country by Peter the Great on the conclusion of the Nordic War in 1721, and they were by no means typical of the country of which they formed the Western confines. The real Russia was as yet a *terra incognita* to me. This may strike one as odd, but the reason was that my father, as I have already stated, was the Commander-in-Chief of the military district of St. Petersburg, and while on duty he had to travel through the length and breadth of his Command. This district was very extensive indeed, and comprised within its radius the home provinces of the Metropolis, Finland, Esthonia, Livonia, Pskov, and Vitebsk. The Baltic littoral and its immediate hinterland, as well as the far Northern regions of Archangel and beyond, stretching away to the estuaries of the great Arctic rivers. My father had taken part in that famous expedition which attempted to investigate the possibilities of the Arctic sea route. It had tried, unsuccessfully, to reach Novaya Zemlya, during the summer months when the sea was not entirely icebound.

The Northern passage along the Arctic Ocean to the Pacific by the Bering Straits has always been an ambition of Russia. The feasibility of such a short cut would save one the tedious voyages from the Baltic to the Far East by way of the Suez Canal, and if ever such a route could be practically realized, it would bring Russia enormous economical advantages.

Thus it was not until the spring of 1893 that I first had an opportunity to visit Moscow, our ancient capital and second cradle of Russia, the very heart of the country and its holy city.

Uncle Serge,[1] was at that time its Governor-General and he had invited Mother and myself to some celebrations and gay society functions there during the season before Lent.

During this short visit—I only remained two days there—I had a very general impression of that most remarkable and entirely unique place, the beauties and treasures of which I was to get to know intimately during the Coronation of the late Emperor in 1896.

Suffice it then to give an impression of Moscow. Whereas St. Petersburg, in its general aspect, is a place of classical severity, efficiency, and majestic grandeur, methodically designed, equipped, moreover, with master works of the eighteenth and nineteenth centuries, it lacks that natural cohesion which alone the unplanned growth of centuries can bestow. St. Petersburg is new and therefore cold. Moscow, on the other hand, is different. For, being the work of many centuries, it provides a panorama of Russian history from the middle ages. It presents a motley ensemble of streets, broad and narrow, crooked and straight. Wealth and poverty are heaped together in natural disorder. Burnt down again and again, invaded, destroyed and rebuilt, Moscow has shared the fate of all great cities, and its destiny throughout history has stamped it with the mark of haphazardness. Unexpectedly, in the centre, one comes upon the Kremlin standing in the splendour of its originality, a blend of many centuries of Russia's history and representative of the glories of her past. Another feature which lends special charm to this city is the

[1] Grand Duke Sergey Alexandrovitch, brother of Alexander III.

many houses belonging to the nobility and merchants, surrounded as a rule by extensive gardens and grounds. That Moscow abounds in an unusual number of churches, with their differently shaped and coloured cupolas is a well-known fact. This city, then, has an atmosphere which is at once congenial and inviting. Conveying an impression of intimacy and welcome, it is the true personification of Russia—an expression in material shape.

This then is the general impression one gleans of Moscow on one's first visit. Later on I was fortunate in being able to witness Moscow in its most gorgeous apparel, a festive city adorned in its most festive robes, a great and last flare-up of a candle, which thereafter was to be extinguished.

In the summer of 1893 I again went to sea, but this time on board the Training Ship *Prince Pojarsky*. She was an ancient three-master ironclad, steam and sail, of antediluvian design. Owing to her size and tonnage, she carried a veritable forest of yards and rigging, into which, except up the mainmast, we were forbidden to go because it was considered definitely dangerous.

However, in spite of this cumbersome world aloft, we cruised a good deal in her under sail, but only in the Gulf of Finland.

There was the same seemingly entirely indispensable and continuous flow of abuse, and the commander of the *Mariak* had thoroughly worthy rivals in our captain and commander when it came to venting their tempers on the crew. They, too, were addicted to crew beating.

There was something new on the *Pojarsky*, which we had not experienced on the *Moriak*, and it was a truly interesting experience, something that had to be seen to be believed; this was her horizontal engine and the boilers—veritable museum pieces.

When I went to sea, engines, and those that dealt with them, were still considered by the older men as an unwelcome invasion, a wanton incursion into the hallowed and pure realm of sail. They were looked upon in the light of uninvited strangers, men who had filtered in unasked, bringing with them vapours, smoke, and pestilential odours.

To some degree they were justified in their attitude, as I was soon to experience, and sail and steam did not in fact enter into any kind of harmonious partnership at any time; they interfered with each other, they did not 'hit it off,' as they belonged to different worlds.

Steam has taken much romance from the sea, it has broken her mystery and captivating glamour for ever. The art of the ancient craft of seamanship has retreated before the onslaught of progress. The sea, once a proud and domineering mistress, cruel and condescending, vicious and caressing to those who fared upon her, and lived by her, has become a liquid expanse, all planned out into lanes, along which steamers ply according to timetables, like trains, to gather in merchandise from the uttermost ends of the earth. Every now and then the sea will rise and levy her toll, but she is being defied progressively not by art, but by soulless calculation and ingenious cunning.

Our living quarters were amidships and situated around the engine loft, into the mysterious gloom of which we could see quite easily like people looking over the parapet of a theatre gallery. And like in a theatre, we were occasionally treated to strange performances.

When her engines were started, and it took twelve hours to raise steam in her archaic boilers, there could be heard metallic clangs and the hissing noises of steam issuing forth from cylinders. Bright levers were moved, wheels turned, coppery tubes would flash in the yellow light of lamps, reflecting against mysterious clocks and cranks, among the deep shadows of that hellish and gloomy region. Figures moved, hurried, fled hither and thither in the steaming, oily vapours of this inferno. There were rumbling sounds, whistling sounds and sighs as from the lungs of an all-metal giant. There were the shrill ringings of the engine telegraph, whereon the hurrying shapes below could be seen turning more wheels, moving more levers, and then, with a jerk, moving first slowly forward and then falling heavily and retreating, the cranks might be seen sliding forward and backward, sallying forth and withdrawing smoothly in the unequal rhythm of a mechanical witch dance, faster and even faster. The whole procedure had the semblance of some fantastic ritual, 'of a sordid farce enacted upon a sombre background,' of a hellish fetish. This 'rite' of starting up the engines, quite appropriately had its sacrifices and its archpriest, for they were considered so dangerous that there was only one man in the Russian Navy who was deemed initiated enough in the esoteric secrets of this engine to start it.

Meanwhile the waist, amidships, would be filled with the hot vapours of steam and oil. A fog would arise that shrouded us with its clammy and malodorous embrace. No wonder engines of this early design were unfavourably considered, as were also those who tended them, a greasy and dirty gang of men, who, whenever one of the ship's officers drew into sight, would scurry away and down into the innermost depths of their regions, like frightened rabbits into burrows.

We carried with us four nine-pounder guns, which might have delighted the heart of Nelson—they were breech-loading affairs—but apart from that they differed little from the guns of his times, and were at most a danger to life—not, of course, to potential enemies, but to ourselves.

It was quite seriously considered right and fitting—and this was by no means intended as a practical joke—to teach us rudimentary gunnery with these things. The 'things' stood on wheels, and were nothing else but infernal machines. They had an eight-foot recoil, in which they were restrained by ropes. Every time they were fired they jumped viciously, as did the gunners—but for their lives, right out of the way, for one could never tell where these 'cannons' would land, and the ropes might burst too. Quite rightly, they were left alone as much as possible.

We had to work very hard on the *Pojarsky* from after breakfast in the early morning till night, and for that reason were excused night watches as we were much too tired. We continued with our theoretical and practical courses of the Naval College programme. They overworked us.

When she manœuvred under sail, one of her funnels was lowered, so as not to interfere with the main royal of her mainmast. I do not now remember whether the Russian equivalent of the English command was given: 'Down funnel, up screw,' but it is likely. This, too, was one of the curiosities of those transition days.

When she moved under sail and the engines were not needed her propeller acted as an impediment to her speed. On such occasions it was disconnected and taken up through a special shaft which existed for that purpose aft.

This shaft provided us with much fun. It was narrow and deep, a kind of well at the bottom of which the sea gurgled and foamed. The motion of the vessel, specially in rough seas, her upward and downward pitch, strongest aft, of course, created a violent draught. We used to put our caps on this well and the draught blew them up in the air, throwing them about like a volcano ejecting rocks.

The conditions on board were exceedingly primitive, and although I had my own bunk, I felt the absence of the necessary comforts with which every ship of our navy at that period should have been equipped. There were neither baths nor electric light on board.

For our baths we had to go on shore with the crew, and in the few spare hours which were allowed bathed in the sea.

As young cadets we were taught the traditions of our navy. When entering the quarter-deck and during the midday ceremony of sharing out vodka to the crew, hats had to be removed. When in foreign waters the crews were served rum.

Before the midday meal, the food, which was excellent in our fleets—there was fresh bread every day—was tasted by the captain, and was presented to him by the commander and the chief cook. On Sundays we were piped to the quarter-deck for divine service, after which the 'old man' read out a chapter from the naval regulations.

When all this was done, the crew and the rest of us were given shore leave, and when at sea we were dismissed.

The only official punishments in the Russian Navy were confinement to the ship's prison and cancellation of shore leave. This latter held the greater terror for us. When the Navy had been completely reorganized on a modern footing, and sail had gone the way of all things on earth, brutalities to the crews ceased entirely, but this in no manner reflected itself unfavourably on the excellent standard of discipline on board our ships.

No matches were allowed on board and no knives, unless specially attached by a thin cordon to our tunics. A knife dropped by accident from aloft has its obvious dangers.

As for matches, there were fusees kept in special brass-containers; we used to play with these fusees, chasing each other with them in the hope of giving one another hearty whacks with them.

When the crews were allowed to smoke, these fusees were lit by special command from the bridge. We did not have to do any manual work, except, of course, our drill aloft, sailing, rowing, gunnery, and the usual splicing, together with all the rest that belongs to the sphere of ropes. Deck scrubbing was the province of the crew, who incidentally went barefoot on these sailing-ships. They never wore boots and suffered much from sore feet as the result of climbing up and down the stays.

In August 1893 I left *Prince Pojarsky* and joined my parents at Tsarskoe Selo.

In the autumn of the same year I accompanied them and my brothers and sister to Spain. On my previous two visits there I had only had the opportunity of seeing a small portion of it—the Basque country—and, in any case, was too small to appreciate the great historical treasures, the monuments of its glorious past, which make Spain one of the most interesting countries in Europe.

Father was the best possible guide, as he had a predilection for that country, the history of which he knew intimately.

Moreover, we were specially privileged in being able to see many of the treasures and works of art, which were jealously guarded by the clergy, and only shown to royalty. The ordinary visitor to Spain was not admitted to see them. How many of these, I wonder, have been spared from the blind outrages of hatred and destruction, from the appalling lust to annihilate the things which are beautiful and sublime when the bestial nature of man has broken the bounds of restraint?

We visited Valladolid, Saragossa, Barcelona, Valencia, and much else of interest, all of them names which then belonged to history, and now to the tragedy which is taking place in that country of sorrows—*tierra de los dolores.*

It was during this visit that I had my first impression of bullfights, which in their passion, death-defying courage and cruelty reflect better than anything else the true nature of the Iberians.

While on this Spanish tour we availed ourselves of the opportunity to go over a number of schools, institutions, and factories which gave us a general impression of its social and economical conditions at the close of the last century.

In order to complete our expedition, we crossed over to the Balearic Islands, the luxuriant and ethereal beauty of which made a very favourable impression on me. I remember especially our visit to the vast stalactite caves of the southern coast of Majorca.

After this very impressive and pleasant holiday I continued my studies partly at Tsarskoe and at St. Petersburg, where I remained alone for a few months, to make it easier for my instructors to attend to me.

I had to work very hard indeed, from nine o'clock in the morning until the evening, and then again after supper. The syllabus consisted of marine engineering, engines and boilers, electricity, mechanics, deviation of compasses, land fortifications, and nautical astronomy, and of much else besides. At the same time I continued with other lessons, not belonging to the Naval College programme. In spite of this crowded schedule, I found time for social functions, and physical exercises. About an hour before supper, Shaeck and I used to perform in our gymnasium at the Vladimir Palace.

I have always been a very keen tennis player, and during the winters of 1893 to 1896 I played frequently in the courts of Uncle Nicholas[1] and of Count Shouvaloff, whom we used to call 'Bobby.' These courts were, of course, not in the open, but had been improvised in their houses. We had another court in one of the large storehouses in the naval yards.

Father and Uncle Alexey[2] frequently joined us in our games, as did also various foreign diplomats.

These were happy gatherings, carefree and merry.

How well I remember Uncle Alexey with his handsome figure accoutred in a strange garb of his own choosing and invention, which gave him the appearance of a real showman. It was a kind of red-striped flannel suit—a

[1] Grand Duke Nicholas Nicolaevitch (the younger).
[2] Grand Duke Alexey Alexandrovitch, then Grand Admiral of the Russian Navy. Brother of Alexander III.

Mephistophelian affair—of which he, alone, among all men on earth, was the proud possessor. He was pleased with it and liked to be seen about in this fantastic get-up. "I am better dressed than any of you fellows," he would say to us.

When we had our tea in this storehouse—the tea incidentally was brought to us from Uncle Alexey's house nearby—the small boys from the Naval Training School, who were our ball-boys, would seize the opportunity to fool about with the tennis balls. When the 'hullaballoo' and din became too obvious, Uncle Alexey would thunder at them with his huge naval voice from the other end of the large building.

A fascinating part of my syllabus, fascinating because it was practical, was the making of nautical charts and survey work in the open, which I did on the lake at Tsarskoe with the able tuition of Youri Shokalsky.

Another equally absorbing part of my syllabus was nautical astronomy, taught me by M. Shulgin.

In the summer of 1894 I joined my third training ship, the *Vovin*.[1] She was a fully-rigged frigate, then of quite modern design, having been built in the Motala works in Sweden in the 'nineties. She was equipped with excellent engines, electric light, cabins, and baths. This was a welcome change, indeed, from the rough and primitive conditions to which I had hitherto been accustomed.

One day I was told to report to the captain. I presented myself to the old man accordingly, foreboding evil, but was to be happily disillusioned.

"Your Imperial Highness is to report to His Majesty," was his pronouncement. "There is a torpedo-boat alongside which will take you to the Imperial yacht."

I was delighted! This meant two things—an interruption of board routine and a thoroughly pleasant time with Uncle Sasha (Emperor Alexander III), who always thought of everything and everyone.

[1] Warrior.

He was on holiday at the time, cruising in his English-built yacht, the *Tsarievna*, in the Gulf of Finland.

Off I went on the torpedo-boat and clambered up on to the deck of the *Tsarievna*. There I met Uncle Sasha and Aunt Minnie with some of my cousins.

I spent two delightful days with them, and had, to use the schoolboy expression, a real treat. I was to distinguish myself, too. Uncle Sasha arranged a boat race for cousins Misha, Alexey Michaelovich, and myself. The race was to be rowed in dinghies, one dinghy to each of us with naval officers at the tillers. I won easily by several lengths, and on our return to the yacht received a handsome prize from Uncle Sasha.

Alas, this was to be the last occasion I was to meet him. Cousin Alexey,[1] too, was to pass from us. He caught a severe chill during a gale and died soon after.

The circumstances which led to his death were interesting. Cousin Alexey was in the Navy, where he was finishing his training period afloat. He was of delicate health, and when he caught this chill it was suggested to his father, the Grand Duke Michael Nicholaevitch, that he should interrupt his course of training to get over his illness. Grand Duke Michael, however, who had a great, and possibly exaggerated, sense of duty, would have none of it, and insisted that the boy should finish his course. As a result cousin Alexey developed double pneumonia, of which he died. The first time he wore his midshipman's uniform was in his coffin.

When I returned on board my ship I found myself an object of general envy among my young shipmates.

Death came to us and to all Russia, for in October of 1894 the Emperor Alexander III passed away.

The premature death of the man who had carried so admirably on his broad shoulders the heavy responsibilities of his vast empire, and during whose reign, for the first

[1] Grand Duke Alexey Michaelovitch, son of Grand Duke Michael Nicolaevitch (Uncle Micha).

time for centuries, there had been no war, was an appalling disaster and a fearful calamity.

While he reigned all felt safe, because a strong man was known to stand at the helm of the Ship of State. His great and handsome frame of a blond giant held a character of iron and an absolutely truthful nature. He hated untruth and the crooked things of life. He was no subject to flattery. In everything he was straight.

In his body as well as in his spirit, he was the veritable personification of a 'bogatyr,' the legendary national heroes of the early Russian chroniclers, like the Arthurs and Siegfrieds of other peoples. He was in all this an admirable pattern of what a Russian Emperor should be.

Had he lived, and he died when he was only forty-nine, there would have been no Japanese War and no revolution of 1905, and possibly also no World War either, nor the deluge of blood that followed in its fearful wake. Russia, and possibly the world as well, might have been spared from their Calvaries.

His death was a sunset, thereafter the sombre shadows of the dusk, preceding that fearful night which was to cover all things Russian with its ghastly gloom, advanced relentlessly. His death was the beginning of the end.

All the happy reminiscences of Gatchina, of the Anichkov Palace, of Peterhof, and the merry occasions also at which he and the Empress Maria Feodorovna had presided and which they had inspired with their personalities, all these were to end abruptly.

It was his policy, in which he was helped by his beautiful and charming wife, to keep the Imperial Family united in a bond of friendship and peace. He was the father of his family, as well as of his people, and all looked up to him as such.

I remember all the charming balls and dinners made bright by their presence. We were then a big, united family.

There were the winter balls, for example, periods

of great festivities that came to a close when the rigorous fasting began, ascending in its severity the nearer it drew to Easter. This ball was usually held at the Anichkov Palace, where all of us would gather. It brought the season to its conclusion.

On those jolly occasions there would be a great display of flowers, adding to the informality of them, because they were in pleasant contrast to the severe and formal atmosphere of the great Court balls.

During the intervals the older people would play cards, while we amused ourselves splendidly with all sorts of bright diversions. A start, as a rule, was made with figure dances, which were followed by quadrilles, with interludes of cotillons and finished with mazurkas. Viennese waltzes were not allowed at that time, except the two-step waltz.

Uncle Paul would occasionally conduct these dances, not an easy task by any means. One had to be very efficient to ensure good order and to maintain the harmony of them.

During the great Court balls, cavaliers presented their partners with coloured ribbons that had little bells attached to them. The ladies vied with each other for these, for the one who collected the most was naturally the heroine of the occasion. They used to wear them, during the balls, slung over their shoulders. This was a very old tradition of our Court.

I remember distinctly, when quite a small child, how mother used to give us her ribbons when we came to her dressing-room in the mornings. We used them as reins when we played horses.

My parents and all the members of the Imperial Family were near Uncle Sasha at his death in Livadia in the Crimea.

Never again was there to be that same spirit of understanding among us, that easy fellowship and gay merriment. All that had come to a final conclusion. It was a harsh stroke to Aunt Minnie, whose personality had been ideal for the exalted position which she had so admirably occupied. She had been an excellent consort. It was, I repeat, a dismal tragedy for Russia, the full extent and the real nature of which is clearer to me now than ever before.

His funeral was attended by a bevy of royalties and the representatives of foreign countries. The Prince of Wales represented England, and among the many others present were the Duke and Duchess of Edinburgh and the Duke of Connaught, who later represented his country at the Coronation of the late Emperor.

While everyone was away at Livadia, I had remained at Tsarskoe, and found myself in the somewhat awkward situation of senior Grand Duke there, having to cope in that position with a crowd of officers, who were anxious to make certain of what they had to do concerning the oath of allegiance to the new monarch. They pestered me from morning till night.

On 14 November 1894, old style, my cousin, the late Emperor married Alexandra of Hesse. The Court was still in deep mourning for his father. Cousin Michael, my two brothers, and I officiated at the matrimonial rites as his best men in the Cathedral of the Winter Palace. I wore my Hussar uniform for that occasion, the right to which, as well as to those of three other regiments, Grandpapa had conferred on me at my birth.

The whole affair was very simple; it was entirely a family function, and was not, of course, followed by any festivities.

During the rest of that year and in the early part of 1895 I devoted myself entirely to my studies, and spent some months alone, for the first time, in the capital, to make it easier for my instructors to attend to me.

In the spring of 1895, the dread experience of the examination was at hand. My nerves were on edge. The expectation of the uncertain weighed upon me like a ghastly nightmare. One can get used to most things, but never to examinations. The memories of them pursue one throughout life, when many of the other recollections and experiences of childhood have been forgotten. I did not go to the examination—it came to me, to the Vladimir Palace.

When the great day came, I found myself faced by the formidable and forbidding array of my inquisitors, a board of Areopagites, with the director of the College presiding, and what made things considerably worse was that my father was in their very midst.

State examinations in Russia had a curious feature. To some degree one held the scales of one's own fate, quite independent of how much or how little one knew. It was a matter of luck. The questions were written on slips of paper which contained every conceivable conundrum which the inventive genius of the examiners could devise. They covered all the subjects, and were piled up on a table, covered, of course, with that seeming indispensable feature of all examinations—the banner of them all—the green cloth.

One could only see the blank reverse side of these slips, the other side of which contained the 'terror.'

One had to draw the tickets in this gruesome lottery, and ponder over them for a time before being admitted to the hall of judgment. My rank as a member of the Imperial Family made not the least difference to my chances of success or failure. I was treated equally with the rest, and I passed.

My joy was great, like appeasement after expectation of possible disaster.

Having acquitted myself well of this test, I was promoted to the rank of Petty Officer. There were no acrobatics of promotion for us. We all had to go through the mill with the rest, taste of their experiences and learn the lessons of the world as it presented itself to us in its natural and cold aspect.

Therein lay the wisdom of our traditions.

Before I joined my fourth and last training ship, the *Vernyi*,[1] in the summer of 1895, Uncle Alexey,[2] who was

---

[1] Staunch.　　　　[2] Brother of Alexander III.

then Grand Admiral of our fleets, decided that his young nephew should have a little fun to compensate him for his hard work.

Germany was about to celebrate the completion of the Kiel Canal.

The Russian squadron was led by Admiral Skrydlov's flagship, the *Rurik*, the latest and most up-to-date of our battleships at that time.

Hitherto I had not had an opportunity to see the Baltic proper, as all our activities on board the training ships had been confined to the narrow seas of the Gulf of Finland, between Kronstadt and Helsingfors.

It was on board the *Rurik* that I had my first impression of the open sea.

Arrived at the German Baltic Naval Base of Kiel, I took part in the procession through the canal on board the Russian gunboat *Groziashchi*. The procession of warships was led by Emperor William II on board his yacht. We were greatly impressed, not only by this amazing masterpiece of engineering skill but also by the excellent state of the German Navy. I must admit that at that time, in the late 'nineties, our fleet was in poor condition, most units being quite out of date and of no practical use whatever, but all this was to be subjected to a very thorough reorganization.

On our return to Kiel, the *Rurik* was inspected by the Kaiser, who always showed a very keen interest in all things Russian. He was a sincere friend of our country, and believed in the value of friendly relations between the two empires; a strong bond between them was always his cherished ambition.

On being informed of my presence on board, he sought me out specially. I was lined up on the immediate right of the petty officers of the *Rurik*. After he had shaken hands with the officers he came up to me, shook my hand and said some kind words. Later on I was invited to a big luncheon, a gorgeous affair indeed, at which nearly all the

German princes and many other Royal personages were present. The Kaiser drank my health. This was the first, and somewhat alarming occasion of the kind I had experienced. I got up and bowed, and was decorated then and there by the Kaiser with the Order of the Black Eagle.

The rest of this summer, which was cold and damp, we cruised on the *Vernyi* between Reval, Helsingfors and Baltic Port. There was much fog and the sea was grey and uninviting.

This monotony was interrupted by a pleasant and quite informal diversion when we lay at Baltic Port for a few days. We got up a dance with the local girls in one of the harbour sheds and amused ourselves splendidly in this easy and popular atmosphere.

Baltic Port was in the military district of St. Petersburg, and as my father was just then inspecting this particular region, he came to see me.

The term was brought to an end with a practical examination on board the *Vernyi*, where a committee of examiners, who were always on our heels, tested our knowledge, in navigation, torpedoes, and a number of other practical subjects. On the last day of the term we had a boat race, and thereon I left for good the realm of sail, which is now almost a memory of other days, in so far as the great ships are concerned.

In the autumn of the same year I paid my first more or less independent visit abroad, with my good friend and tutor, de Shaeck. We went to Switzerland, where I had my first experience of climbing mountains. We did not attempt anything out of the ordinary, but did some mild climbing. This tour was a great success, and after a thorough inspection of that remarkably attractive country, we returned to Russia, stopping a few days in Coburg, where we stayed with Uncle Alfred and Aunt Marie,[1] the Duke and Duchess of Edinburgh (later ruling Grand

---

[1] Daughter of Alexander II.

Duke of Saxe-Coburg and Gotha), my future parents-in-law.

My final examination was due in the early spring of 1896. There was the usual hard work and pre-examination feeling caused by excited nerves and by the hope of success and fear of failure. I succeeded, however, once more, and passed into the top class of the Naval College, where we were the nearest Russian equivalent to midshipmen. This entitled us to wear an anchor on the shoulder plates of our tunics. When later the Navy was reorganized an equivalent rank to midshipman was introduced, but at that period it did not exist as such.

There was yet much that would have to be learnt on board the various battleships in distant waters of other hemispheres, but that would be practical, and what made me feel relieved, delivered, and thoroughly appeased, was the knowledge that the almost unbearable humdrum of theoretical study had been left for ever behind. I suppose that at no time in life, except in very special circumstances, so much is demanded of the brain as during the period of one's early studies.

It was spring; and spring in Russia is the loveliest season of the year, for it is Nature's gradual awakening to new life.

I experienced the joy of having achieved, of having done the thing well, which comes to one after a great effort, when the brain is exhausted.

My friends who had gone through the same experience gave me a party. It was held at Sheremetieff's parental home and was a splendid occasion, made very jolly by the carefree attitude to life which had just held one in the grip of its severity. There was a choir of gypsies, an almost indispensable feature at Russian parties of those good old days.

By the time our celebration drew to a close we were well in 'our cups,' and poor Sheremetieff got into trouble later.

In the spring of that same year the late Emperor was to be crowned at Moscow. There was feverish activity in both capitals. St. Petersburg was preparing for a general exodus, and Moscow was organizing a brilliant reception.

There was a general *déménagement* in all the palaces of the members of the Imperial Family in St. Petersburg.

Uniforms were being fitted, and everything was being got ready. We were to take our own horses and carriages as well as our domestic staff.

At last, when all was ready, we left for Moscow, where the Nikolaevsky Palace within the walls of the Kremlin had been specially set aside for our family.

There we stayed during the Coronation with our parents. We had the whole palace to ourselves.

Everything in Moscow was strange to me. It was like arriving in a new country, which at the same time was still one's own. I have already given my first impression of Moscow, but now I was to see it and to get to know it intimately in all its exquisite beauties, with the guidance of Father, whose love for history made the past of that city live again.

We went over museums, saw the historical rooms of the Czars of Muscovy, the Granavitaya Palata,[1] the famous churches, and much else that breathed with the spirit of old Russia.

Moscow wore its most brilliant apparel. The streets of it and the houses were decorated, and there were special structures erected for the occasion to add to its already lavish gaiety. The whole place was like a city of fairyland.

The organization, barring one disastrous oversight, was quite unimpeachable.

On the day of the Coronation we assembled outside Moscow at the Petrovsky Palace for our entry into the

[1] A large hall in the Kremlin built in 'Muscovite Style' and used during the fifteenth, sixteenth, and seventeenth centuries for ceremonial occasions.

capital. Everyone had been allotted his special place. The procession teemed with royalties from all over Europe and the East. We mounted our horses, and the Royal ladies stepped into their gilded carriages. I was riding a grey charger, a present to my father from the Emir of Buchara. It was a high-spirited animal, not easy to manage. I remember the beautifully embroidered saddle-cloth, a veritable *chef-d'œuvre* of art. Everything on that occasion, from the very smallest detail to the highest and most sublime of them all, the climax of this unforgettable episode, was a blending of the best that art can produce with the dignified proportion of exquisite taste. The whole *ensemble* of the component parts of that ceremony was a drama acted in complete harmony with the surroundings.

The Emperor entered Moscow on a white charger, heading a brilliant cavalcade. He was followed by his uncles all in the different uniforms of their regiments, next came we and the Royal delegates from all the monarchies of Europe. There was among them a group of our Asiatic vassals, adding to the kaleidoscope of colour with the gorgeous costumes of the East.

This brilliant array of horsemen preceded a chain of golden carriages, flashing brightly in the sun of this warm spring day. The very weather, the blue sky and the sun seemed to collaborate with the effort of man to excel even Nature in a special and unique act of creation.

The line of carriages, most of which were of the period of the empresses of the eighteenth century, conveyed to the Sacring the Royal women of Europe, all of them radiant in their festive apparel. Among them were some of the greatest beauties of the time.

There was the carriage of the Empress and the one of Maria Feodorovna, always majestic, in spite of her bitter bereavement. There was another which contained the lovely daughters of the Duke and Duchess of Edinburgh,[1]

[1] Queen Marie of Roumania, the Grand Duchess Kyrill.

who were both striking beauties, and all the others who enhanced the charm of this occasion by their presence.

This procession proceeded along the streets of Moscow, among the enthusiastic cheering of the crowds that had gathered from the ends of Russia, from its colossal expanses, to witness this great event.

The climax of the great day was at hand. It took place in the Uspenski Cathedral of the Kremlin.

In spite of the fact that the Cathedral was packed with humanity, that the religious rites seemed interminable, and that one had to stand the whole time in a stifling atmosphere of heat, the general impression of the experience was altogether unique. It was a thing once and only once seen, a flash, as it were, of the beyond, only a sudden flash— and an enlightenment.

Whether it be in the smallest village church of our vast country, or even in some railway carriage eastward bound, or in the solitudes of the forests, Russian singing is a thing unique in this world, because it is almost celestial. It is a national gift and entirely original. And on this occasion a choir was gathered, composed of the finest known male voices in the whole land. The waves of harmony rose and fell, rolled and broke like the sea in tones which were scarcely of this world, vibrating throughout the length and breadth of the cathedral, filling it to its smallest recesses.

From sudden thunder it would dwindle to a still whisper. It implored, it triumphed, and it sorrowed, it conveyed an idea of the infinite, and while it lasted brought heaven down to earth.

The intricate rites of the Anointment followed each other in an uninterrupted flow of gorgeous ceremonial. The air was heavy with incense, the Cathedral resplendent with the flash of golden vestments and the sparkling of precious stones.

Upon this brilliant array of the officiating clergy, on those who were the objects of these rites and all those present, the icons looked down severely from their gold

THE AUTHOR
As young Naval Officer.

THE LATE KING GEORGE V WITH HIS COUSIN,
THE LATE EMPEROR NICHOLAS II

and silver screens, upon which the eternal lamps cast their coloured lights.

The mystery was great, and inscrutable, being in accord with the infinite.

The Coronation over, we took part in the brilliant gaieties that succeeded it. There were great balls, great gatherings of the cream of European Society, of royalty, and the representatives of the Great Powers. We had our first impression of the night life of the city, its cabarets and brilliant shows.

It was as though the past and the present had combined in a last great effort of joy before the gloom was to fall upon them. It was like the last great flare-up of a candle before it was to be extinguished.

The foreign princes who had come to Moscow provided us with much scope for merriment and pleasant buffoonery.

There was one of them, for example, who, after a very gay night, complained to me that he was "Alas, unable to make the best of the good time owing to the beastly education his grandfather had given him."

There was another, too, a Siamese prince, who became the butt of our friendly teasing.

The music, the singing, the dances, and all the charming women there, the great dinners at the palaces of the Moscow nobility, the very cream of Russia's ancient families, and of the merchant patriciate, the jolly, carefree hours of late nights, and many gallantries, too, all this has remained an unforgettable episode.

England was represented by the Duke of Connaught, a delegate of Her Majesty the Queen, and the Royal Family by the Duke and Duchess of Edinburgh, who had with them their daughters and their son, Cousin Alfred.

Of all the Royal beauties the daughters[1] of the Duke of Edinburgh were among the most radiant.

I was included in the list of Coronation honours, and

[1] The Crown Princess Marie of Roumania, Grand Duchess Victoria of Hesse and Princess Beatrice of Cobourg.

was to be promoted to the rank of sub-lieutenant of the Imperial Navy, to which the passing of the final examination entitled me. I was given a year's seniority over my contemporaries in the Navy, but before I received my first commission I had to go through a somewhat grim proceeding.

When members of the Imperial Family received commissions in the services, they had to take two oaths to the Emperor, the first was the oath of members of the Imperial Family, and the other was the ordinary service oath.

This ceremony took place at the Tchoudov monastery within the Kremlin, in the presence of the Emperor, his Court, and foreign royalties. I stood under the standard of the Corps of Naval Guards, which was held by a petty officer, with a naval officer on my right.

When the great festive gathering had dispersed, and things once more resumed their natural routine, I accompanied my father to the fair of Nijniy Novgorod, Russia's great emporium on the upper reaches of the Volga.

Nijniy Novgorod, which means the Lower Novgorod, succeeded its more historical namesake, the mediæval City Republic of Novgorod the Great as a place of great commercial importance. The power of Novgorod the Great was broken by Ivan IV, 'The Terrible,' who also put an end to the flourishing Oriental trade of Kazan, the Tartar city on the Volga, then Europe's most northerly outpost of Islam. Their monopoly of trade passed to Nijniy Novgorod. This famous town had also the distinction of having been the birthplace of Minin, the Russian national hero, who, in the chaotic period of the interregnum during the early part of the seventeenth century, had been among those who led a national rising against the Polish invasion.

It has often been maintained that Russia knew no middle class. This is an erroneous assumption. The middle class of the country were the merchants, from the small shopkeepers to the great merchant dynasties.

When on this visit I first came into contact with our

merchants, who entertained us lavishly both here and in Moscow. They were a highly cultured and thoroughly European lot. I remember especially Sava Morozoff in Moscow, a member of that famous trading family.

These merchants of Nijniy Novgorod gave us an excellent time, which often resulted in a feeling of ' the morning after the night before.' After this visit we returned to Tsarskoe Selo.

It was my father's wish that I should also experience the duties of an Army officer. Thus during the summer of 1896 I joined the Infantry Regiment of the Imperial Family's Own Rifles, as an infantry officer. While I was in camp at Krasnoe, the Russian Aldershot, I was allotted a small timber-built house for my quarters—each officer had one to himself—of the same pattern as the ones which we had occupied with mother when we were quite small, during our visit to the military camp at Tsarskoe in the 'eighties.

During this camp season at Krasnoe I remember especially the splendid performances by the actors from the Imperial Theatre. These people lived their parts, and there was not the least trace of artificiality in their acting. In theatre technique Russians are unrivalled, as, I believe, the actors are unaware that they are doing anything unnatural; they live their parts, whatever these may be, and hence succeed in bringing real life to the stage.

There were comedies and ballets, with short ballet turns at the end of the performances.

So as to finish my education with an impression of the artistic beauties of Europe, my father decided that I should go to Italy. Thus, in the autumn of 1896, to conclude that year, which had been so full of splendid impressions, my friends Misha Cantakouzene and Ushakoff accompanied me on my Italian tour, during which we visited everything that was worth seeing there from the Lakes in the North to Sicily. We took our time, and had a very thorough impression of that country.

The winter season of 1896 was one of the most brilliant

that could be imagined. The young Imperial couple entertained much, and there was an uninterrupted succession of balls and parties.

It was during this winter of 1896 that I started my service with the Naval Guards by joining Her Majesty's first Company. I remained with them for twenty years—until the Revolution—and in 1916 was appointed their commander by the late Emperor.

III

Eastward Bound

In the early spring of 1897 I went to Cannes with my brother Boris.

I have special reason to mention this visit to the South of France, because it was on this occasion that I met Queen Victoria for the first time. She was staying at the famous Hôtel Cimiez in Nice.

We called on Uncle Alfred, the Duke of Edinburgh, at his Château Fabron, and on his suggestion we accompanied him to be introduced to the old Queen. Uncle Alfred, incidentally, was very proud of his Russian relations, and liked them to meet members of the English Royal Family. We lunched with Queen Victoria, whom we found very amiable. She made a very favourable impression upon me—there was something quite distinctive about her, which only a strong personality can convey on the first acquaintance. I believe that Princess Beatrice of Battenberg was one of those who took part at that luncheon, and there was, of course, her indispensable Indian servant. More than this very general picture of that first meeting has not remained in my memory.

On my return to Russia I joined the *Rossya*.[1] She had been just commissioned, but was not yet out of the hands of engineers and workmen. My appointment to this latest

---

[1] Russia.

addition to our Navy was most welcome, as she was not only brand-new but a complete novelty in marine engineering at that time.

She had been built in our shipyards by Russian engineers, and was the prototype of many famous ships in Russia and abroad which were improvements of her type. Moreover, it was on the *Rossya* that I was to have my first experiences as naval officer.

Her special features, the ones which made her at that time unique and the first of her kind, were her long range of action, her heavy armaments and speed, all ingeniously combined. In every way she was a masterpiece of skill.

As the units of the Russian Navy were stationed at immense distances from each other, from the Baltic to the Pacific Ocean, and in the Black Sea, long-range ships were essential to us; that was the object of her designers, who had provided her with unusually large bunkers. These bunkers, however, in no way interfered with the other features of the ship, nor did they disturb or affect her general purpose and utility. And in this lay the secret of her success.

She was armed, moreover, with 8-inch and 6-inch guns, and had two excellent engines of the reciprocating pattern and boilers of the Belle-Ville type. In addition she carried a smaller auxiliary engine, which was of little use to us, apart from providing us with much fun in the mess. It was jocularly suggested that this 'appendix' should be removed, and its vacant space made into a swimming-pool. On board a man-of-war every inch is valuable, and for that reason this auxiliary engine was later on dispensed with. The *Rossya's* comforts were great. We were, I believe, the first man-of-war to carry a meat refrigerator and an apparatus for making ice. Apart from this, we had our bakery, which supplied us with fresh bread every morning.

The *Rossya* made a great impression in the world, and I believe that the *Terrible* and *Powerful* were Great Britain's reply to her.

There was an unholy din from morning till night on her decks and in her innermost parts. A constant hammering, clattering, and banging, amplified by the rattling of pneumatic drills and the clatter and thuds of steel against steel, gave one the impression that a legion of devils had been let loose on her. There were painters, engineers, and workmen running and bustling each other—an impossible noise and feverish activity! They were in a hurry to put the last touches to her, as she was to be our emissary to the Queen's Diamond Jubilee. We were new to her and to each other, everything was new, and it took some time to get used to this environment. Her captain, whom I will have occasion to mention later, had chosen his officers and crew from among the very best elements of our fleet.

At last all was ready and we left on our maiden voyage, our mission to England. After an uneventful passage by way of Jutland, we put in at Devonport to receive a new coat of paint to make us spick and span for the Spithead review.

A few days after our arrival, I left for London, where I stayed during the Jubilee celebrations with Uncle Alfred and Aunt Marie at Clarence House. They had with them their daughter Victoria Melita, then Grand Duchess of Hesse, who was to become my future wife, their son, Cousin Alfred, and my uncle the Grand Duke Serge[1] and his beautiful wife, the Grand Duchess Elizabeth, sister of the late Empress. I occupied rooms on the same floor as Cousin Alfred, and remember performing to him on a very ancient piano which he had in his drawing-room, for we both had musical tastes.

The Jubilee procession to St. Paul's impressed me as a magnificent affair; it reminded me not a little of our Coronation at Moscow, although it was, possibly, even on a larger scale.

[1] Brother of Alexander III.

There was the usual great concourse of foreign royalty all in their special and brilliant uniforms, to which the exotic dress of the Indian princes lent an air of pleasing variety; all this, together with the magnificent line of carriages and the mounted escorts, was a picture representing the glories of Britain at the time of her great splendour.

The weather, too, was perfectly suited for this great occasion. The crowds were immense—millions of them lined the route along which this brilliant array pursued its course to the City. The cheers of those crowds were overwhelming—they resounded like thunder.

I would have enjoyed the occasion considerably more had it not been for a very violent attack of hay fever, an evil to which I have always been prone. It made things difficult for me, as I had to guide my horse with one hand and hold my handkerchief with the other.

The late King Edward VII, then Prince of Wales, led this cavalcade.

Jubilee Day was succeeded by a continuous series of parties and balls. I found the great Court balls at Buckingham Palace a little tedious and somewhat too pompous, but I will always remember them for one thing which made them outstanding. There was the *élite* of English beauties there, the names of only a few of whom I now remember. There was the Duchess of Sutherland, with whom I danced—she was my senior in years, but I was struck by her magnificent appearance—and the ladies Dudley and de Gray, all thoroughly representative of the just reputation for beauty with which British women are endowed.

All these and many of the others whom I saw on these brilliant occasions, the flower of Society and of the late 'nineties, made an unforgettable impression on me. I danced a great deal and amused myself excellently at all these official and unofficial social functions.

When the time came for foreign royalty to be presented to the Queen, I was led up to her by Uncle Alfred, who said,

"May I present to you my young nephew, who is on a Russian battleship." The Queen said a few kind words, and I remember that I had to stoop very low, as she was seated on a low chair and was so very small. Once again, I left with the impression that this little woman had something very distinctive about her—a very definite and striking personality.

During this visit to England, which was my first, I did not see much of either London or the country, except that I went to Ascot with the Royal Family. The various and uninterrupted social functions absorbed all my time.

There was yet much to be done on board the *Rossya* before she could be put into proper condition for her trial voyage to Far Eastern waters, where our Admiralty intended her to proceed later on during the course of the same summer.

When we fetched up with the shores of Holland we got into a dense fog. There was very poor visibility, and we might have been in the very midst of some mountain of cotton wool; that was the impression it gave. The fog stuck to us obstinately, covering and penetrating everything with its clammy dampness. We were proceeding, however, on our course in spite of it, but dead slow, when all of a sudden, as if from somewhere in space, there was the sound of splintering wood. That we had struck something was obvious, but what, precisely, was impossible to say. The noise vanished as suddenly as it had come upon us, into the cotton-wool atmosphere. We had reversed our engines and then dropped anchor. There was nothing but the stillness of fog and a sea the presence of which had to be presumed, as it could not be seen. The whole impression was one of floating in mid-air.

When at last the fog lifted, we called at the nearest port to find out whether we had run anything aground, and if so, what?—This port was Weymuiden, and I presume that the harbour authorities were strangely surprised, if not alarmed, to behold a great battleship of Russian nationality coming upon them quite unexpectedly, out of the blue, as it were. Soon, also, our victim put in with broken masts and spars, but with no loss of life.

The rest of our voyage home passed without any incidents, and the *Rossya* behaved splendidly in every way. She proved a great success and worthy of the skill of the Russian engineers who had built and designed her. Her successors, of the *Gromoboy* type, were even better. They were fine and proud ships.

Arrived at Kronstadt, there remained much to be done. There were the usual overhauls and adjustments; ammunitions and stores were being loaded, and all this took some time. We had to acquaint ourselves with every detail that concerned us. It is extraordinary how much of every conceivable thing such a great vessel needs for a long voyage. While loading up, she reminds one of a veritable Noah's Ark, taking on board her all manner of things, from shells to soap, and from coal to potatoes.

The night before we were due to put out to sea my friend Kube and I paid our farewell calls in the capital. It was a merry night, filled with the expectations of the unknown, with the glamour that youth alone can give before the setting out on a venture to strange latitudes, to the seas of the East on a voyage of many thousand miles!

We caught the last train to Oranienbaum, and from there took a small steamer to Kronstadt.

The next day we cast off and sailed for the Pacific and the Far East.

Portsmouth was our first port of call; there we remained for about ten days. We received official visits from a number of British admirals and senior officers of the Royal Navy, and were entertained by them in their mess on shore, where I had my first taste of whisky.

We must have been an attraction to the public whom we admitted on board during certain hours, and I wonder whether they considered us in the same light as did the

British Admiral who commanded the joint British and Russian squadron which destroyed the Turkish fleet at Navarino. He is reported to have said on one occasion, when a dispute had arisen between him and our Admiral over going to sea on a Monday: "The Russians are an uncouth and barbarous people, they are superstitious and backward, they refuse to go to sea on a Monday, when every sailor knows that Friday is the unlucky day!"

While we lay at Portsmouth, I received shore leave and availed myself of this opportunity to pay a visit to Uncle Alfred in London. I stayed with him only one day and then rushed over to Paris, where my parents were at the time. My father was a very frequent visitor to France, where he was better known than any other member of the Imperial Family, and, possibly, even more so than any other foreign Royal personage. He was an associate of many of the most exclusive societies in that country.

I spent a few days with my parents in Paris, and looked up a number of my friends, and then returned to join my ship.

We next proceeded to Vigo, that very dismal and uninviting coaling station on the north-western extremity of Spain.

The British Atlantic Fleet was there with Prince Louis Battenberg on board the flagship *Royal Sovereign*, I believe, although, at this distance of time, I cannot be quite certain. He was her flag-captain then, and I accompanied our captain to call on him. He apologized to us quite unnecessarily for receiving us in a rough get-up, as *Royal Sovereign*, together with the rest of the fleet, was coaling at the time. He wore sea boots, had a muffler wound round his neck, and was dressed in an old uniform. I remember that he turned to us and said: "I am sorry to be receiving you in such a fearful mess, but you can see for yourselves, we are coaling."

I was greatly struck by this distinguished and very handsome sailor, of whom I had heard it said that he was later generally considered to be the best and most able officer in the Royal Navy. He combined the most typical characteristics of an English gentleman with the thoroughness of a German. Later I heard from my mother that our good impressions of each other had been mutual. It appeared that he wrote a letter to her in which he said that I had made a very good impression on him, and much else in my favour.

We did not go on shore for two reasons, nor were the crews allowed to do so either. We had been warned by the harbour people that the place was diseased, and, secondly, we did not want our men to meet any of the British crews, as such meetings are apt, in such a small port as Vigo, to result in 'free fights' and broken bones over the *señoritas*.

The monotony of the coaling operations, which did not take long, was pleasantly interrupted by a number of visits by the British officers to our mess.

When we put out from Vigo we were glad to see it recede in the distance of that sombre and savage coast. We directed our course due south.

When we drew close to the African coast, near Algiers, I had that curious experience which comes to those who for the first time meet the East. It came upon us suddenly like a faint puff of wind laden with the aroma of spices, pleasingly odorous and very sweet to smell. Algiers, where we called, appeared to me to be in no way different from any of the seaside towns of southern France, and yet, in this spice-laden breath, there was a world of difference, that very abyss which lies unbridgeable between the East and the West. Two worlds, indeed, that are for ever apart, in spite of an exterior appearance of resemblance.

Thence, we put our course on Malta, the Melita of the ancients, and the birthplace of my future wife, whose second Christian name, Melita, was derived from that island.

What a sequence of historical prodigies it had experienced! It enclosed within its limited confines the marvels of prehistory, the work of Phœnicians, Greeks, and

Romans, it had witnessed the contest between the knights of Malta and the tawny Corsairs of the Barbary Coasts. English and French had fought over its coveted possession. I understood all this well when I saw its magnificent harbour, an impregnable place, forsooth, made so by very Nature. Whether it is still so very safe in these days of aircraft I know not.

While at Malta, we had a very gay time with the officers of the Mediterranean squadron. We visited each other and went to the opera and dances. I remember that we were greatly struck by the excellent and smart evening kit of British naval and military men, and by the elegant dresses which their ladies wore at social functions. We had nothing of the kind in our navy, no mess jackets at all, and must have appeared a pretty poor lot to them.

A compatriot of ours, a Mme Rylova, was performing at the opera. She played the leading part in *Aida*.

We stayed from five to six days at Malta, and on an occasion during this period the British Admiral in command of the Mediterranean squadron paid us an official visit.

Our captain was in need of some naval stores, I think it was paint, and asked the Admiral whether he could provide us with some of this. He proved most affable and kind and gave us all we wanted.

On this occasion I witnessed a phenomenon of Nature which struck me then as very odd indeed. Later on, when I was in the Caucasus, I was to have a similar experience, but then I had never seen anything of the kind before.

I had just stepped on board one of our steam-launches and we were proceeding on our way to the *Rossya*, expecting no evil whatever, especially not one from the sea, vicious element though it be, when all of a sudden a strong wind blew upon us, violently and in gusts, as though from nowhere, but actually, as I discovered later, from the shore. The impression was that it had been let loose upon us specially, by some malignant spirit of the place, to impede our progress. The sea in the harbour became dangerous and we reached safety only with considerable difficulty.

It was so sudden and unexpected that it seemed quite uncanny, seemingly lacking all cause, as the sky was perfectly serene all the time. Later, my surprise concerning this strange prodigy of Nature was dispelled, when I was told that it was quite a usual occurrence in Malta, but I have not been able to discover to this day the causes of this strange outburst. I am not in the least surprised that the Apostle St. Paul suffered shipwreck on the coasts of this strange island.

In those days we had a part of our fleet stationed in the Mediterranean, where it was based on Crete and Greece. There we proceeded on leaving Malta.

We met with our ships at Crete and were inspected by the Admiral in Suda Bay. The *Rossya*, as I have already pointed out, was the most modern unit in the Russian Navy, and for that reason presented an object of special interest to the Admiral and to the rest of the squadron.

Queen Olga of Greece was the daughter of my great-uncle Constantin, Grandpapa's brother, who, as already mentioned, had been the High Admiral of our fleet. As an Admiral's daughter, Aunt Olga took the keenest interest in everything that concerned our ships, and whenever one of these hove in sight off the coasts of Greece she hurried to meet it like another Iphigenia in exile.

She was, indeed, like another Iphigenia, having left her native country for a strange land at the age of sixteen, and Russia had remained to her the ideal of her life. She patronized our sailors and was like a mother to them. She would have them at her palace at Athens, where she chatted with them for hours, while her old Russian maid served tea, providing them with all manner of good things to take back on board ship.

Soon after our arrival at the Piræus she came on board

accompanied by her sons. She did not confine herself to one visit, but came frequently, and would stay so long that we were at a loss to know what to do. Our ships were the only link with Russia which Queen Olga had.

I paid a visit to Athens and its Acropolis, and found the latter in very pleasant contrast to the town which it dominates as the sad and aged witness of the glory that was Hellas. Athens, on that visit, struck me as a disorderly, ill-kept, and pretentious place, quite unworthy of the name it bore. All this, however, has changed since. The country, on the other hand, gave me the very best impression with its pleasant and wooded aspect.

I called on my relatives at the Royal country residence of Tatoy; it was a jolly place, and in its surroundings more in tune with all that Greece stands for.

Peterhof has some grounds which were known as 'Alexandria'; they contained 'The Cottage,' where Uncle Sasha liked to stay. Passionately clinging to the reminiscences of her childhood, Aunt Olga had an exact replica of it erected in the grounds of Tatoy.

We had an excellent band on board, and decided to give a ball for the Royal Family and the members of Greek Society. It proved a greater success than we had anticipated. We became the lions of the place and left the Piræus regretted by all.

Through the waters of the Aegean, past the isles of Greece, famed in legend and great names in history, we ploughed our way towards prosaic Port Said and the Canal.

We spent a few days at Port Said, which gave me an opportunity to pay a hurried visit to Cairo and the pyramids of Giza. The climbing of the great pyramid proved a somewhat exhausting effort in the heat. I even penetrated into its uncanny interior. Did it contain some esoteric mysteries known to its builders, or only the dry conclusions of mathematics?—I know not. However, there they stand, and are far more of a riddle than the famous Sphinx—a personification of the duality of man, half man and half beast. The passage of time has sealed the *raison d'être* of these expressions in stone of more than human genius.

I had little time then to see much else of what this strange land contained, for we had to keep our watches.

The displacement of the *Rossya* was twelve thousand tons, a mere trifle, when compared to modern battleships, but in those days she was considered a great vessel of her kind, and it required much skill on the part of the pilot and ourselves to see her safely through the Canal. I believe, although I am not certain, that she may have been the largest ship at that period to pass through the Canal. We proceeded along under our own steam, and all went very smoothly indeed.

Our hull was painted black, and those unfortunates who had their quarters on the starboard side were being roasted by the merciless glare of the sun.

Soon the tropics came upon us with their usual features of phenomenal heat, sudden darkness that dropped upon one like a screen of inky blackness after sunsets of great splendour, and the night skies with the multitudes of stars, all very clear and resplendent in the awe-inspiring vastness of space. Those skies were more eloquent of the endlessness of things than anything else in Nature.

And then there were the usual emissaries of the tropical seas, the flying-fish, which for some quite unfathomable reason made for the portholes, and might be found flopping and beating about on one's writing-desk.

We called at Aden for coaling. A parched and deadly place, it struck me as one which required real valour to live in it—an inferno of heat. I remember that I went on shore to see the water reservoirs.

Down the Indian Ocean we went, past Ceylon, on our way to Singapore, where we remained for a few days.

Kube and I went ashore to see some of the night life. As an experience of the East it was worth while. But it was of a dubious nature—to the full extent of that word, even when applied to the ports of the East. The place itself is excellently planned, and makes a favourable impression as a tropical town; moreover, it struck me as being splendidly suited for a naval base.

Wherever one went a spicy odour of burning wood pursued one. This, too, was one of my first impressions of the Tropics.

Our Russian Consul took us to the mainland, to Johore, where I had my first taste of Indian curry, which I liked.

Whether we touched Hong Kong on our way or not I do not now recollect; we may have done so, but I remember little of it now.

Our course lay to Port Arthur.

It would be appropriate at this juncture to mention what led to our occupation of Port Arthur as well as some of the causes of the unfortunate friction between Russia and Japan, in which I took part in the capacity of mediator, as I will have occasion to mention later.

China had been for some time in a state of disintegration, and the Powers were quick in seizing this opportunity to take advantage of the situation.

Japan had been watching these doings uneasily, and was determined that, whatever happened, she would not allow herself to become a pawn in the hands of the Powers in their game for supremacy in the Far East, nor to fall under their domination as China had done.

She set to work feverishly to prepare herself to meet the growing danger which threatened her, too, by adapting herself to those standards of the Western World which had enabled the Powers to establish their influence so easily over the Celestial Empire.

With immense foresight, and leaving nothing to chance, she pursued systematically the process of assimilation. Her statesmen knew perfectly well that it was not enough to content oneself simply with building up one's dykes against the rising tide from the West, and hiding behind them, but that the best way of defence was one of aggressive tactics.

She anticipated the others by going to war with China, and, by a brilliant campaign, pursued with clocklike accuracy, she baffled the Powers, with whom she now put herself on par in her influence in Chinese affairs.

Japan did not content herself with that victory, but pursued her path along the ambitious course which she had planned for herself, a course which she deemed would finally lead her to become a great force in the Far East. That was her goal.

In the execution of this ambitious scheme Japan was bound to come into collision with the Powers sooner or later, and the first of these was Russia. Russia, too, had a Far Eastern policy of an ambitious kind. Her steady and advancing expansion to the East, which had begun in the sixteenth century, had never ceased. It was a spontaneous and quite natural movement, and this fact, together with her geographical features, made her naturally into a dual power of European and Asiatic greatness.

The linking of our Far East with European Russia through the Siberian Railway, our naval base at Vladivostok, our growing interest in Manchuria, all this led to a state of nervous anxiety in Japan, which reached a climax over Korea in the late nineties of last century. Our Korean policy left much to be desired. It was clumsy in the extreme and defeated its own purpose by giving rise to a series of very regrettable incidents of a most provoking nature, which finally led to the war of 1904–1905.

Vladivostok is icebound during some winter months, and as we were beginning to extend our influence over Manchuria it was considered necessary to find a more suitable naval base nearer to our new field of activity.

In the choice of such a port great care had to be taken not to accentuate the already charged atmosphere of animosity and impatience in Japan.

There is an ideal harbour on the coasts of Korea. This is Masampo, the naturally protected anchorage which could hold the fleets of the world, and the small islands which surround it make it excellently suited as an impregnable naval base. Korea, however, then an empire in nothing but name, had for a long time been Japan's sphere of influence, and as Masampo controlled Japanese waters, the occupation of it by us would have led then and there to a war with Japan, for which we were in no way prepared.

For this reason, as well as to counter Germany's move in her occupation of Weihaiwei, Port Arthur was chosen. But this served to assuage the fears of Japan only for a very short time, and in any case wounded her self-respect, for Port Arthur had been won by her from China in 1894. The Powers, with Russia among them, forced Japan to return this place to China, the latter ceding it to us. This transaction was unwise, to say the least, for it provoked Japan.

It follows from this account that the relations between the two Far Eastern powers were strained to a dangerous degree at the time when the *Rossya* arrived outside Port Arthur. It was this situation which later on led to my official visit to Emperor Mutsu Hito.

In the early spring of 1898 we anchored outside Port Arthur. At that time it was nothing but a place on the map of the world which had created a short-lived stir on the political horizon. It was a cluster of bleak, stony hills, with no grass, no trees, not even a harbour except at high tide—nothing!—It was the most dismal and forbidding place which I had ever seen!—It seemed as though very Nature had designed it in order that millions should be spent on it, and thousands should die on its dismal slopes, in a deadly and gruesome contest fought against its parched background.

Admiral Dubasov had found it utterly unsuitable for a Russian naval base. At low tide the inner harbour was empty of water—a waste of grey sand. Ships had to be anchored in the open, where they were deprived of all natural protection, and became easy targets to any potential enemy.

He had reported all this to the authorities in Europe, but his warning had fallen unheeded on deaf ears. They insisted on Port Arthur, although there were many spots on the coast far better suited for a naval base—all to no avail. It had to be Port Arthur, and we occupied it. I myself, accompanied by the appropriate ceremonies, hoisted the flag of St. Andrew on its highest summit after the dragon flag of China had been hauled down.

It was a bleak and bitterly cold day with an icy wind, quite in tune with the surroundings.

The Chinese Governor ceded it to us on behalf of his Government, or as Li Hung Chang, the great Chinese Premier put it, it was leased to us for a long term of tenancy, 'to save face,' as the Chinese have it.

The Governor, a mandarin, was a true gentleman, whose speech was translated to us, as were ours to him, by Kollisev, our expert interpreter from our mission in Peking, who spoke fluent Mandarin Chinese. This ceremony of handing over had been preceded by a gala luncheon on board the flagship of a detachment of our Pacific fleet. China was represented by a small cruiser.

Two weeks were spent at Port Arthur in fleet exercises and various necessary activities, and when finally, bound for Japan, we saw it receding quickly astern, I was not in the least sorry.

Nagasaki was my first impression of Japan, and an excellent one, too, especially after that deadly place Port Arthur.

The bay is sprinkled with tiny islands. They are rotund and rocky, overflowing as it were with vegetation and covered with pine woods, among which, every now and then, a tiny shrine can be seen, often nothing more than a place for burning incense.

Everything seemed small to me, like a toyland, a place from the pages of a fairy-tale, with small men and women, small animals, little houses and temples, all exquisitely neat and clean. This was, of course, before the modern god of 'progress' and 'enlightenment' had sprawled all over the world, making it ugly, discontented, and more rapacious than ever. There was harmony there and it was pleasant to behold, because the work of man was so perfectly adjusted to these pleasant natural surroundings. Japan struck me as a charming place with friendly, cultured, and polite people.

The town of Nagasaki was not, possibly, very typical of the country, in so far as Japanese towns are concerned—not at that time, at any rate. It had been strongly influenced by Russia, and more resembled one of our Far Eastern settlements. There were Russian restaurants, tea rooms, and houses. Even the 'geishas' who served us spoke Russian. There were pictures of our men of war on the walls. These were relics of the times when the two countries had been on normal friendly relations, although even then there was not the least sign of hostility to be noticed.

And when the dusk of night came the little gay paper lamps would be lit and, with the little houses on the shore, the whole was a picture of great contentment and peace.

There were no fights or excitement on shore, no perturbance, and no noise. Sampans would come noiselessly alongside, gliding fast over the water with the forward stroke of their nimble oarsmen.

The sampans were useful, as we could dispense with our boats to a certain extent. They were clean, moreover, everything was clean and tidy, and had little deck-houses aft, where one was protected from wind and rain.

To remind their clients of their existence, tea-houses would send their emissaries with the typical yellow cakes of the country—a custom as charming as it was practical.

In great contrast to this land of miniatures stood the vastness of Siberia, a glimpse of the unfathomable depth of which I was fortunate to have next, when we left Nagasaki and took course for Vladivostok.

Vladivostok, in absolute contrast to Port Arthur, is one of the world's most perfectly suited spots for a naval base. It possesses an immense inner harbour, where many fleets could find anchorage together. It is a natural stronghold, protected on all sides, towards the sea as well as towards the land, by hills, and its narrow entrance is guarded by a number of islands.

At that time it was nothing but a very primitive outpost of Russia on the Pacific coast. It had no fortifications of any kind, dry docks, workshops, coal, stores for ships—absolutely nothing at all except its great future possibilities and the immense natural resources that its vast hinterland contained. This, without any exaggeration, is a continent in itself, stretching away as it does to the confines of North America, of which it has the natural features.

When I visited a tiny section of this enormous territory it had scarcely been as much as scratched by explorers. It lay there, vast and imposing, dark in the gloom of its primeval forests, and silent with the silence of first creation. It was virgin land then, and probably much of it still is a land of mystery.

As Vladivostok contained none of the things we needed, not even the most essential of all to ships of those times—coal; everything, from a belaying-pin to a ship's anchor, and from rivets to boiler tubes, had to be got through the agency of the Jew, Baron Günzburg. The latter had all these things; everyone knew of him in the Far East. He was one of the only representatives of the outer world which lay outside these regions. He had his agencies and stores all down the China coast and in Japan. If a ship had fouled and damaged a propeller, or a cylinder was leaky, or if one wanted to be sure that one's letters would reach their destination safely, the Jew Günzburg would do it. One had simply to lodge one's order with his agents and everything would be promptly and unfailingly delivered. He was a boon to us, an indispensable institution on whom the whole of our fleet in the Pacific depended, until our authorities provided us with dry docks, wharfs, and all the rest.

Vladivostok at that time was primitive to say the least. Its streets were unpaved, its footpaths made of wooden planks, many of which had rotted away leaving gaping holes. In autumn its streets presented a dismal aspect of quagmires, where such vehicles as plied along them sank up to their axles in liquid mud. It was untidy, sprawling, and planless. It had, however, one hotel of a primitive 'Wild West' kind, two schools, and a music-hall. But all this was long ago, and was a stage in its development. The closest general resemblance, as much else, indeed, in this country, is to Northern Canada, in its pioneering days. A regiment was stationed there to protect it—from the wilderness and robbers, and, in spite of this rough atmosphere, it boasted an excellent officers' mess with a good up-to-date library.

When, now forty years ago, I visited Vladivostok there were still some people of the early pioneering period alive, and the town contained among its population an interesting and very special class of people in its Siberian merchants. They traded with Japan in the wealth of the country. There was old Lindholm, for example, a Swede, of whom it was said that he had 'traded generally' upon the seas—in other words, that he had been a pirate. Vladivostok had, indeed, been in its early days a place of buccaneers who had made the seas unsafe. They were the last European sea-rovers of their kind. Old Lindholm had two pretty daughters—Tully and Lully they were called, and with them the whole fleet flirted.

There was another interesting specimen—the merchant Starzev, and others, too, whom I now no longer remember. We visited them often. They had gone through much, had seen much, and had let others feel their power. The only great drawback which this ideally suited harbour of

Vladivostok has are two of nature's visitations. The port is icebound during a few months of the winter, as already mentioned, when it blockades itself, and during the summer it is frequently subject to heavy fogs of the London kind. They are laden with dampness and penetrate everything with their dripping shrouds. They come suddenly upon one, and when caught by them on shore the ships in the harbour vanish from sight, only their bells give one an indication of their whereabouts. These fogs are caused by the polar and southern currents meeting in a manner similar to the ones off the coasts of Labrador and Newfoundland. On such occasions, we had to get back to our ships 'by guess and by God.'

The arrival of the *Rossya* at Vladivostok very nearly coincided with the completion of the last link in the immense chain of the Trans-Siberian Railway. The last stretch which linked Vladivostok to European Russia, to Moscow and St. Petersburg and all Europe, had been nearly finished by the construction of the Chabarovsk-Vladivostok line, and was known as the Ussuri Railway.

General Grodekov, who was commanding at the military post of Chabarovsk, played an important part in such developments as were being made in those immense regions. He proved a capable and efficient administrator as the Governor-General of the Ussuri Territory.

He asked me whether I would do him the favour of paying an official visit to Chabarovsk and of inspecting the railway. I was only too glad to accept this proposal, and set off in the company of some officers into this *terra incognita*.

We went to Chabarovsk by train, or at least tried to do so. The rails had just been laid and parts of the line were not yet sufficiently strong to carry the locomotive and the few carriages attached to it. When this was the case, the journey had to be continued on a trolley. They were still hard at work everywhere, putting the finishing touches to the line. The Ussuri territory came upon me with the whole of its unexplored immensity. Everything there was on a vast scale, its forests and giant trees, its lakes and rivers, the very mineral resources which its mountains and rocks contained. Everything was to be found there: gold, silver, rock crystal, coal, and precious stones of all kinds. The forests were teeming with game and the waters with fish. There were the long-haired Siberian tigers, bears, deer of all kinds, and boars, as well as the smaller creatures of the ermine and weazel race, and beavers, the furs of all of which are world famous. They abound, moreover, with multitudes of strange birds.

All this and more, the great, sombre forests untrodden by man and in the silence of their primeval nature contained within their unsurveyed depths. This region knows no frontiers. It stretches away from the Pacific to the uttermost north, to the polar wastes, and to the Bering Strait. There is the whole of volcanic Kamchatka with its fabulous wealth in gold, with its hot mineral springs and untouched resources, inhabited only by the creatures of the wilderness and by a few tribes of Red Indian origin. It is a veritable El Dorado of the north. These endless forests are sombre and forbidding and very ominous in their silence. Puny we seemed, as did our work, in comparison with what lay around us. Our great northern forests of European Russia are dwarfed by the gigantic proportion of these trees. The only comparison I can find is with Canada and Northern California, but here it was almost completely untouched.

And what struck me as more than extraordinary was that our naval base of Vladivostok, a town which had been founded in the sixties of last century and had had thirty years to acquaint itself, even if only slightly, with its immediate hinterland, had never as much as attempted to supply itself with coal. And there was coal in plenty on the very surface of the earth. It protruded in seams in the railway cuttings, one only needed to scoop it into trucks, and yet coal had to be imported—from Cardiff, when it was on the very threshold, in the wilderness that lay around.

Arrived at Chabarovsk after these amazing impressions, I was made the centre of social activities there. There were official presentations in the Governor's Palace, which had been put at my disposal; uniforms, banquets, speeches, and receptions, and social functions of many kinds, all very well done, in spite of the great waste around this settlement.

I was struck by the efficiency with which these social functions had been arranged, and by their brilliance. There was, for example, a military band which was quite as good as that of any of our Guard Regiments in St. Petersburg. They played a piece from Wagner, as though they had been accustomed to play him all their lives. And yet these were rough men, completely isolated from civilization in the very bowels of the wilderness.

Whether in harsh exile and poverty, scattered in their bitter diaspora throughout the length and breadth of the world, or in these lonely outposts of Siberia, Russians always contrive to create around them, on occasions, an atmosphere of pleasing social gaiety.

The celebrations in my honour terminated with a shooting expedition in the forests, where we resembled tiny beetles attempting to crawl into a great haystack—that was my impression. We boarded a comfortable steamer, belonging to the Ministry of Ways and Communications and steamed up the great Amur River. After a number of days, we reached the great Hanka Lake, where we got into boats and were rowed across to the place where a shoot had been arranged for me. Our beaters were all soldiers belonging to the Siberian Rifle Regiment, and were all born shots. The shoot had been poorly organized. I saw some fine game on this occasion, but most of it was small. One of the soldiers had been placed behind me for my protection; one never could tell what might come upon one out of the depths of that darkness, it might be anything from a tiger to a boar. Nothing, however, troubled me, except the general impression of still immensity.

During this expedition, General Grodekov showed me some natives of this region. They were the 'Golds,' a people of Mongolian origin, who live by trapping in the forests, and I was treated to a tribal dance, a most primitive and ritualistic affair, weird and uncanny, made even more so against the mysterious background of the forest.

I asked the Governor-General how I could express my pleasure to the Chief, and was told that he would appreciate nothing more than the gift of a modern rifle, as this is an essential tool in the daily struggle for existence of these children of nature. We used army rifles for the shoot, and I presented the Chief with a brand new one. He was immensely pleased.

On crossing Lake Hanka I was amazed by its wealth in fish.

A part of the early summer I remained at Vladivostok and had ample opportunity to get to know it and its immediate surroundings.

The town, though ill-equipped with some of the more essential things, contained a Sports Club which organized a number of expeditions to shoot stags on the outlying islands. They are very pretty creatures, beautifully spotted and small. The antlers of the young stags are greatly prized by the Chinese, who prepare an aphrodisiac from them which they sell for fabulous sums.

I greatly regret that I had no time to see at least a little of the immense and untouched regions to the north of Vladivostok with Petropavlovsk and Nikolaevsk, its only ports, and the vast continent which lies beyond. Kamchatka and the Tchukche peninsula, with its great mountain ranges, aroused my curiosity. Even Alaska had been ours once. It was sold for a trifling sum to the United States.

They are stormy and sinister seas that stretch away to

the farthest north; cold they are, forbidding and gale-ridden, with savage and uncouth coasts which are known to few.

We kept a flotilla of gunboats which patrolled those waters to protect our possessions from Japanese and American poachers. The Aleutian Islands were famous for their seals. I would have liked to have known these regions, but this was not to be.

It had been decided that I should pay an official visit to the Emperor of Japan, as a friendly gesture to his country, in which feeling had reached a dangerous degree of hostility against Russia, as I have already explained.

I could do no better than to quote the words of Baron Rosen,[1] then our Ambassador at Tokyo, concerning this visit. This is what he says:

'... early in the summer they' (the Russian Government) 'thought it proper to instruct the Grand Duke Cyril (first cousin of the Emperor and next in order of succession after the Emperor's brother and the yet unborn Tsarevich), who was serving as sub-lieutenant on board one of our Pacific squadron's vessels, to proceed to Tokyo on an official visit to the Japanese Court. When I learnt of it I suggested by telegraph to Count Mouravieff[2] that the Grand Duke's visit had better be postponed for some months, as popular feeling in Japan was still such that the Japanese Government might feel embarrassed to undertake the responsibility for the Grand Duke's safety, remembering the attempt on the life of Emperor Nicholas when as Tsarevich he visited Japan, in spite of all the precautions taken to ensure his safety. No attention, however, was paid to my suggestion, and a couple of weeks later the cruiser *Russia* (sic), with the Grand Duke on board, arrived at Yokohama.

'During His Imperial Highness's stay in Tokyo the usual round of official functions took place. A State banquet at the Palace, dinners at the palaces of some of the princes, at the Legation,

[1] *Forty Years of Diplomacy*, by Baron Rosen, pp. 159-160. George Allen & Unwin, Ltd., 1922.

[2] Foreign Minister.

and so on. The young Grand Duke—I think he was in his twenty-first year—produced everywhere the best impression.'
... 'On the day of his arrival I had a long conversation with him and acquainted him fully with the political situation, its significant gravity, and the great importance for us of the maintenance of the friendliest relations with Japan. The Grand Duke listened with the greatest attention and interest, took in the situation at once, and conformed his behaviour to it with unerring tact. In short, his visit, to which I had been looking forward with some apprehension, turned out a complete and socially very marked success. So much so, that Prince Arisugawa made him promise that on the next visit of his ship to Yokohama he would come to spend some days with him and the Princess quite privately at their Palace at Tokyo, a pointedly intimate kind of hospitality such as had never yet been extended to any Royal visitor by any member of the Imperial Family.'

In June of 1898 the *Rossya* hove anchor and set out from Vladivostok to Yokohama.

We anchored some distance from the shore. My arrival was heralded by a fascinating display of day fireworks, or they might be called smoke-works, as there is nothing of the kind in Europe. It made an excellent effect with its continually changing colours.

On landing, I was officially received and taken to the station, where a special train was waiting for me. On my arrival at Tokyo I was met by Prince Kanin and a guard of honour. Accompanied by the Prince, I was driven to a palace which was specially set aside to receive foreign Royalty when visiting the Emperor. It was built in traditional Japanese style, but contained the most modern European comforts. Its cuisine was excellent, according to the best standards of French cooking; the servants were dressed in European Court liveries, everything, in fact, had been organized with the most thorough efficiency and foresight to make my stay as pleasant as could be.

Two days, I think, were spent in showing me the various places of interest. I was entertained with displays of wrestling and juggling, and with a Japanese version of polo, which was played in the traditional costumes of the country worn for that game.

The heat was torrid, and wherever I went I found that the Japanese, with that foresight which is typical of them, had prepared iced drinks, cigarettes, and fans for me.

I was received by the Emperor Mutsu Hito and his Court. I wore full naval uniform on that occasion, and the Emperor and his Court were dressed in European clothes. I was introduced to him by our Ambassador, Baron Rosen,[1] who had arranged my visit. My interpreter was Baron Madenokosi, who spoke fluent Russian. He was in attendance on me during my stay in Japan.

The Emperor was a striking and historical personality and an exalted figure who played a great part in the transition period of his country, which owes much to his wisdom and character. During his rule Japan adapted herself admirably to Western standards in so far as the material greatness of civilization is concerned, but she did not lose her traditional culture. That was due to the great wisdom of those men who directed her course.

Later there was a banquet in my honour, during which the Emperor pointed to an exquisitely worked silver table set, a *surtout de table*, and explained that it was a gift from my Emperor. He asked me to tell my cousin how very pleased he was with it.

I sat next to the Empress, who possessed the exquisite, lovely charm of Japanese women, and found her perfectly sweet. Later I was told that I had made a more than favourable impression on her.

The Emperor decorated me with the Imperial Family Order of the Rising Sun, and presented me with a number of splendid gifts of rare Japanese craftsmanship. There were cloisonné vases, swords and rare screens, and much else of great value. Later I had them all at my palace

---

[1] Later Russian Ambassador at Washington.

in St. Petersburg, where the great vases made excellent lamp stands.

The town of Yokohama gave me a collection of charming dwarf trees, which unfortunately perished on the voyage back.

A few days after the banquet I received the members of the Diplomatic Corps in Tokyo. The reception took place at the palace where I was staying and was somewhat of an ordeal.

I have another very pleasant recollection of this visit to Japan in the reception which the first secretary of our Embassy, M. Poklevski-Koziell, gave me at his private house in Tokyo. It was very informal and absolutely Japanese. We sat on the floor while Japanese dishes were served to us by the 'geishas' who danced and entertained. It was a pleasant evening in an atmosphere in tune with the surroundings, and a welcome interruption of the official routine. Before leaving Japan I paid an official visit to Japan's ancient and sacred City of Kioto.

It is a place of temples and of beautifully kept gardens and parks, with all the sights that are now familiar to tourists. I went over a number of interesting temples, where I was received by the clergy. Whatever shrine or temple I entered I was offered a cup of refreshing blossom tea. Strongly made, it was an excellent 'pick-me-up' in the glaring heat.

This hospitable and charming country impressed me deeply, and even if I had seen none of its glories, there would have remained one thing indelibly in my mind—the children of Japan. They are a very special feature of the country. Like little dolls they looked to me. I had never seen anything quite so charming before, except possibly the women of the country. In their love for children, the Japanese are unique among nations. There are no societies there for the suppression of cruelty to children, and if Japan has learnt much in the way of 'progress' from the West, the West has still much to learn from them.

Before the *Rossya* sailed, I had still time for an expedition to some famous stores, where, among other things, I bought some silk kimonos for my sister Helen.

Before I left Japan I visited Kobe and Nagasaki, whence the *Rossya* proceeded to Port Arthur for fleet exercises.

The rest of the summer and early autumn was spent at Vladivostok.

The time had come when I had to bid farewell to the *Rossya* and to my shipmates. We had been a united group on board.

The night before I was to bid good-bye to my fellow officers a farewell dinner party with toasts and speeches had been arranged. It was a great occasion accompanied by lively scenes. I addressed our captain, Damajirov, expressing my gratitude to him for the experiences and training which I had received while in his care, a duty which I knew was the more onerous inasmuch as it entailed a great responsibility for my personal safety and welfare.

The dinner was followed by singing and music and a very pleasant and original side-show, when our torpedo officer, Kerber, with a number of other officers dressed up like savage 'Golds' in leather jackets, performed some kind of ritualistic witch dance, Kerber beating a round drum, just like a real *shaman*.[1] He did it very effectively indeed.

This party was a great success although I was partly an invalid, for shortly before this occasion I had had a bad accident on board, and had injured my foot, which I had to have heavily bandaged. I had lost much blood and was not in the best of health. None the less, I shall never forget the touching way in which my friends smoothed over my regrets on leaving *Rossya*, which had been my floating home for such a long time. Apart from Lieutenant Kerber, I wish to mention Admiral Russin, who at that time

---

[1] Native Siberian witch doctor.

was one of our gunnery officers on board. They all played an outstanding part in our Navy.

In the sad events which followed, many of my shipmates found a sailor's grave. They were the bravest of the brave.

The *Rossya* had taken me to Yokohama, where I boarded an American passenger boat that was to take me across to the United States, whence I was to proceed back to Europe.

I will not forget the touching farewell which my shipmates gave me as they followed the liner out to sea in one of the *Rossya's* steam launches, waving to me, until distance began to separate us.

IV

Return to Russia

WHILE I had been acknowledging the farewell ovations from the officers of the *Rossya*, a little group had gathered near me which took in these doings with particular interest. An old man with a white beard disengaged himself from this group and said to me: "You must be feeling pretty proud about this, sir?" It was Mr. Bell of Telephone fame, who was returning to the United States after a business visit to Japan. He had his wife and two very pretty daughters with him. Apart from the Bell family and my two companions, Lieutenants Kube and Pusanoff, the *Rossya's* paymaster, the latter being in charge of my finances, there was a Russian doctor proceeding to Honolulu.

This little intimate group was all the Society on board.

The steamer belonged to an American company and was by no means a luxury liner. She carried five masts for emergency purposes in case her engines should break down on the way, but in spite of this cumbersome burden, she did a steady fourteen knots all the time.

The voyage passed without any untoward incidents. There were the usual deck games, and the ship's doctor added to the monotony of a quiet sea and the rhythmic thud of the engines by singing sentimental German songs. Every morning he and the captain would be seen ' shooting the sun.'

When we passed the 180th degree latitude, I experienced the curious time freak of two consecutive Fridays.

Eight days after leaving Yokohama we reached Honolulu, which at that time presented none of those attractions for which it is now so famous as a Pacific resort. It had then, I think, only recently come under American suzerainty, and apart from the town and a number of sugar plantations worked by Germans, it had little of interest for a casual visitor, as there was not enough time to see the interior.

After two days at that island, we continued on our way to San Francisco.

I was greatly struck by the magnificent harbour, which like Constantinople and Vladivostok has its 'Golden Horn,' but apart from the fact that San Francisco, including my hotel, was at that time almost entirely built of wood, I remember little.

I was in a hurry to return to Europe, and my recollections of the trans-continental journey are of the vaguest. At every station where the train stopped I was pestered by journalists who swarmed upon me like bees. They wanted to know everything. 'What do you think of the Far East situation?' or 'What is your impression of American girls?' and much else was fired at me. About the political situation I knew nothing and cared less—I am a naval officer—and about American women—after all, I had had scarcely time enough to look around. I had met none; I was anxious to get back to Europe as soon as possible.

This farce was repeated again and again until I became thoroughly tired of it all.

I interrupted my journey at Chicago, where I was met by our Consul, Baron Schlippenbach, who took me to the fashionable and magnificently equipped 'Gentlemen's Club.' I think that I spent two days at Chicago altogether, and I had a good general impression of the place and American life.

It was December and bitterly cold, and I just remember having had a glimpse of the frozen Niagara Falls through the windows of my compartment.

The journey across the United States had taken about one week, but the very well equipped and comfortable Pullman coaches of the various railways left one none the worse for this long period spent in trains. I had been well looked after and had all the comforts that could be devised as well as excellent food.

Arrived at New York, I decided to stop there a week, attending Divine Service at our Church and seeing all that could be seen during such a short stay. An excellent impression was made on me by the high standard of acting in the theatres, and by New York's gay night life.

Then I boarded the *Fürst Bismarck*, bound for Genoa, and, I believe, one of the North German Lloyd's steamers.

Here all was very different from the old-fashioned Pacific steamer with its homely atmosphere.

The *Fürst Bismarck* was one of those vessels which foreshadowed the swimming palaces that were to come upon the sea, veritable luxury hotels afloat, which, in a way, take away much of what used to be fascinating and original in a long crossing on board the small craft of other days.

To us sailors these modern liners with all the 'hullaballoo' of their cocktail bars and other 'blessings' of modernity are a wanton incursion of 'landlubberism' into our realm, which has always held us to it with its dangers and uncertainties, has invited us to wrestle with its primitive spirit in a contest of skill and courage.

Moreover, I hate crowds. I have always hated them, and the *Bismarck* was packed like a box of sardines!

Fortunately they had provided me with the ladies' lounge which I had entirely to myself.

While we were mooring at Genoa, I noticed two girls waving to me frantically from the shore. The situation was awkward, as I had not the least idea who they were. I said good-bye to Captain Albers and thanked him for the excellent arrangements which he had made for my comfort and stepped ashore, where I was met enthusiastically by the girls whose salutations had puzzled me so. They were Ella and Marie Naryshkin, the dancing partners of my childhood days who had grown up into handsome young women, and had become pleasantly unrecognizable.

They were staying with their mother on the Italian Riviera, for it was January of the year 1899, and during the severe winters all who could get away to the pleasant warmth of the south did so.

I paid a hurried visit to Cannes, where I met my Mecklenburg relations and a number of others. We played golf, bicycled together and had a very pleasant time.

Thence I rushed home to Russia, where I presented myself to my parents and the late Emperor.

He gave me my well-earned leave, and I decided to return forthwith to Cannes, where I was sure to find many people of interest.

Cannes in those days was a most exclusive winter colony of Royalties. Its villa life was unique of its kind with an atmosphere of exquisite refinement and old-world culture. There were no crowds, no casino, no rowdyism, and no tourists. Everything breathed with the spirit of that inimitable refinement which belongs to a world the shattered fragments of which have been washed irretrievably by war and revolutions into the sea of history.

It was a welcome change from the strenuous work on board and I intended to make the best of this congenial atmosphere.

My brother Boris, Kube, and I left accordingly for Cannes.

On our arrival we found that the Prince of Wales was staying there. He had his yacht *Britannia* with him.

There were many names famous in the English Society of the 'nineties among those who were staying there at the time. I remember especially Sidney Greville, the Prince's equerry. Occasionally we joined Prince Edward's week-end parties at Monte Carlo, where we took part in all kinds of pleasant social diversions. He attracted around him a very congenial spirit of brilliant gaiety, and it was a real pleasure to be in his company.

At Cannes I found Cousin Michael and his wife, Countess Torby. My Mecklenburg relations were still there and Princess Charlotte Reuss, and a host of other Royal guests who entertained one another and joined in the many social activities of the season. After a pleasant six weeks' holiday I returned to Russia and the sea.

The gunnery school which I joined at Reval consisted of a rare collection of maritime show-wonders, many of which belonged to the immediate post-Crimean period. It was as though these ancient hulks had been specially gathered from a desire to preserve them for a kind of object lesson of how things should not be done at sea.

It was a quixotic armada which I beheld with something approaching a feeling of mingled pity and awe.

They were the scrapings of our fleet, veritable museum pieces of archæological interest.

There was the old *Kreml*, for example, a vessel which was more like a crab than anything else I have ever seen. It was a standing joke in the Navy that she was obsessed with awe of the Island of Gothland, for whenever she drew up with its coasts, she passed it moving sideways as if in terror of some fearful calamity that might lie in store for her if she were to pass it otherwise. The Japanese, I believe, perform some funeral rites before scrapping their ships in the belief that these have souls. Ships may have souls, at any rate some sailors think so, and if any vessel had a spirit of dark superstition in her, it was this one.

And there was another, which when the helm was put to starboard would invariably proceed to meander about, and then move in the opposite direction or turn right round on her course. And some of these museum pieces in that scrap-heap were actually sent out to fight the

Japanese. Their real purpose was that of monitors, but the most they could do was to float.

We have a word for vessels of the kind. We call them 'old goloshes,' and if ever there was a lumber-room containing all the old and useless 'goloshes' it was to be found here. Forty years previously they might have done.

Some of them found it hard to negotiate the easy passage from Reval to Helsingfors. Into these flat-bottom affairs they had built some modern guns, which were to provide us with training in gunnery.

I was appointed to the *General Admiral*, a square-rigged, half-sail and half-steam frigate for which six knots was the very maximum of speed.

To add to the inconsistency of the situation a brilliant man was in command of this gunnery school afloat. He was Rojdestvenski, then a Rear-Admiral, the defamed hero of one of the great exploits in naval annals, a kind of Hannibal of the Sea, of whom I will have occasion to say a few words later. I consider it my duty to pay a tribute to this Russian patriot who sailed to certain doom, about which he had no illusions whatever, with a floating scrap-heap, over twenty thousand miles of sea, unbacked by any base and with the face of the world set hard and sarcastically against him. And when they knew that all was lost, that Port Arthur had fallen, and the armies routed, they met a splendidly equipped enemy born to the sea, and in an unequal contest they perished like men, fighting till the sea closed over them.

In spite of this heterogeneous and obsolete collection of hulks, I learnt much that was useful to me in the way of practical gunnery, and I got to know the Admiral as a man of severe and upright character, one passionately attached to his duty and painstaking, possessed, moreover, with an unflinching will to overcome all difficulties.

It was, indeed, his misfortune that he had such useless material in his hands, but ill luck pursued him throughout his career.

My training in gunnery was interrupted for a brief interval by my parents' silver wedding, which was entirely a private affair and recalled for a moment the very happy home of my childhood.

I rejoined my ship and continued my training until early September, when we all returned to Kronstadt and leave, the fleet being dismantled for the winter. The Baltic freezes in those parts and makes navigation possible only with the aid of ice-breakers, hence we had to continue our service on shore during the winter months until spring recalled our ships to activity from the hibernation which nature had forced upon them.

I intended to go to Paris, but my brother Boris who had been invited to Darmstadt by our cousin the Grand Duchess Victoria Melita of Hesse, as she then was, persuaded me to come with him.

There was going to be a family gathering at Wolfsgarten, near Frankfurt. Everyone was going to be there. I did not regret my decision as I found the occasion one of unrestrained and quite natural gaiety. The late Emperor and Empress were among the guests. It was the home of her childhood. We were *en famille* and lived a normal and charming life among the pleasant and wooded surroundings of the Grand Ducal estate. There were amateur theatricals in the evenings at which all of us performed, rides and drives in the woods and pleasant pranks, and time passed only too quickly. Our hosts were Victoria Melita and her husband, the Grand Duke of Hesse, the brother of the late Empress and of the Grand Duchess Sergey. I have the happiest recollections of this visit, and it must have been a success, for the late Empress was particularly gay and charming, and gaiety was not part of her character. This place contained memories of her youth and she felt at home in these familiar surroundings.

The only official business that came our way was the consecration of our Church at Darmstadt.

THE LATE EMPEROR NICHOLAS II
The Author's first cousin.

THE AUTHOR

Princess Louis Battenberg lived quite near at Schloss Jugendheim, where we paid her a visit.

Boris and I left this happy gathering for Paris and before our return to Russia we spent a few days with Uncle Alfred[1] and Aunt Marie[1] at Coburg. While we were with them, the Grand Duchess Victoria Melita came to see her mother.

Uncle Alfred's estates had some excellent shooting, a pastime of which I have always been particularly fond.

On my return to St. Petersburg I served with the Naval Guards in the dual capacity of Lieutenant in Her Majesty's first Company and of A.D.C. to the late Emperor.

The winter season at the capital pursued its uninterrupted course of brilliant gaieties, with great Court Balls and private social functions. These episodes of a sunken world are like a series of kaleidoscopic pictures, with their colours and movement and unmatched splendour;—a last great and spectacular effort, before the fall of the curtain. The 'grand finale' of an epoch.

The Princess Hohenlohe-Langenburg, who was to be my youngest sister-in-law, joined in all these festivities, entering into their spirit with the charming elegance and grace which was hers. She was very popular among society and with us, who called her 'Sandra.'

I cannot pass over this occasion without paying some tribute to the efficient organization of the Court. It was a model institution of its kind and worked with clock-like precision. Of all the official institutions in Russia, I think, without exaggeration, it was the best organized.

It was entirely self-contained, had its minister with his department, and was, in fact, a State within a State.

Quite apart from its splendour, which at no time was permitted to become overloaded or to stick blindly to a military discipline or pedantic ceremonial, it combined,

---

[1] Duke and Duchess of Edinburgh, then Duke and Duchess of Coburg and Gotha.

as it were, the best points of all the Courts of Europe. And it had charm!

We were an enormously rich country, the wealthiest in the world at that time, but in spite of this its wealth never expressed itself in vulgar show. A spirit of culture and refinement pervaded the Court representing the best traditions of eighteenth-century Europe in a modern setting. Its organization left nothing to be desired. This clock beat rhythmically, when, alas, so much else was allowed to lag behind in the other spheres of the machine of State.

One occasion during this gay season, especially, stands out among all these fascinating but now hazy recollections of Court and Society life, and this was a fancy dress ball which we gave at the Vladimir Palace, when men were dressed in the dashing Polish uniforms of the Napoleonic era and the women wore classical 'Empire' dresses.

This ball was such a conspicuous success that the late Emperor had it repeated at the Ermitage Palace.

In the early spring of 1900 I paid a visit to Cannes, where I met all the usual *habitués*, and on my return to Russia was appointed to the *Rostislav*, one of the units of our Black Sea fleet.

The Captain of the *Rostislav* was Grand Duke Alexander Michaelovich, whom we called Sandro in the family. He was the husband of my cousin, the popular and very charming Grand Duchess Xenia.[1]

I visited them on the conclusion of my service with the Black Sea fleet, at their Crimean castle of Aitodor, where for the first time in my life I saw vineyards. All kinds of wines were produced in the Crimea, even champagne, which was so excellent that it was served at Court banquets.

The Crimea and the Caucasus, in fact, the whole of the Black Sea littoral, are a veritable paradise of nature, abounding in vegetation and natural beauty.

[1] Sister of the late Emperor Nicholas II.

For that reason, service with our Black Sea squadron was a pleasure. Curiously enough, and for no apparent reason at all, our fleet in those hospitable regions only went to sea in the summer, possibly out of sympathy with our Baltic squadron, which, for reasons already mentioned, had no alternative to remaining ice-bound at its base. The Black Sea is open for navigation during the whole winter and yet our men-of-war were confined to port. Only skeleton crews were left on the ships, the others occupied naval barracks and for the time being became Marines. The whole thing was amazing, and needed, as did the whole of our Navy, stringent measures of reform.

The *Rostislav* was a new vessel, but in spite of that a failure. As a man of war she did not want in comforts, but from a practical point of view she was of no use. Slow and insufficiently protected, she had but one redeeming feature, and even this at first defeated its own purpose —she was our first oil-burning naval unit.

When I joined her in the late spring of 1901 she was still in the hands of her builders and our engineers were trying to get used to her boilers and to the various gadgets attached to them. This took time and, what was worse, instead of producing as little smoke as possible, the *Rostislav* was covered with a cloud of black soot like a volcano in the process of eruption. Thick and oily smoke hung over her; it got into everything, our white summer tunics were covered with it, the white paint and everything that was not already black became so in due course, and the engineers were cursed.

After a month of experimenting they had made themselves more or less familiar with the firing process, and we proceeded along with a smaller pillar of smoke in our wake.

After the usual course of gunnery and fleet exercises and all the rest that belongs to the ordinary routine of navies, we started out from Sebastopol on a cruise along the shores of the Black Sea.

When we passed the yards of Nikolaïev I saw a number of 'Popovkas,' in all probability the most exotic of naval freaks. They had been designed in Russia and built in England. Their purpose was that of monitors and their appearance was that of a mixture between giant armoured pancakes and jelly fish. They were quite round and like a sphere cut in half, being designed to move in all directions, sideways as well as forward or astern, and carried a heavy gun. The early monitors proved too low in the water, and were dangerous in heavy seas. To counteract this, the 'Popovkas' were built in such a way that, even if they were awash in 'dirty' weather, they could remain afloat like submarines. The total result of this ingenuity was that they were unmanageable and unseaworthy in the extreme. As they were armoured islands afloat, and almost hermetically sealed, the sun beat down mercilessly upon them, and owing to lack of proper ventilation they were infernally hot inside. And in conclusion, they were, of course, dismal failures. But as a curiosity they were worth seeing.

Our first port of call was Odessa, and what I saw during this Black Sea cruise was like a revelation.

At Odessa there were receptions by the Governor, Count 'Pavel' Schouvaloff, and a number of the usual social activities, only one of which I now clearly remember because it was marked by something which, had I not actually seen it with my own eyes, I would have thought impossible. The Odessa fire brigade gave a display, during which its chief, whose physical strength was reputed to be enormous, demonstrated his Herculean prowess by tearing a strong towel in half. Not content with this, he took the torn towel up and putting the two halves together tore them once more, so that four separate pieces remained in his hands.

Thence we directed our course to the coast of Turkish Asia Minor without, however, entering any port. The first port at which we called was Batum, where we interrupted our cruise for a while. The climate there is sub-tropical and the vegetation luxuriant.

I am thoroughly familiar with the French and Italian rivieras, but this Black Sea coast and its mountainous background are by far superior. Along the west coast there were scarcely any ports, no railways, and no modern roads. It was a wilderness and paradise, a land of plenty left to itself.

Not only had Nature been generous to this region in every conceivable way, where mountains and sea and cliffs, heavy with verdure and mineral wealth too, are heaped together in lavish proportions, but even history had left the fascinating imprint of ancient civilizations on the coasts of that sea which the ancients had called 'the Hospitable.' At Batum I was given short leave and went to Tiflis, the capital of Georgia and Vice-regal seat of government for the Caucasus. The train passed through the splendid Caucasian scenery—a land of wild mountains and forests, more imposing than the Alps, numbering among its snowy heights Mount Elbrus, the loftiest peak in Europe.

From Tiflis I visited Cousin Nicholas[1] at his place at Borjom. He was an eminent man of learning and the historian of our family. Apart from this, he was a world authority on entomology and had the best collection of Caucasian butterflies. Even the gates of the drive which lead to the castle were surmounted by a butterfly of wrought iron. The scenery, which unfolded itself around Borjom, was one of savage grandeur—an ideal spot, moreover, for a lover of nature and sport, and there was excellent shooting to be had in that region.

During my return journey to the ship, I spent another day at Tiflis, where, I remember, I tried the Kachetian

---

[1] Grand Duke Nicholas Michaelovitch, son of Grand Duke Michael and of Olga Feodorovna, princess of Baden, executed by the Bolshevists on January 30, 1920, in the fortress of Petropavlovsk.

wine of the district—very heavy and white wine which the natives drink like water, but on the uninitiated it is apt to have sad effects. It belongs to that family of wines which, although they leave one quite sober, possesses the unfortunate propensity of affecting the power of movement. One simply remains 'anchored,' so to say, to the spot—a foolish situation indeed.

The Caucasus made an unforgettable impression on me, for its glens are inhabited by a motley crowd of mountaineers, and practically every major valley across a pass has a different people with a different language, traditions, and dress. It is as though the Caucasus had acted like a magnet throughout the ages of human history, attracting to it the representatives of all the races that have ever passed from East to West and from West to East in the great ebb and tide of human migration. There are tall, fair-haired people of the purest Nordic stock and Iberians of Spanish type. There are the Ossetians and Chevsurs, the Georgians and the Svanetians, Tartars and Circassians, Armenians and many others. There is one people, for example, which to this day wears the chain mail armour of the Crusaders. Tall and fair-haired men, they seem to have come straight from the expeditions of Richard Cœur de Lion or St. Louis. Their language and religion are one of the many puzzles of this racial backwater, and even their dwellings resemble the architecture of medieval strongholds.

The Caucasus provides for all tastes, and here the nature lover and mountain climber can share his happiness with the mining engineer and archæologist.

A grand and savage and a very imposing land it is, and the rich mythology of its peoples runs in line with that of ancient Greece. It is the country of Prometheus and the Golden Fleece, of the quest of the Argonauts and of Iphigenia's exile, of St. George and the forty martyred legionaries. Greeks occupied parts of it as did the Romans and the Parthians. All passed along that way—a land of promise which invites exploration.

We continued our cruise along the West Coast, saw New Athos, a monastic settlement, and anchored at Novorosiisk. There were the usual official receptions with dinners, speeches, and toasts.

While lying at anchor there I witnessed the same natural phenomenon which had puzzled me so at Malta. All was perfectly still when suddenly a violent and vicious wind descended from the mountains upon the harbour and turned it into a cauldron of foaming water, while the sea beyond remained quite calm.

Not far from Novorosiisk was the famous castle of 'Gagry' which Prince Oldenburg had turned into a sanatorium for consumptives.

I visited Abrau Durso, a place famous for its vineyards. The property belonged to the Imperial Family, the members of which were the beneficiaries and the late Emperor its trustee. The vineyards of this estate, under the able management of an old Frenchman, produced all the better-known French wines, including excellent Russian champagne.

From Novorosiisk the *Rostislav* took course for Kertch, where were excavations in progress under the auspices of the Ermitage. The tombs of Kertch contained the treasures of all the stages of Greek civilization and are now as famous as Troy, Minos, and Mycene.

During the period of my service with the Black Sea fleet I had an opportunity to visit a number of castles along the Crimean coast. Those of them which belonged to members of the Imperial Family were in pleasant contrast with many of the other residences of the kind which, together with the grounds in which they stood, had been allowed to fall into a state of disrepair and presented a picture of sad neglect.

But the Imperial residences were thoroughly worthy of the magnificent landscape with which they were perfectly matched. I visited Livadia and Yalta. In Livadia, Uncle Sasha had died and a new palace had been built for the late Emperor.

My captain's[1] place at 'Aitodor,' which I have already mentioned, was a pleasant and very comfortable edifice, beautifully situated on the cliffs which descended abruptly into the clear waters of the Black Sea. Its rich orchards and vineyards were famous.

On the conclusion of my duties with the Black Sea fleet I returned to the capital, whence my sister Helen and I set out for Wolfsgarten once more.

This was to be my fourth meeting with my cousin Victoria Melita. During the occasions on which we had met before we had become good friends, and our friendship grew into a strong mutual affection. The three weeks which I spent at Wolfsgarten in the autumn of 1900 were decisive for the whole of my life. Thereafter we were to meet as often as possible.

I was accompanied by Ilia Tatishchev, my father's A.D.C. I mention him specially because later he was attached as A.D.C. to the late Emperor, whom he accompanied to his exile and martyrdom in Ekaterinburg. He remained with his Imperial Master to the very end and perished with him. A better and more loyal man than he it would be hard to find.

Helen persuaded my cousin Victoria to come to Paris with us, where we had planned to go next. It proved an excellent idea as we enjoyed ourselves enormously in the gay and carefree manner of youth.

They returned to Germany, but I paid a hurried visit to Cannes.

On my return to St. Petersburg I was appointed to the *Peresviet*,[2] which at the time was still building. It had been decided by our Admiralty that her first voyage should be to Port Arthur, and this, as far as I was concerned, meant an absence of at least two years.

[1] Grand Duke Alexander Michaelovitch, Captain of the *Rostislav*.
[2] Legendary Hero.

The Emperor gave me leave and I again returned to Cannes, where I found Aunt Marie[1] with her three daughters, Marie, the Crown Princess of Roumania, Cousin Victoria, and the future Infanta Beatrice. Cousin Marie had her husband and children with her.

Boris and I took our cousins for drives in our motor car, or 'automobile' as they were then called, and we went through the length and breadth of the French Riviera.

Motor cars were then a complete novelty and we belonged to the small group of pioneers.

Our 'machine' was a Panhard-Lavasseur and boasted twelve horse-power. Its engine had to be started up like a primus stove, spluttered, shook and made fearful noises. The brakes were dangerous, its front wheels smaller than the back, and one had to get into it from the rear. In spite of this protoplasm in the evolution of cars, it negotiated all the steep inclines of this mountainous region, and proved itself quite reliable and efficient.

The *Peresviet* lay at Kronstadt undergoing her finishing touches, with workmen and engineers still on board. There was the usual concert of pneumatic drills, bangings, and hammerings. The living quarters on board had not been completed and I had obtained the Emperor's consent to establishing myself meanwhile on board his yacht, the *Poliarnaya Zvezda*.[2]

Every day I reported for duty on the *Peresviet*, where, among other matters, I had to supervise the electrically worked munition hoists, which, more often than not, broke down.

The *Peresviet* was a strange vessel, as strange as was her ultimate career and those who were to be her officers.

---

[1] Previously Duchess of Edinburgh, then Duchess of Coburg and Gotha, for the Duke of Edinburgh succeeded to the title of Duke of Coburg and Gotha.
[2] Polar Star.

She had been designed as an intermediary type between a cruiser and battleship, but succeeded only in missing the advantages and purpose of both, being too heavy and slow for a cruiser and too weak for a battleship.

The reason for some of our failures in naval construction lay with the Admiralty and not with the designers. The former was too anxious to produce new types of ships, lacked sobriety of purpose and were prompted by a spirit of extravagant innovation, which only succeeded in defeating its own object. Our designers were excellent, and when things were left to their initiative they were always entirely successful. They were perfectly capable of producing such excellent results as the *Rossya* which surprised the world and, in a way, gave rise to a revolution in naval construction in so far as long range ships were concerned.

The career of the *Peresviet* was ill-fated. She fell into the hands of the Japanese after the capitulation of Port Arthur: they raised her from the sea and incorporated her in their Navy. At the outbreak of the Great War she was bought by us from Japan and was sunk by a mine in the Mediterranean. There is a memorial to those who perished on her at Port Said.

Her sister ship, the *Pobieda*,[1] was sunk at the battle of Tsushima.

The officers who had been commissioned to the *Peresviet* were, barring a few, a hopeless crowd of incapables. They had been chosen at random by the Admiralty and apparently without any reason whatever.

Few of them knew their jobs. The captain, who knew nothing at all, came from the Black Sea squadron, and had to learn all his navigation during the voyage. It is quite possible that his appointment to the command was an accident, for it was said of him that he had been in charge of a 'light ship'!

[1] Victory.

There may have been some confusion in one of the Admiralty's offices—a clerical error, a mix-up of names, for there was something definitely wrong with the rest of them, who were not far behind their captain in inefficiency, and this was quite contrary to the usual practice of appointing first class officers and men to new ships.

The captain was helpless and so entirely ignorant that he had to be taught the use of the engine telegraph. Everything had to be done by the commander, who together with a small group of others was our salvation. We owed it to this commander that we succeeded in getting to the Far East. Without him and Lieutenant Kube, Gunnery Officer Dimitrieff, and Navigation Officer Dournovo, we would certainly have come to grief outside Kronstadt, as we did, in fact, soon after leaving.

This atmosphere of inefficiency on board, the continuous noise and other things, too, of an unpleasant nature, did not encourage me to look to the future with particular optimism. Such a voyage had its sudden as well as continuous dangers. Anything might happen, not, indeed, through the usual perils of the sea, which every seaman expects and is trained to counter, but through the stupidity of man which is incalculable and, therefore, by far, more alarming.

The evil emanation of amateurism and rank inefficiency was as pronounced on the lower deck as it was on the quarter-deck. The engines were bad, as was everything else on board—all was dismally chaotic.

I had no illusions about the nature of this voyage, and three weeks before I was to set out upon this East Asiatic odyssey of several thousand miles, in such pleasant company, I took leave and went to Wolfsgarten, taking Ilia Tatishcheff with me.

I was glad to have gone, as it proved a great success, as had, in fact, all the occasions on which I had visited Wolfsgarten. The place was admirably run by Cousin Victoria. Everything, from the castle to its grounds and stables, was of the best. She was, incidentally, the most accomplished, graceful, and daring horsewoman I have ever known.

I will mention the names of some of the guests who were present. There was Princess Helena and her daughter, 'Tora' of Schleswig-Holstein, and Prince Arthur of Connaught with his equerry, Captain Wyndham, who was an excellent horseman.

We amused ourselves immensely. There was tennis, riding, and drives among the splendid pinewoods in the evenings. We danced and performed amateur theatricals and played all kinds of amusing games.

Before leaving Germany we went to Mainz for the German Army manœuvres.

It was not on this occasion but, I believe, during one of my previous visits to Wolfsgarten or Darmstadt that I met the Kaiser for the second time. He has a way of singling out someone during luncheons and dinners to whom he generally addresses himself for a while, the others having to listen.

On this occasion his choice fell on me, and as my German was by no means fluent, I felt like a victim.

His knowledge of naval matters is that of an expert, and I remember that during this luncheon he expounded to me the technical moves of changing a fleet from one of the ordinary formations into a line of battle. He did not generalize but went into details. Every now and then I was able to fire a rapid charge into his continued broadsides in German which left much to be desired. The whole situation was awkward in the extreme.

On another occasion I was taken on a special visit to the Dowager Empress Victoria, the wife of Emperor Frederick. She was a striking person to meet and had in her time played a political part. In character she may have taken after her father, the Prince Consort. She ruled her castle near Frankfurt, and all those that belonged thereto or entered its precincts, with a severity which approached that of military discipline.

She would not tolerate anything which came upon her black list of 'taboos,' of which there was a formidable array. She would have no smoking, and woe betide the culprit who dared to throw a cigarette stump upon her immaculately kept garden paths. My cousins told me that whenever they wanted to smoke they had to do so in the large fireplaces where the smoke of their cigarettes would be caught up by the draught of the chimneys.

Relatives, casual visitors, and domestics, were in awe of her.

Arrived back in Russia I joined in the efforts of putting the *Peresviet* into final shape. It proved a strenuous process, as much had to be done in the short time which was left before putting to sea in the early autumn of 1901.

Her builders had arranged my cabin in a very homely manner. The iron walls had been covered with chintz attached to wooden brackets.

Following my family tradition of sleeping on camp beds, as my ancestors had done since my great grandfather Nicholas I, I slept on one during the whole of this voyage. It proved far more suited to the movement of the ship in heavy weather than an ordinary ship's bunk. When the *Peresviet* rolled in heavy seas, I was never thrown out of bed as were the others.

At last all was ready for the venture. I bade farewell to parents and friends, and with mixed feelings of anticipation of certain but unknown calamities and of anxiety for the welfare of the one for whom I cared, I went on board not in the best of spirits.

V

Service at Sea

THIS may sound like a passage from the chronicles of the early navigators, but it was our tradition and a good one, too, that before starting a long voyage there should be a religious service first during which the ship is hallowed by the sprinkling of holy water. A Te Deum was accordingly celebrated on board, and after a big luncheon which followed, we cast off. Twelve thousand miles of sea lay before us.

One of the things that had to be done on leaving was to teach the captain not to come to the mess unasked. The poor man was not familiar with the naval tradition that the captain takes his meals by himself and joins the mess only when invited by his officers.

The part of the Baltic which joins the North Sea between Jutland and the Danish Islands is known for its dangerous currents, a feature which narrow seas share more or less in common. Here they are especially dangerous, and to avoid any unpleasant incident we had picked up a local pilot to guide us through them. In spite of his presence on board, which according to the laws of the sea does not shift the burden of responsibility from the captain in case anything should go wrong, we ran aground off the coast of Jutland.

Every effort was made to get the *Peresviet* off into deep water, but she remained stubbornly fixed. We could not shift her, and fearing that she might have been damaged below the water-line we sent our divers down to investigate.

These Russian divers were splendid and enjoyed a world-wide reputation for their efficiency. I have been told by English Naval officers that our divers were considered superior to any. There were certain specialities in our Navy which were excellent and, generally, our fleet, though leaving much to be desired as a working whole, was excellently developed in some of its details, among which divers and compasses were predominant. The theory of compasses had become a special study with us and we were acknowledged as experts.

When the Baltic squadron of Rojedestvenski performed its prodigy of a twenty thousand miles voyage, it had to rely entirely on its own resources, and all its repairs had to be done mostly while afloat. Owing to the obsolete types of 'tin box' vessels which he had been ordered to drag over the seas into battle at the other end of the world with his base about 18,000 miles away, there were a great number of breakdowns.

Thus, for example, one of the small destroyers broke its rudder in the Indian Ocean during a heavy swell. The divers attended to their work while their shipmates kept the sharks away. The rudder had to be repaired at all costs as the Admiral was determined not to lose, except in battle, even the smallest of the ships which had been entrusted to his charge.

One of the divers was carried away by a huge sea and plunged like a stone into the fearsome depths of the ocean, followed by the sharks. Another took his place at once. The upward flight and fall, while the destroyer's stern was raised sky high and sank deep with the sea, produced sea-sickness among the divers. In spite of all they worked on till the damage had been repaired. Every time they were raised to the deck of the small craft they had to be restored to consciousness, and then they returned to their work.

Such were the men who sailed consciously to their doom and fought until the last of their guns had been put out of action and their 'tin boxes' had turned turtle in the waters of Tsushima.

We had not been damaged, but as we could not get off the reef with our own engines, Danish tugs were called for, and, after some strenuous efforts, succeeded in hauling us off into deep water.

Nothing of any particular interest happened until we got into the Bay of Biscay. It was calm, and just because of that an idiotic incident happened which might have brought about a calamity. I was resting in my bunk at the time when all of a sudden I felt that our engines were put full astern. As we were on the wide ocean, this strange manœuvre amazed me. I rushed to the bridge—and what did I see?—I beheld a mysterious sight which seemed to lack natural explanation, and yet had all the appearance of intention. . . . A strange farce seemed to be in progress, with the ocean as the stage and a great man-of-war and small tramp-steamer as the actors. It looked as though this meeting had been specially contrived by elaborate calculation.

The *Peresviet* and the tramp-steamer were head on to each other, and when I came on the bridge were receding with their engines reversed. Then both stopped and lay becalmed, bowing politely in a friendly counter-dance on the swell of the wide sea around them. Neither of them seemed willing to get out of the way of the other, until, finally, we had gone sufficiently far astern to alter course a few points to starboard and pass by the tramp.

What had happened was very typical of the persons we had been condemned to drag with us.

One of them, who later on was to get us into trouble again, had been on watch when he sighted a tramp-steamer ploughing its way harmlessly and slowly on a totally opposite course to ours.

Instead of giving it an appropriate berth, he lost his

head completely like a person learning to ride a bicycle and making straight for a tree. He continued relentlessly on his course and straight at the steamer. Had it not been for the vigilance of others, he would have taken us full speed into her. What they thought and especially what was said on board that steamer has not been recorded. I think that they were so amazed that they were completely dumbfounded. What, after all, but an attempt at piracy could be the intention of a man-of-war bearing down upon them on the open sea until the very last moment and then suddenly reversing its engines. The whole affair must have given them the impression of an act inspired by malevolent intention on our part.

The result of this incident was that the officer in question was mercilessly jeered at in the mess. Even then he seemed not to understand that he had done anything out of the ordinary, and I presume he considered it his duty to sink anything that chance brought on our course. He was in every way typical of the kind of person we had to contend with, and the result was that those of us who understood our jobs had to do the work of two or three.

We were bound for Toulon, our next port of call after Vigo.

In the Gulf of Lyons we ran into heavy weather. A howling gale had turned the sea into a foaming mass, through which we ploughed our way at twelve knots. It was pitch dark when I came on the bridge for my watch. The air was filled with the sound of the gale, with spray and sleet which drove at us pursued by the force of the elements. The only things which could be seen were our binnacle lights and the white foam of the seas that rose and fell, hurling themselves upon us.

Suddenly out of the darkness and the din of the storm a red light appeared dead ahead. It was the port light of a vessel which was coming straight at us. Instinctively I ordered the helm hard a-starboard. For the moment, only for the flash of a few seconds, I stood holding my breath. A large barque driven by the full force of a following gale passed within a few yards of our port side.

She was swallowed up in the darkness of the raging storm as quickly as it had come upon us. I had avoided disaster just in time. A few seconds later it would have been too late. The sleet and rain which the gale chased in continuous curtains at us had made it impossible to make out the mast-light of the barque.

It was fortunate for all of us that one of our hopefuls had not been on duty at the time.

At Toulon we received a visit from Aunt Anastasia—the Grand Duchess of Mecklenburg—who, like Queen Olga of Greece, patronized Russian warships. She, too, was ever on the look out for them, and whenever one put in at a port anywhere within easy reach of her whereabouts she would always gladly visit them.

We interrupted our voyage for five days at the French Naval base of Villefranche, where I met Cousin Victoria, to whom, from now onwards in this account, I shall refer as 'Ducky,' which was the name by which she was known in her family.

She was staying with her mother and her sister Beatrice at their castle, Fabron, near Nice. She was in exile. The circumstances which had led up to this had their roots in an unhappy married life.

In marrying the Grand Duke of Hesse she had complied with the wishes of Queen Victoria. It was no love match and her feelings in the matter had not been consulted. It was dynastic duty.

Their married life was doomed to failure owing to the incompatability of their characters. The step of divorce had been suggested to her, but she had turned it down. The Hessians adored her.

When, however, real love finally came to her she took this step, and became an exile from Hesse, bitterly regretted by her people, as a consequence.

She came to look me up on board ship and was entertained to tea by the officers. I remember that Dimitrieff sang and that I accompanied him on the piano. He had a splendid voice and was an excellent fellow.

Later I showed Ducky over the ship and my cabin, as she was particularly anxious that I should be well lodged on this long voyage.

My shipmates had proved splendid fellows on this occasion and had arranged this reception with great care and much taste.

I was given a short leave and went to Château Fabron, where Aunt Marie[1] had decided that on the last night Ducky and I should have dinner by ourselves and that we were to be left alone as this was a farewell occasion.

She was in exile and I was going to the unknown, to the uncertainty of a blank future. About one thing both of us had no illusion whatever, that a mountain of obstacles to our happiness would arise, that every conceivable wheel of intrigue, coterie and vetos would be put into motion against us, and that we would be left to fight that sea of troubles alone with thousands of miles between us. By that time I would be at the other end of the world and the woman I cared for would have to defend herself as well as she could and I would be unable to come to her aid.

All this we knew and more. But that the future had a happy solution in store for us, that we did not know. With the feeling that this might be the last farewell, I plucked up courage and left to join my ship.

I drove to Villefranche in my little car. A steam launch awaited me at the quay. I sent the car back to Fabron with its French chauffeur. I wanted Ducky to use it.

The next morning as we were casting off I noticed a carriage driving up to the quay. Ducky and her sister, the Infanta Beatrice, had come to see me off. The propellers churned up the water, the *Peresviet* moved slowly out and

[1] The Duchess of Coburg and Gotha.

the quays receded. I stood on deck and watched them until distance hid them from sight.

While rounding the proverbially storm-infested Cape Matapan a gale was blowing, the night was pitch black and no stars were visible. The officer who had nearly got us into trouble in the Bay of Biscay was on duty on the bridge. Little could be seen. Suddenly a steamer's lights appeared out of the night right on our course. Our friend lost his head completely and began to zigzag wildly, taking us completely off our course, so that in the end no one knew where we were, and as there were no stars to put us right, the navigation officer had a pretty problem in trying to calculate the right course from the maze of zigzags which had been indulged in. In the end, ' by guess and by God,' he established what he considered might be the right course. When I came on the bridge for my watch early in the morning I saw a lighthouse appearing out of the mist high up on shore. It was a well-known landmark and proved the navigation officer's calculations to have been dead reckoning—no mean achievement.

At the Piræus we received the usual visit from Aunt Olga with the King of Greece and her sons 'in tow.' On a later occasion I made use of one of our visits to the Piræus to look up my sister Helen, and her husband Prince Nicholas of Greece,[1] at their charming house in Athens which they had just occupied after their marriage.

From Crete we went straight to Port Said, where my brother Boris with his friends, the Chevalier de Shaeck, Constantine Grews, with his brother, and Captain Nicholas Strandmann joined us. They were on a world tour, a 'globe-trotting spree,' and Boris had received special permission from the Emperor to be taken to Colombo on the *Peresviet*. They were a merry company, and were welcome to me as I was not in a happy mood. I was

[1] Father of the Duchess of Kent.

neither on a pleasant cruise nor did I take kindly to the world around me at the time. Their noisy and carefree attitude to things in general brought with it a jolly atmosphere, and for the time being relieved me a little of the burden which I was dragging with me.

I joined this lusty company on their visit to Thebes, where we went by train. We saw the sights of Memphis, Luxor, and Karnak, where there are some almost perfectly preserved temples, which made a special impression on me because they looked as though they had been built quite recently instead of over four thousand years ago. The two colossi of Memphis towered high and imposing, as the appropriate witnesses of the uninterrupted civilization of millenniums which had flowed steadily like the waters of the River Nile, its centre and *raison d'être*, to become a unique and colossal achievement of the human race.

The Khedive had provided Boris and his company with his private yacht, which took us back to Cairo.

The merry company which had joined us was somewhat rowdy, and as they were not under naval discipline they over-indulged in libations. In the end the senior doctor, who, in any case, was an addict to liquor of all kinds, broke absolutely loose. He lost control over himself completely, with the result that the commander had him locked up. We all thought that he would sleep it off and that for the time being he was out of harm's way, but suddenly there was a fearful commotion accompanied by the noise of splintering glass. He had broken loose, had smashed the skylight of his cabin and stood before us with his white summer tunic and his face smothered in blood. At Colombo he was dismissed ship.

In the Indian Ocean we met some homeward-bound units of our Pacific squadron with which we exchanged compliments. There is always much excitement when one meets one's own people on the immensity of the sea.

One day we sighted a British Naval sloop bound from Colombo to Aden. She was flying a signal in the

International code, which read something like: 'Please send us your doctor—bad accident——' then followed the long Latin name of some medicine for eye trouble.

We hove to and sent our steam launch with our junior doctor, the other being, as already mentioned, under lock and key. Fortunately we had the medicine required, as the case was one that needed urgent attention.

Our Navy was on excellent terms with the British and, although we were on friendly relations with the fleets of other countries, barring one which belonged to a certain European power, our relations with the Royal Navy were the best possible, and better than with any others.

When chance brought us into ports where British men-of-war were lying, we could be sure that a good time would be in store for us. The English commander would generally send an invitation to join in boat races with them. We invited one another to our messes and, generally, there was among us a spirit of true fellowship. That fellowship, which was one of the sea and of our calling, was shared with the others too, but the ships of one particular navy had a name for their aloofness and lack of hospitality. They were proverbially mean.

Colombo and the coast of Ceylon when seen from the sea makes an unforgettable impression on one—a picture of dark green on red against an incredible blue.

I accompanied Boris to see a little of the attractions of the place, but I had not much time to spare. We visited the Temple where one of the teeth of Buddha is kept, and had an impression of a Ceylonese temple dance at night in the light of torches. This dance was, incidentally, not arranged by the Temple authorities as one would have expected, but by the Hotel. The drums beat to the accompaniment of a strange and discordant ritual music while diabolical figures were whirling round in a mad dance until they either were on the point of running amok or else collapsed from exhaustion. The tropical night and the uncanny sight in the red light of torches gave the performance a truly infernal aspect, and the exotic odour of the lotus flowers near by added an air of mystery which belongs to the unfathomable depths of the East. The whole show was more like a dream than reality.

Before leaving Ceylon I joined Boris and his companions on an expedition to Newara Eliya in the hill country. It was comparatively cool up there, so much so that at night fires had to be lit. This looked somewhat out of place in these tropical regions, but it was necessary.

The tea planters of the district invited us to a stag hunt. They hunted with beagles on foot—a strenuous exercise in the heat of the day, and none of us felt inclined to continue after the first efforts.

Returned to Colombo, I bade farewell to Boris and his merry company. I did not know then that our next meeting would be in somewhat awkward circumstances.

On our way to Port Batavia in Java we had a distant view of Krakatoa and the sea was still covered with pumice stone from the eruption or rather explosion. We took some of this useful commodity on board, which Nature had scattered so generously—it came in handy for scrubbing decks.

From Port Batavia—I call it so because its real name, 'Tanjong Priok,' is more than double Dutch—I paid a hurried visit to Batavia. I called on the Governor and was very favourably impressed by the way in which the Dutch had turned this town into a reproduction of their native country. The great neatness of the place and its canals gave this tropical region an almost Dutch aspect. Everything appeared well organized and efficient in the extreme. Of all the European colonies which I had occasion to visit, the British and the Dutch made by far the best impression on me. There is order and efficiency in their outer aspect as well as in their administration. I cannot say the same of some of the colonies belonging to some other European nations. The British and the Dutch are born colonizers.

One curious feature which I had not noticed anywhere else was that whenever one met a native in the street he would kneel down. I do not believe that this conduct had been forced upon them by the white man. The Malays are a proud race and consider themselves equal to Europeans, but this token of respect, for such I think it was, was not the outcome of servile submission but one of esteem, a form of politeness and an acknowledgment of valour.

These Malays are a splendid race of men with an ancient civilization to their credit, the remarkable achievements of which are to be found further inland, and I greatly regret that I had no time to see them.

The botanical gardens at Buitenzorg are quite remarkable; they are world famous and justly so. I do not know much about flowers and trees, but the general aspect of the magnificent collection of tropical flora which I was fortunate in seeing would please any lover of beauty. For all the benefits and material profits reaped in their colonies, the Dutch have given much in return. This is the right spirit for colonization.

On our way from Java to Hong Kong one of our engines broke down. We proceeded along very slowly while our engineers repaired the damage. These engines had done splendid work hitherto, considering that they were quite new. Engines, like living things, take some time before they settle down in their environment and begin to work smoothly. After twenty-four hours of tinkering our engineers successfully repaired the damage.

Outside Hong Kong harbour we took a pilot on board who nearly got us into very serious trouble with a small British cruiser which was lying at anchor in the port.

We seemed to have been doomed to get into trouble through pilots during the course of this voyage. Their presence on board defeated their very purpose and invited disaster.

On entering the lovely harbour we were carried straight at this cruiser and a collision seemed imminent.

There was the sound of bugles and a commotion on board accompanied by the rattling of anchor chains as they paid out their anchors to enable them to swing away from us on the current. Had it not been for the prompt way in which the British cruiser had dealt with the situation, serious damage would have been certain. As it was we just missed her by a narrow margin.

The captain of the British cruiser told me later that we had given him a frightful shock and that he thought that it would be impossible to get out of our way in time. We were invited on board by him and parted the very best of friends, as we always did with those on British men-of-war.

Hong Kong made an excellent impression on me and I have seen few places more beautifully situated on hills surrounding a splendid harbour.

When myriads of lights are lit upon the hills and dusk descends on the town, it is really worth seeing. Its night life is of the gayest, and the Chinese quarter of the old town with its bright colours, curious shop signs, and narrow streets, in which the East pursues its immutable course, add much to the fascination of its natural beauties.

We called nowhere on our way from there to Port Arthur, as we were in a hurry to join our Far East squadron which had assembled there.

Soon after our arrival we were received with a 'bang' by Admiral Skrydlov, who was in command of our Far East squadron. He pounced upon us, making 'heavy weather' about our inefficiency and uselessness!

It was an infuriated admiral's visitation. He let his thunder and lightning loose upon our captain, who, in spite of his inefficiency, was a 'decent fellow,' and popular with all of us. The Admiral raved and stormed in front of the whole crew. This was an error and a dangerous one.

Everything, in his opinion, which he vented in non-Parliamentary language, was wrong with us and with the ship. We were the most inefficient and hopeless beggars that had ever sailed upon the Seven Seas and the captain was the worst of all! He found fault with everything. We were no earthly good to anyone. How could they in Russia have dispatched such a vessel with such incapables. He would report this at once. Yes, he would wire to the Admiralty. Something had to be done about it. It was an unheard-of and an unprecedented piece of infernal cheek. He would not have it! No, not he! He would dismiss the captain. And he did.

While these pronouncements of doom, accompanied by violent abuse, were pouring over our poor captain, he stood like one petrified, a sorry figure at the salute. All of us, officers and men, looked on dumbfounded. We felt really sorry for him. He was no Drake, but many of Skrydlov's comments would have been more in place had they been addressed to the Admiralty. Much of it was manifestly unjust. To me, however, the Admiral behaved with the greatest circumspection, and he was genuine in this. Ours was a brand new ship which had come straight from the builders and we had had no time to get used to formation exercises with the rest of the fleet. How could he have expected us to take part in the exercises successfully and smoothly straight away? Such manœuvres require a team spirit and that needs training in unison with the rest. The instruction which one has had previously in other ships does not enable one to collaborate successfully and at once with other units of a fleet which have had ample time to work together and create an individual harmony. All this takes time. Every ship and every fleet possesses a marked individuality of its own, which have to be brought into unison with skill and patience.

This frightful row was a most unpleasant experience, and I felt really sorry for our 'old man.'

It was a very different Port Arthur which I saw in February 1902 from the one on whose bleak heights I had raised the flag of St. Andrew four years previously on that bitterly cold December day.

Then it was a lonely wilderness; now it resembled a beehive of activity. They were feverishly at work everywhere. The hills were being fortified. A town had been built and the harbour-works had almost been completed. Everything was being done to make it into a first-class naval base, and all had been taken into consideration except the most essential thing of all—that the place was a death trap and not only no good at all but even fatal for a fleet.

And what is more, although the forts later proved that they could ward off armies indefinitely, yet the courage of their defenders was of no practical avail. Port Arthur has only a strategical *raison d'être*, if its hinterland is controlled by one's own armies. If these are defeated, as ours were, and the enemy is in full command of such regions as lie in its rear, Port Arthur is like a rock in the sea, when all else has been covered by the high tide.

I found the place teaming with life. There were hotels and restaurants and a good hospital; the streets were filled with soldiers of Siberian regiments and Cossacks. There were Chinese and, of course, crowds of Japanese who said nothing but saw everything. They had established themselves as laundry men, but all of them were connected with their Intelligence Service. Nothing escaped their notice while our good people took no serious precautions to conceal their activities under a cloak of secrecy.

All this motley array hurried hither and thither. Engineers and soldiers, merchants and agents of foreign firms, all were jostling each other, some eager to make as much money as they could and others putting finishing touches to the place.

There was constant hammering and the din of work in full swing, and although this sudden activity had brought life to the grim hills and their savage bleakness, yet it had not in any way reduced their fearsome and moody aspect. They appeared like silent and disinterested spectators among the ants which laboured around them, and seemed to forbode the evil, the fearful tragedy that was shortly to come upon us all.

In the early summer of 1902 I was instructed by the late Emperor to pay an official visit to the Empress of China at Peking. The purpose of this visit was to express our sympathy to China for the trouble into which the Boxer Rising had plunged her, but considering that this calamity had been brought about to no mean a degree by the conduct of foreigners whom the Chinese in their exasperation had vainly tried to eject, this expression of sympathy was of a dubious nature from the ethical point of view, as was, in fact, the behaviour of Europeans in China generally.

It was rather like expressing one's commiseration to a person in hospital whom one's own gang had knocked down and injured.

I boarded one of our sloops which took me to Taku, whence a train conveyed me to Peking. At every station which my train passed a guard of honour belonging to one of the foreign contingents of the 'punitive' force had been turned out for me.

On my arrival in Peking I went straight to our Legation. I stayed there a few days, during which I received very careful coaching in the elaborate and thousand-year-old ceremonial of the Chinese Court. It was a most intricate procedure in which every step, every gesture, and every movement of the body in general had its special function and meaning, not unlike the elaborate sacerdotal rites of the Orthodox and Catholic clergy. I was initiated only into the most essential of these, but even then it was not easy, for the Chinese Court had not adopted European Court ceremonial as had the Japanese when meeting foreign royalty.

On the day which had been fixed for my interview I was carried to the Imperial Palace in a sedan chair. My retinue consisted of our Minister, the Legation Interpreter, Kolishev, whom I have already mentioned in connection with the occupation of Port Arthur, and a number of officers.

Before one reaches the innermost and sacred part of the Imperial Palace several courts have to be crossed. They were absolutely empty. Except myself, our minister, and the interpreter, the rest had been dropped in one of the exterior courts, beyond the threshold of which they were not permitted.

When we reached the inner court we got out of our sedan chairs and were ushered into the reception hall of the Palace. When I entered its temple-like interior, which was shrouded in a mysterious gloom, I made a deep bow. The whole Court stood at the other end, the ministers on one side of the Empress and the ladies of the Court on the other. She was seated like a female divinity on a beautifully worked gold and blue chair, and everything in that great hall was in a gold and blue scheme; possibly this, too, like the rest of the Palace and its courts, was intended to convey some esoteric meaning of which these outward signs were the symbols.

Before her stood a table laden with the Regalia of China, which was intended as a bar between her and us.

The hall in which I found myself was just like a Chinese temple into which daylight was admitted sparingly from the ceiling. It was exquisitely furnished with the treasures of China's millennial cultures and arranged with the greatest of taste.

The little woman on the throne, her hair dressed in the most elegant Mandshu fashion, was perhaps the most powerful and certainly the most absolute ruler of her time. Five hundred million people were under her sway. She was endowed with formidable intelligence and was credited with a masterly talent for State-craft. Little in her huge country was done without her ken and authority; she held in her hands all the strings of government. Her will was absolute, her orders law, and if anyone was in her way she would have such a person promptly dispatched.

When I reached the centre of the hall I bowed and once

again when I reached the table. Beyond the table I could not go.

The whole Court was dressed in ceremonial attire of which every colour and insignia of office and rank were as complicated and important as the ceremonials themselves.

The Empress addressed a few polite words to me about my journey, my health, and the usual Oriental politenesses of the kind. She did not address me directly but whispered them to one of her ministers who knelt down at the side of her chair. The minister repeated her words to Kolishev, who translated them to me. Then my words, such as, "I hope Your Majesty is well," returned to her directly by way of Kolishev. We were, of course, standing all the time.

The Empress ruled the country for her son, who was Emperor only in name. Later, so, at any rate, the story runs, she had him put quietly out of the way.

This exchange of politenesses did not last long, and on their conclusion after another succession of bowings we were taken to the Emperor, whose apartments were in the same 'holy of holies'—just a few doors away. He was a pale and distinguished-looking young lad of about eighteen or nineteen years of age, and I was favourably impressed by him.

My interview was of a quite informal nature, the only other person present being our minister and Kolishev. The young Emperor conferred the Dragon Order of China on me, and tried hard to overcome his natural shyness during the interview. He did his best to be amiable, but one could not help feeling sorry for him as his unenviable position had given him a marked inferiority complex.

After a series of the usual 'exit' ceremonials I returned to our Legation.

During my stay at Peking I was entertained to dinner by the British Minister, and on another occasion by the German Minister, Herr von Mumm. These occasions had no political significance but were quite ordinary social functions. They were well done and, what is more, amusing.

In between my various duties I saw all the sights of the Imperial City, and before leaving Peking called on Prince T'Sin at his palace.

He was a member of the Imperial Family and a very interesting old man whose hobby appeared to be collecting watches and clocks, of which he had a great many of considerable rarity and value. They ranged from the earliest to the latest models, among them were some of which any European museum would have been proud.

Prince T'Sin asked me whether there was anything which I would like to be shown in particular. I had often heard of the palace dogs of Peking which I understood differed considerably from their European version. A whole basketful of these delightful creatures was brought. There were eight of them—all puppies. The Prince asked me to choose some. I gladly availed myself of this welcome opportunity and picked out three. Exquisite little creatures they were, with glossy coats and far more delicately shaped and dainty than their descendants in Europe. I intended to take them to Europe as a present to 'Ducky,' but, alas, they perished on our return voyage from distemper and had to be thrown overboard. The crew had made pets of them and had taught them all kinds of tricks.

At Peking itself the Temple of Heaven made a striking impression on me, as did the Imperial summer residence in its surroundings.

The Court had arranged a special luncheon in my honour at the Summer Palace where I and my escort went on horseback. This palace and the fabulously beautiful grounds among which it stands are well known as one of the great marvels of China, and it will suffice for me to say that in everything they are an expression of that amazing civilization which has no rival of its kind anywhere, both in its continuity and longevity. They succeed admirably in conveying an atmosphere of repose and perfect tranquillity about them which was exactly the object for which they were created. It was the wisdom and the understanding of things beautiful and the exquisite refinement of a noble and peace-loving race which made itself apparent in all these dainty and patiently worked details, and in the grand simplicity of the whole.

This attractive picture had been sadly marred by the activity of those who at the same time had sent emissaries of 'Light' to a people who had nothing to learn from them save, possibly, the art of destruction.

The European contingents had looted all that could be carried away and had destroyed much of what could not, and in the streets of Peking the most precious articles of Chinese art were being offered for sale by members of the 'punitive' force, and not all of these amateur salesmen were soldiers. In the face of this blatant audacity one could have nothing but a feeling of shame. Barbarians, the Chinese called the men from the West, or 'foreign devils,' who had come upon them like a scourge. I was told that the only members of this shameful visitation of might who had not participated in this orgy of destruction and looting had been the Japanese. They had looked on silently and had kept aloof.

I was entertained to a splendid Chinese Court luncheon on the lower platform of the famous marble junk on the lake of the Summer Palace. It consisted of, I think, thirty courses and the names of the various dishes were written on red paper menus. I asked our interpreter to translate them for me. There was every conceivable thing there. Shark's fins and bamboo shoots and fried duck, all well and pleasantly spiced. There was not a single dish which was unpalatable, not even the putrid eggs with their piquant taste of good gorgonzola, which after all is really a form of putrid milk. We were served champagne and some of the Chinese ministers and courtiers became quite merry. The weather was beautiful as were the palace grounds with their rivulets, dainty bridges, and pavilions.

It was like a picture from fairyland, a never-to-be-forgotten impression of exquisite human skill merged with the resources of nature. The only unpleasant thing which I had experienced in Peking was the dust which pursued one wherever one went.

I left for Newchwang, near the Great Wall, where we had a contingent of troops stationed which I had been asked to inspect as part of my official duties. Then I left for Port Arthur on the small sloop which had brought me.

From Port Arthur the *Peresviet* accompanied Admiral Skrydlov on the *Petropavlovsk* and a number of other ships to Vladivostok by way of Hakodate.

Shortly after our arrival at Vladivostok the Admiral called for me and handed me a telegram from the Emperor. It read to the effect that I was to stay on in the Far East, but for how long was not clear. What was quite obvious, however, was that pressure had been brought to bear on my cousin[1] to keep me and my future wife apart and to ruin any chance of meeting her. The Emperor's dispatch was followed by one from my father to the effect that I should submit for my own good. This made matters considerably worse. I was furious, not so much with the contents of these pronouncements as with the manner in which plots were being hatched behind my back. My situation amounted to exile.

I was desperate and great gloom fell on me, life seemed to have lost its purpose, there was nothing but a completely blank future bereft of all expectation of happiness and achievement. It was a dismal and sorry state to be in, made more unbearable because I had no means of knowing what stringent measures of suppression would be brought in my absence against the woman I cared for. Twelve thousand miles separated us. To disobey the Emperor never entered my mind at any time. I was a naval officer pledged by my honour to do my duty, that was the main

---

[1] Late Emperor Nicholas II.

thing, and which personal interests, however strong, had no right to interfere with.

When the situation of complete uncertainty had reached its climax sudden appeasement came to me. One man at home had had the sense to realize that all this fuss was an ado about nothing, and that this treatment was most unfair and undeserved. His truthful nature and straightforward character could not abide these continuous coteries and whisperings at home. In his capacity as the head of our fleets, Uncle Alexey Alexandrovitch, ordered Admiral Skrydlov to appoint me as Lieutenant-Commander to the *Nahimov*, a cruiser of our squadron. It was more than kind of him and typical of this splendid giant of a man who had a kindly and understanding heart and a great open nature.

This was a great joy and the unbearable burden of anxiety and dismay fell from me. The *Nahimov* was shortly bound for home and was manned by officers and men of the 'Naval Guards,' to which I myself belonged, and I felt at home with them, for they were my own lot.

Admiral Skrydlov was greatly pleased and I believe that he took the credit for this promotion on himself. At any rate, he congratulated me on my appointment, which really amounted to my being second in command. He had shown a keen interest in my career and, so I was told, considered me an efficient officer.

Life assumed once more a pleasing aspect as the future seemed more certain. I found a very congenial atmosphere on board my new ship, and this, wherever human beings are herded together, depends in no small measure on the character of the man who is in charge. Captain Stemann, of the *Nahimov*, was an ideal leader of men. He was quiet, efficient, and just, and possessed all the finest attributes of a thorough seaman. In appearance he was short and stocky, and looked like a real skipper. He was very popular and on his ship everything went smoothly. Captain Stemann was the best man I have ever served with, and what made him specially pleasant to associate with was that on all occasions, even when the burden of responsibility weighed heavily upon him, he always contrived to be in a merry mood. Moreover, he knew no fear, and I do not believe that he had any in his character at all.

No angry word passed his lips and on all occasions he was dignified, and even when joking with us or the men, as he often did, he inspired respect. His ship was a model of efficiency.

As the *Nahimov* had done five years' continuous service in the Far East and needed a change, it had been decided by the Admiral that we were to go on a visit to Japan, where the crew was to be given longish leave.

I paid an unofficial visit to the Emperor at Tokyo, and on that occasion met Prince Arisugawa who, as I have mentioned previously, had asked me to stay with him *en famille* during the next occasion on which I should visit Tokyo. I was the first who was honoured thus by a member of the Japanese Imperial Family.

I accepted the invitation gladly and spent a very jolly few days with the Prince and Princess at their castle, built in old Japanese style, in Tokyo.

In the evenings there were musical soirées at which Japanese musicians performed on their instruments, and there were traditional dances of the country.

The Princess asked me whether I would like her to give me tea in the Japanese ceremonial manner. This is a most interesting and very ancient tradition of their hospitality, which she performed with great elegance and grace. The procedure is a complicated one, and I believe that it requires much training from early girlhood until a Japanese lady acquires this polite art to perfection.

I was fortunate in being honoured with this interesting ritual of hospitality by one who, in her position as one of the first ladies of her country, was an expert exponent.

The castle had some fine gardens arranged in the traditional style of the country. These, too, had some special significance and are planned according to carefully preserved rules. But even to the uninitiated they are a lovely thing to behold, simply from the point of view of beauty, with their pavilions, fish pools, dainty bridges, and rivulets.

During my stay in Japan my friend Baron Madenokosi was my guide as he had been on the previous occasion, and accompanied me on all my expeditions.

Returned to Yokohama, I joined in the gay and easy holiday spirit of my fellow officers. The crew, too, were off duty, and except for the most essential things on board, no work whatever was done, and as most of us were young we enjoyed ourselves greatly on shore.

We had received special permission to go from Kobe to Nagasaki through the Inland Sea, where, as a rule, no foreign warships were allowed. It resembles a large lake and is dotted with islands, with a picturesque background of mountains giving it a very pleasing and quiet effect.

At Nagasaki, which had by now become a very familiar place to all of us, we visited our old haunts and finished what had been an unusually jolly and carefree occasion enhanced by the knowledge that soon we would start on our homeward voyage.

At Port Arthur we continued on our ordinary routine of fleet exercises and gunnery, when one day we received the order to take our Minister to Seoul and his wife on board and proceed with them to Korea.

Seoul, the capital and residence of the Emperor of Korea, is some way up a river estuary and is joined with Tchemulpo, its port, by railway.

I accompanied our Minister to Seoul, where I was received by the Emperor. He was the last Sovereign of that very interesting country, which gave one the impression of being half Chinese and half Japanese, although it had a very ancient civilization of its own. The most obvious peculiarity to a casual visitor, and I stayed there less than twenty-nine hours, is the white dress and black top-hats worn by the men in contrast to the blue which at that time was almost the universally worn colour of the Chinese masses.

The Emperor struck me as a pleasant and well-meaning individual, an easy and amiable man to get on with, whose modest palace was run by an elderly and very portly Englishwoman. I was given excellent tea and was shown some strange native dances. The Emperor was murdered soon after.

The river in the estuary of which we lay at anchor has very dangerous currents which are made exceedingly tricky by the tides, so that the raising of the anchors of a large vessel is an extremely delicate task. We lay on two anchors at the time, and it fell to me, as second in command, to have them raised. The starboard anchor had to be taken up first, but in such a way that the strain on the port one by the violent current and tide should not cause the chain to snap. For that reason the port anchor chain had to be paid out to a considerable length to decrease the strain on it. The whole of this procedure was interesting as a problem in seamanship and mechanics. All went well and we returned to Port Arthur without any untoward incident from wind, weather, or human agency.

The usual routine was interrupted by a short visit to Newchwang. Admiral Skrydlov had given our officers permission to go on a short excursion to Peking.

I remained in solitary command of the cruiser while the rest were away. To give the crew an opportunity of a change from routine on board, I allowed them to visit their comrades in arms on shore and in the evening went out to fetch them back. I took as many as I could on the steam launch and the rest into our long-boat, which I took in tow. I was particularly anxious that while I was in charge of the *Nahimov* nothing should go wrong. The sea was fairly rough but not dangerously so, but when we got out into the open and away from the shelter of the shore I found that the long-boat which we were towing was beginning to ship water.

We ourselves were getting into difficulties through the rising sea, crashing against the oncoming waves with unpleasant thuds while spray flew in all directions. The sea got worse the nearer we drew to the *Nahimov*.

When we had got half-way across, shouts were raised on the long-boat. It appeared that their rudder had been carried away. I ordered them to steer with an oar. The situation was becoming critical. We were struggling hard, going dead slow against an ugly sea. Finally I succeeded in reaching the *Nahimov* and dropped the long-boat alongside, manœuvring the launch to her opposite side. We clambered on deck soaked to the skin and got the boats safely hoisted into their davits, a procedure which was by no means easy in view of the roll of the vessel and the heavy seas on which the boats were tossed about. They might have been smashed to splinters by the waves.

The poor fellows in the long-boat had had a most unpleasant experience, they were wet, miserable and numbed with cold. It was hard to quiet them down. On our return to Port Arthur we received the very welcome order that we were to proceed to Europe. Everyone was delighted. We coaled and took provisions on board, and when all was ready the Admiral ordered us to heave anchor.

We hoisted the long pennant which is used on such occasions by homeward bound units, and steamed half-speed round the anchored fleet to the music of our band. We were cheered out and took course for Mosampo, where we were to pick up our naval picket, which had been guarding our Consulate there.

It was a friendly country which unfolded itself before us, green, hilly, and inviting. The Bay of Mosampo, as I have had occasion to mention before, is ideally situated for a naval base, being naturally protected by little islands

THE AUTHOR AND HIS WIFE

The Grand Duchess Victoria of Hesse and the Grand Duke Cyril at the time of their betrothal.

THE LATE EMPEROR NICHOLAS II AND THE CZAREVITCH
Seen at a regimental review with the Author standing behind them.

It was a veritable temptation to us, but had to be left alone for fear of exciting the Japanese, who would never have tolerated us there. In any case, they greatly resented all our activities in Korea.

When we left that hospitable bay and directed our course towards the China Sea, I felt that every revolution of the propeller was bringing me nearer to the woman I loved. By now I was a commander, and this, too, gave me cause to be very happy and pleased with the world.

We stopped nowhere on our long trek between Korea and Cochin China until we anchored in the Bét'Along in the estuary of a river on the upper reaches of which is Honoi, the capital of this French colony, where they had a colonial exhibition at the time.

This bay has a reputation of being a favourite haunt of sea serpents. I do not know exactly what to make of these monsters, but am sailor enough to believe that they may exist. I saw none on that occasion nor at any time during my voyages, but others have seen them and, in any case, the sea is huge and deep and who knows what uncanny horrors lurk in its uttermost depths.

We went up the river to Honoi in a small steamer to see the exhibition, but I was not at all impressed by it. There were a few pavilions among the palm trees, and there was nothing that was particularly attractive, and besides I had no knowledge of this colony, and so could not compare its products with those of others.

The place was stiff, official, demoralizing, and I was glad to leave.

Our next port of call for coaling was to be Singapore, but great disappointment awaited us.

When we had reached the latitude of Saigon, Captain Stemann called me to him. He lay in his cabin when I entered. With a smile on his face and in a joking manner he said to me: "I am sorry that you should find me in this state, but I have been laid low by something which has a nasty resemblance to a stroke. I shall have to transfer the command to you. Here are the keys to the safe; you will find all the secret papers inside."

We were all dumbfounded by this disaster which had come upon us so entirely unexpectedly. The captain had seemed perfectly well, and this calamity was deeply felt by all on board. He had been loved and admired by everyone without exception. For the time being we were in a dilemma. I called an officers' conference. It was agreed that Singapore was too far and the gravity of the captain's condition made it essential to proceed full steam to the nearest port.

Accordingly I altered course to Saigon, which we reached the following evening. I let the officials of the French Colony know by wireless of our captain's precarious condition and when we arrived a steam launch was waiting to take him off. The captain left his ship on a stretcher. He was never to return. He was well looked after by the French doctors and sisters in their well-equipped hospital. We remained three weeks in the estuary of a tropical river, the steamy and malodorous banks of which were one-quarter putrid water and the rest mud. The hot-house atmosphere, the leaden heat, and the disaster on top of it all made this infernal place a loathsome nightmare—and we were waiting for—death! From the first the doctors had expressed the view that the captain was doomed. He became completely paralysed. Every day we visited him and during the third week he died. We buried him there.

I cannot pass over this sad event without recording the excellent impression which I had of the Catholic Bishop of Saigon.

Captain Stemann was a Protestant, we were Orthodox, and the only church in the place was Catholic. A religious service was necessary and the bishop allowed us to use his church for that purpose. In every way he showed great sympathy and kindness in a truly generous manner.

A funeral mass was celebrated by our priest, whom we

had on board with us, our sailors' choir sang the appropriate liturgy of 'eternal memory' over our well-loved friend and captain, and in a far-off and fever-infested land of the tropics we laid him to rest with the flag of St. Andrew shrouding him.

It was a remarkable occasion—Orthodox funeral rites over a Protestant in a Catholic church.

During the three weeks of our inactivity in this wretched and deadly hole the crew had shown signs of unrest, as I had issued strict instructions that they were not to go ashore.

The authorities had warned us that an epidemic of dysentery was ravaging the district, which was already prone to the visitations of other evils. A case of dysentery on board might have had far-reaching results. The unbearable heat on the ship, the inviting but treacherous aspect of the land which hid its sinister evils beneath a mask of tempting loveliness—all this played on the imagination of my men, and had it not been for the vigilance of my boatswain, there might have been serious trouble. He proved an excellent adviser to me and was most useful in every way. Thirty years at sea and ten of them on the *Nahimov* had made him into a fine sailorman—into an ancient mariner who was familiar with all the ways of the sea and with the men who fared thereon. He had seen all climes and countries and was invaluable as a guide through many of the baffling problems with which one's first command confronts one.

We left Saigon and its unwholesome river with its white residents, most of whom were, as the doctor told me, doomed to perish sooner or later from liver ulcers. They brought this on themselves through excessive drinking, but the poor devils could scarcely be blamed.

As we had lost three weeks already in that dreadful place and everyone was anxious to return with as little delay as possible I wanted to take the *Nahimov* straight back to Europe, stopping only on the way for coaling. I asked for permission to sail at once, but was instructed to put in at Singapore to await the arrival of a new captain. This dismayed me, as I considered it quite unnecessary, and it meant, moreover, that there would be weeks of further inactivity and waste of time. Besides, I had sufficient experience by now to be able to see the cruiser safely home.

Accordingly I took her to Singapore.

It was Christmas of the year 1902 when we got there. I remember the occasion well, because I received a very pretty watch from Ducky as a present.

The three weeks of our stay at Singapore proved anything but dull. The British Pacific squadron was in port with Admiral Sir Cyprian Bridge in command.

There were the usual exchanges of visits between us and the British ships. I met the commander of a British sloop who had served with my uncle, the Duke of Edinburgh, and knew his family well. We became good friends and played golf together every afternoon. On such occasions we often met Sir Cyprian Bridge and his flag-lieutenant, Hamilton.

Every afternoon, weather permitting, because it was the rainy period, I sailed my boat from the *Nahimov* to the quay, for we were anchored some way off shore.

There were jolly parties and entertainments as well as frequent visits to Government House, where we used to play tennis and have tea with the Governor and his family.

Although Singapore was well equipped with every conceivable thing that people are used to in Europe, there was a noticeable absence of a good band.

We had an excellent one on board which had been hired by the mess for the period of the *Nahimov's* service in the Far East and consisted entirely of civilians, who for that reason were not under naval discipline, their only connection with us being that they were in our pay. They were a 'tough' crowd and greatly addicted to drink. At times these artists were a real source of worry to us, but as musicians they were excellent. Some of the large hotels of the place asked us for a loan of them to play at dances and entertainments. This was a special and very welcome opportunity for our musicians and we gladly accepted the offer. They performed very well, indeed, and added greatly to our popularity. To us, however, they proved a confounded nuisance as they invariably returned to ship dead drunk. To avoid any unpleasant incident on shore I used to send our boatswain to accompany them whenever they performed in town, and on several occasions the whole lot of them were locked up for the night in an empty coal bunker on deck. They were in the habit of knocking up such an infernal din that they prevented everyone from sleeping. In the coal bunker they were out of earshot. In fact it very nearly became their more or less usual abode.

When finally, without any casualties, all of them were safely returned by us to Russia, I think it was no mean achievement on our part.

Finally our new captain arrived. I did not feel overzealous in handing the *Nahimov* over to him as by now I had become thoroughly used to my job, but it had to be done. This brought a very happy three weeks to a conclusion, and time had passed quickly in this jolly environment.

We hove anchors almost immediately after the captain's arrival and proceeded straight for Suez, as we had taken sufficient coal on board to make a continuous voyage home.

Our new captain's name was Boukhvostov. I mention this, because he distinguished himself greatly as captain of the *Alexander III*, which perished heroically, not one man being saved, and fighting until the last gun was put out of action, against, in turn, practically every one of the great ships of the enemy at the battle of Tsushima.

As a man he was very different from our old captain. He was a very efficient naval officer, but a hard man of the old school. He knew his job and that was the main thing.

At Singapore we had stocked ourselves with cattle for our supply of fresh meat, and as we would be fifteen days at sea between Singapore and Port Said in the blazing heat of the Indian Ocean and the Red Sea, our paymaster, Lieutenant Kube, had devised a refrigerator of his own invention. The ship's carpenter made a remarkable success of it. It worked to perfection and we had fresh meat until we reached the Mediterranean.

At the Piræus, and by now she has become a regular and recurring feature in this account, Queen Olga with her sons 'in tow' was there to welcome us back, and what is more, I was surprised to see my brother Boris with her. I learnt, to my complete amazement and became thoroughly indignant as a result, that he had been sent there to prevent me from deserting ship, which the good people in St. Petersburg verily believed I was certain to do. They had sent him as ambassador to me, knowing how much I cared for him. This was his mission. This was the first welcome from my own kin, which they had deemed it proper to bestow on me on my return to Europe after my services abroad. Boris only acted according to instructions from home, and knew perfectly well the absolute futility of these absurd anxieties. At no time had I intended to do anything rash, yet at the same time I had not the least intention of giving up the woman I cared for, and the more pressure was brought to bear on me, the more adamant I became in my attitude. Fortunately the attitude of those at home changed completely later on and was replaced by one of great kindness and sympathy, but this condonation took years in coming.

We took Admiral Makarov with us to Naples. A short-lived and brilliant period of activity was in store for him as the leader and hero of our Far East squadron. I was to come into very close contact with him and nearly shared his fate. But of that later.

We spent a few days at Naples in a delightful atmosphere of brilliant Society life. Our consul was well in with the 'smart set' of the place, and soon we found ourselves in a whirlpool of social activities among the lovely surroundings of the Bay of Naples.

While still at Naples, a message arrived that at Villefranche the *Nahimov* was to be put at the disposal of my father. I saw through the idea at once.

Father arrived in due course and tried, but by no means enthusiastically, to persuade me to give up my future wife. When he saw that I was going to do nothing of the kind he discontinued his efforts. I went to Ventimiglia to meet her train. She had been staying in Switzerland and was on her way back to Nice.

It was a happy reunion when at last, after this period of uncertainty and unbearable anxiety, we met in the express.

Father was splendid and a really good friend to me, and kindness and parental sympathy personified in his treatment of us.

We spent a delightful few days at Nice, where we were left to ourselves whenever we liked. At other times Father entertained us to suppers and luncheons. Everything he did was done with love, for he wished us happiness.

All this was, however, strictly contrary to the purpose for which he had come, and I do not think that at any time he had shared the exaggerated views of the clique that had formed around those who were unfavourably inclined towards us.

He visited the ship, looked at my cabin, was very pleased with everything, and in the best of spirits. I will always remember Father's great sympathy in this matter and the helping hand which he had stretched out to us during this difficult period of my life.

We called at Lisbon on our way back, where I presented myself to King Carlos[1] of Portugal and his family.

[1] Carlos I, King of Portugal, assassinated in 1908. He was the son of King Luiz I and of Dona Maria, daughter of King Victor Emanuel I of Italy.

I took to the King at once. He was amiable, jovial, and very pleasant.

The passage had been a stormy one, and when we entered the fine harbour of Lisbon with its town magnificently situated among the fresh verdure of its setting, it was a welcome and very pleasing impression. Unfortunately I had no time to see anything of that interesting country, but what I did see at Lisbon spoke of the great power that Portugal had once been. Among the buildings which left a special impression on me are the churches, for they have a very attractive and special character all their own.

That interesting country, richly endowed with natural beauties of a rare kind and with the relics of succeeding civilizations is fortunate, too, in the man who at present guides her along the course of her destiny.

Our passage along the coasts of Portugal and Spain was rough, and when we had got half-way across the Bay of Biscay we became anxious about our coal, of which we had very little left. We had to decide as to whether to turn back to Vigo or make for the nearest port on our course. We decided to take the risk and took course for the Cornish coast. It was touch and go. We reduced speed and succeeded in reaching Falmouth without being driven to the desperate measure of using our furniture for fuel.

I had never been to Falmouth before. This old-fashioned Cornish seaport and the lovely country made a homely and quiet impression on us.

We found that the *Osborne*, with Princess Victoria on board, was anchored in the harbour. I called on her and later she was officially received by us.

From Falmouth we went without stopping to Kiel, where the crew was given a few days' rest.

Arrived at our Naval Base of Libau, I supervised the repainting of the *Nahimov*. She looked a poor sight after this long voyage and needed a new coat of paint badly. In my zeal to have her return to Kronstadt spick and span I exceeded the bounds permitted by the scheme which had been worked out by her paymaster, Kube. Painting a large vessel is a very expensive item. The *Nahimov's* hull was white and her funnel yellow, both of them very uneconomical colours as they are apt to be soiled by smoke, sea, and weather.

I had somewhat of a row with Kube for having given a new coat of paint to a part which he had not included in his scheme. He assured me that he was certain to get into 'hot water' about it—but he didn't.

We left Libau looking very smart and arrived at Kronstadt the next evening on the last lap of our twelve thousand miles' voyage.

There was the usual inspection of home-coming units of the fleet, after which I supervised the dismantling of the *Nahimov*. She had been five years in commission and needed a very careful overhaul.

It took some time to finish my duties on board, as much, beginning with the smaller guns, had to be removed from her.

When all had been done there were some very touching farewells. Officers and crew, we all had been like a great family and had shared the hardships, dangers, and surprises of the sea together. I was sorry to quit those with whom I had done my duty, and the ship which, in a way, had been my first command.

I did not know then that in a very short time I would loose many of my comrades for ever.

I remember especially that I embraced our old boatswain in the traditional Russian way—he, too, was to perish at sea. When I left there were cries of "Good luck to you, sir, and God speed to you on your way."

VI

War and Marriage

I SPENT a few very quiet weeks with my parents and then with Boris at Tsarskoe.

My brother had had an English country-house built for him there by Maple and Company and kept an English butler and an English coachman, both of them very true to type.

During this period, I had an interview with the Emperor, who did not, however, give me any clear indication as to the future prospects of Ducky and myself, beyond that there was some hope that things would, possibly, straighten out. He was very affable and showed much sympathy.

I obtained his and Father's consent to pay a visit to Coburg. I may mention here that no member of the Imperial Family, unless in the service of his country, was allowed to leave Russia without obtaining the Emperor's permission to do so. This was a well-established rule, which applied to State functionaries as well.

The rest of the summer I spent at Castle Rosenau, near Coburg, where Aunt Marie, Ducky, and Cousin Beatrice were at the time.

Ducky and I enjoyed our freedom and made plans for the future. The making of such plans is one of the consoling things of life, because they are based on hope, and although they may never mature the very making of them is a pleasant pastime. We rode and drove much in the forests near the castle and motored a great deal. I had two cars with me—the small one which I have mentioned already and a large six-seater touring-car which resembled a clumsy kind of omnibus. It had six cylinders, but was far less efficient than the other, breaking down with an enervating regularity. It was equipped with a silver service for picnicking.

Motoring in those pioneering days was accompanied by continuous trouble either from frequent breakdowns or from people and animals which one met on the way. Besides, cars in those days were the 'rich man's pleasure' and anyone having a car was naturally marked down as a capitalist, and therefore as an enemy of the people. I often met with some who manifested their outraged feelings in various ways of indignant behaviour as I passed by them. Apart from offending people politically there was another side to the unpopularity of motor cars, one, indeed, which had a more reasonable cause. They terrified human beings and all manner of beasts. Chickens were scattered in all directions, dogs run over, horses shied, upsetting carts into ditches. There were claims for damage done; road tolls had to be paid. Frequently one was stopped by the police and things had to be explained. In my exasperation I had the number plate replaced by a crown and fixed a special flag on the bonnet which made things easier.

In spite of such episodes, we enjoyed our trips immensely. We went through the length and breadth of the lovely Thuringian Forest, visited Nüremberg, Bamberg, Gotha, and much else of what is old and fascinating in that part of Germany which I had not seen before. We picnicked together out in the open, in nature's solitude and far from the busy world. Life was full and inviting. There was hope and the joy of living which comes to one on such occasions with the whole vigour and entirely carefree spirit of youth. It was an appeasement after much anxiety and sorrow.

In the autumn of 1903 I paid a visit to Palermo for

my health, and on my way to Russia spent Christmas at Coburg.

It was a thoroughly international Christmas, and the manner of keeping this feast was as effective as it was a well-matched combination of the best features of the English, German, and Russian way of celebrating it.

During the course of this very jolly period, the storm which had been gathering ominously for some time over Asia had reached the climax of its pent-up force. Silently, and imperceptible save to those who knew, it had spread until it suddenly broke over an unsuspecting Russia with all the shocking violence of surprise.

On the night of 9 February 1904[1] the Japanese, without declaring war on us, had attacked three of the best units of our fleet while these were lying in the outer roads of Port Arthur. The *Pallada*, *Retvisan*, and *Tzarevitch* were badly damaged by enemy torpedoes and put out of action for the time being.

On 10 February[2] the *Variag* and *Korjcetz* were destroyed at Tchemulpo and at the same time, two days only after the commencement of hostilities, the *Boyarin* and *Yenissei* were sunk by our own mines. Two days of war had cost us seven ships.

Baron Rosen on page 235 of *Forty Years of Diplomacy*, from which I have quoted previously and which I recommend to those who are interested in the events which led up to the Russo-Japanese War, speaks thus of the fight between the *Variag* and *Korjeetz* and the Japanese squadron.

'Real feeling was shown by the foreign sailors who witnessed the tragic destruction of our two small vessels by a powerful Japanese squadron in the harbour of Chemulpho on 8 February 1904. Officers of the French cruiser *Pascal*, which brought to Shanghai part of the survivors of the battle, related to me with profound emotion how the *Variag*, followed by the gunboat *Korjeetz*, having accepted the challenge, slowly steamed, colours

[1] 27 January, old style. [2] 28 January, old style.

flying, officers and men on parade, past the foreign men-of-war anchored in the roads, saluted by our national anthem, heroically going to meet certain destruction at the hands of the enemy who had spread the numerous and powerful vessels of his squadron in a wide semicircle, rendering escape a matter of utter impossibility.'

I was a naval officer and as such had no intimate knowledge of the real story of the drama that had so suddenly unfolded itself. There is nothing I personally know which I can add to the history of this war. As I have already said, I was taken by surprise. Not, indeed, that I had not suspected the possibility of war—that was always likely, due to the conflict of ambitions in the Far East—but the tragedy was overwhelming in its suddenness.

I will, therefore, quote from Baron Rosen's book, who, in his capacity of our then Ambassador to Tokyo, is in a unique position for giving a clear and absolutely authentic account of the events which led up to that war.

First, however, I may mention that Japan considered Korea as her sphere of influence in the same way as we looked upon Manchuria as our field of action.

I have already mentioned that we were embarking on an extensive East Asiatic policy. Japan, too, was pursuing such a plan. The plane upon which the two opposing currents came into contact and produced the spark which caused the conflagration was Korea. Great historical events are more often than not caused by petty incidents. The incident in this case was a timber concession in the region of the Yalu River in Korea. This concession had been granted by the Korean Government to a Russian company, and this is what Baron Rosen says concerning it on page 211 of his book: 'It appears that he (M. Bezobrazoff) had submitted to the Emperor a grandiose plan of the acquisition for Russia in the Far East of an Empire similar to Great Britain's Indian Empire by a similar process of gradual expansion, begun and effected by an organization framed on the lines of the defunct East India

Company. The timber concession on the Yalu obtained several years before that from the Korean Government, by a merchant from Vladivostok, was to have served, so to speak, as an entering wedge.' On page 213 he continues: 'They seemed to have obtained, under a pretext of needed protection, the dispatch to the Yalu of a considerable body of troops who had begun the construction of earthworks which looked very much like future batteries.—Now the absurdity' (p. 214) 'of a power like Russia, possessing on its own territory in Europe and Asia an almost untouched forest area of more than two million square miles, needing a timber concession at the far away mouth of the Yalu River on the Korean-Manchurian frontier—defended by earthworks and Cossacks—was too self-evident not to give rise in the minds of the Japanese to the unshakable conviction that we were preparing for some armed aggression against the Japanese interests in Korea. All these provocative proceedings were welcome to the large and influential party which was in favour of bringing the chronic conflict with Russia to a decisive issue by force of arms.'

Of Plehwe, our then Minister for Foreign Affairs, Baron Rosen says: 'As a very intelligent man, he could not have failed to realize that our whole Far Eastern policy, of which the Yalu enterprise was one of the most disquieting features, was bound to land us in the end in an armed conflict with Japan.' And on page 219: 'In Japan, however, everything seemed perfectly calm, at least on the surface, until two events occurred in Russia which produced in Japan an impression reflected in a remarkably alarmist undertone, perceptible in the utterances of the Press. These events were: the fall from power of Witte,[1] and the creation of a Viceroyalty of the Far East with Admiral Alexeeff as Viceroy.' And then—on page 222: 'Their immediate aims' (i.e. the Japanese) 'were the ousting of Russia from Korea and, if possible, from Manchuria as

[1] Finance Minister.

well, and the establishment of a Japanese protectorate over Korea, leaving to the developments of the future all ultimate aims such as the final annexation of Korea, the gradual absorption of Manchuria, and other ambitious plans in regard to China.' On page 226 he continues: 'I told the Viceroy frankly that as far as I could judge the Japanese Government were determined to secure the exclusive control of Korea by negotiation, if possible, if not, then by force of arms; that they were sure of moral support of the Western powers for whose benefit they were pretending that they were defending the independence and integrity of Korea and China against Russian aggression; that we could not possibly hope to retain our position in Korea as well as in Manchuria; that in my opinion the only rational thing we could do now would be to stick to Manchuria and scuttle from Korea.' Finally he refers to the naval position (pp. 230 and 241): 'The fate of the whole campaign rested on one slender and uncertain thread—the possibility of securing at the first stroke absolute command of the sea—the night attack on Port Arthur deprived us from the outset of the use of a most important arm of defence, as well as of offence, and thereby practically determined the issue of the campaign.'

From all the above it is evident that our refusal to withdraw from Korea as the Japanese had requested us to do during the course of the summer of 1903 up to the beginning of the hostilities led to the conflict.

I can throw no light on why the frequent warnings of Baron Rosen, who in his position as Ambassador to Japan had his hand on the political pulse of that nation, remained unheeded, unless the reason was that we grossly underestimated the military strength and efficiency of our enemy. We did not take them seriously, and this was an unpardonable error.

This, in my view, is the only explanation of our nonchalant attitude to what ought to have been a manifest danger to us.

So much was this the case that, when war came to us, we were entirely unprepared and allowed the Japanese to take the initiative everywhere.

One of the very few men, however, who did take the initiative against the enemy was Admiral Makarov. Japan's success, unlike ours, rested entirely, as the Baron has pointed out, on the control of the sea, as all her troops had to be moved to the Asiatic continent from her islands. If their fleet could only have been destroyed or crippled we might have won, as then the Japanese Army would have found itself cut off from supplies in men and munitions.

When the news of the sinking of our ships reached us, Russia was moved to violent indignation, and I think that this was possibly the only time when this war had the enthusiastic backing of the whole people.

I presented myself to the Emperor and to the Grand Duke Alexey Alexandrovitch and reported for active service. At first it was suggested that I should join the staff of Admiral Alexeeff, but on Uncle Alexey's advice I decided to report to Admiral Makarov at Port Arthur for service afloat. He had just been appointed to succeed Rear-Admiral Starck in the command of the Far East squadron at Port Arthur.

Until the appearance of the Admiral on the Far Eastern horizon, our fleet had not yet recovered sufficiently from the first onslaught by the enemy. With his arrival everything changed completely. This shows how the character of one man can instil hope and courage and the will to overcome all obstacles when all seems to have been lost and beyond repair.

The Admiral was a remarkable man not only as a naval officer but as a personality. His opponent, Admiral Togo, knew his value, and that he had in him a formidable enemy. The peculiar features of Makarov's character were quickness in seizing a situation and making immediate use of his advantages, absolute fearlessness, which sometimes amounted to dangerous audacity, an unshakable will power to carry out his plans unflinchingly and never looking back once he had begun an enterprise. His arrival at Port Arthur had almost a magic effect and ushered in a spirit of energetic activity and of hope. He was the kind of man with whom it would be a privilege to serve.

Before leaving for the Far East and plunging right into the midst of the witches' cauldron, I obtained the Emperor's consent to pay a farewell visit to Nice where Ducky and Aunt Marie were at the time. I stayed there four days and when the hour of departure came it was hard to tear myself away—desperately hard.

I returned to Petersburg via Vienna. On the day of my leaving for the front, I took Holy Communion in our chapel and bade farewell to my parents and to the staff of the Vladimir Palace. Then I left for the great unknown—for death maybe.

I interrupted my journey for one night at Moscow, where I stayed with Uncle Serge and Aunt Ella.[1] Uncle Serge, as I have already said, was Governor-General of that city.

The next day I boarded the Trans-Siberian express for Port Arthur. I believe that the length of the journey from St. Petersburg to Port Arthur in miles is approximately the distance between London and San Francisco.

It was a dreary trek across very monotonous country except for some diversions at the Urals and the Baikal Lake: the latter is really a kind of inland sea called by the local people the 'Sea of Baikal.' We passed small stations where the train halted for hours at a time because the whole line, which was then a single track, was crowded to its utmost capacity with eastward bound troop trains. We were held up at sidings, and whenever we stopped delegations came to my carriage wishing me good luck and expressing their loyalty with enthusiasm. I did not know then how much I stood in need of their good wishes.

[1] Grand Duchess Elizabeth.

The train compared very favourably with the American ones on the other side of the Pacific. It was comfortable, well-heated, and the food and the wines were of the best. We fed well and slept much. I had Kube with me as my A.D.C., and Ivanov, my sailor batman; there were also a number of other officers on the train. Occasionally we made merry to pass time. Small stations were passed on the way where crowds stood on the platform and shouted. They knew that I was on the train and that I was going into the hornet's nest. They seemed pleased that I had thrown in my lot with the rest.

And so the journey dragged on until we reached Irkutsk and the Lake of Baikal.

At that time the track of the Siberian Railway which now passes along the shores of the lake was not yet built. It was completed in 1905 and most of the way had to be blasted through solid rock. It holds the record for tunnels among Russian railways, and is a master work of skill.

The lake was frozen from end to end and the journey to a point roughly half-way across was accomplished in a fast *troika* drawn by sturdy little Siberian ponies. The Governor-General of Irkutsk accompanied us across the lake.

For Siberian conditions the weather hitherto had been mild. There was a temporary inn half-way across the lake where we all alighted. During a short rest in this tavern, we took refreshment and warmed ourselves up with some vodka.

The Ministry of Transport had built a railway line across the ice to facilitate troop traffic; we got into one of the carriages and completed the rest of the journey. The few carriages of which the train consisted were drawn by horses as it would have been unsafe to allow a locomotive on the ice. Even then it shows how heavily the lake freezes. It was a curious sensation to be sitting in a railway carriage and be drawn across a lake, which is famous for its enormous depth. Arrived at the other side, I boarded the all-steel Manchurian section of the Trans-Siberian express, where I had a special car with a small kitchen in it, as, for some unknown reason, that section of the express had no restaurant car attached, all the feeding having to be done in station restaurants on the way.

On the other side of the lake the congestion of the line greatly increased and progress was difficult and slow.

At last, after crossing some of the dreariest landscapes I have ever seen—an endless, mutilated forest known as the 'taiga,' here and there interrupted by bleak snow-covered plains and frozen rivers, a picture of grey, black and white—we approached hilly and then mountainous country.

We were nearing the Manchurian frontier and the Chinga ridge across it.

A halt was made at the frontier station 'Manchuria' and thence the train climbed laboriously up the steep incline of the ridge, helped by an auxiliary engine from the rear. We passed through the long tunnel of the Hingan Pass and thence into the dreary and endless Manchurian landscape, passing Harbin, Mukden, and Lao-Yan. At Mukden I was met by the Governor-General, Admiral Alexeeff. There was feverish activity everywhere. The line and stations were teeming with troops, munition transports, and every conceivable thing connected with the War. A human river flowed continuously from Europe to the Pacific along the narrow steel thread of railway.

Towards the early part of March I arrived at Port Arthur. The journey had taken two weeks in all, which, considering the unusual conditions, was by no means bad.

Port Arthur looked like a human ant heap. I did not concern myself with the fortifications which were being completed, but only with the fleet.

Immediately after his arrival Admiral Makarov had started repairing the damaged units of our Navy. Expert workmen had come from our yards at St. Petersburg and were hammering away at the ships. They worked efficiently and lost no time about it. As there were no dry docks for the battleships the local engineers had improvised some on the spot. Considering the enormous difficulties of their work, our people produced surprising results. After about a month of hard work most of the ships had been put into a condition which made them fit to meet the enemy.

Much has been written about Russia since the Revolution, more of it stark nonsense than truth. Our engineers and workmen were equal to any.

When the War broke out on that fatal 8 February, Port Arthur had not been completed as a naval base. Its inner harbour had only one basin where ships could float during low water, while the rest had to lie high and dry on mud like a lot of ducks. Space was cramped and the entrance to the harbour was only about a hundred yards across from end to end, allowing only one ship to pass at a time. A more awkward place could not have been chosen. It was, as I have already said, a death trap.

Admiral Makarov's predecessor had taken twenty-four hours to move his squadron out into the open, a manœuvre which could only be done during high tide—Admiral Makarov took only two hours and a half, and within two days of his arrival our destroyers were already engaging and worrying the enemy. The demoralizing inactivity of our fleet had been broken as though by a spell through the energy of that remarkable man. He was a great psychologist and knew perfectly well that results could only be achieved by showing his officers and men what they could do. He broke the atmosphere of defeatism entirely and on 11 March the whole squadron engaged the enemy. Very unfortunately three of our best cruisers had been cut off at Vladivostok by the outbreak of War, but even then we had something with which to oppose the Japanese grand fleet, even though we were outnumbered and outclassed by them. We could worry them and impede their troop transport, and although in fact we were doomed, yet so long as our squadron remained active, we could help our land forces by delaying the enemy's landing of troops, and give our armies a chance to accumulate.

The Japanese fully realized our importance and made a number of efforts to block the inner harbour by sinking ships across the narrow entrance as the British succeeded in doing at Zeebrugge during the Great War.

Our forts were built along the hills encircling the inner harbour, and a good view could be had far out to sea. If anything suspicious was seen moving about at sea during the night searchlights would comb the darkness with their beams.

The vigilance of our forts prevented the Japanese from blocking the entrance. They were always surprised by us. If anything suspicious was observed, searchlights were switched on to the scene of the enemy's activity and a fearful din would shake the night, as the shore batteries opened fire from their heavy guns. Long and uncanny beams, flashes of red and orange, and rockets of varying colours lit up the night, in which the Japanese went about their business of bottling us up as though little were amiss, as a firework of destruction. Nothing could stop them. They did sink their ships all right, but never across the harbour entrance, and on one occasion several of their vessels ran on to some rocks with the loss of their crews. At other times, the Japanese would bombard us from the sea in the hope of disabling our ships in the inner harbour. Their projectiles were fired across the surrounding hills and our shore batteries joined in the concert. As we were right among these steep hills, we could not at first get a sufficiently high angle of elevation for our guns to fire projectiles across the intervening hills at the enemy out at sea, and thus had the demoralizing experience of lying about inactively like a lot of clay pigeons and allowing ourselves to be shot at without being able to reply.

Finally the Admiral devised a way of getting over the

difficulty. He had his ships tilted over to a certain angle which increased very considerably the furthest angle of elevation attainable under ordinary circumstances. Our observation post in the forts would communicate to us the particular squares in which the enemy vessels were and, as with this new device we could fire clear of the hills, we succeeded in scoring hits on a number of occasions. So successful, in fact, did this method prove, that two of the Japanese ships were badly damaged and thereafter they left us alone.

About a week after my arrival I was appointed to the Admiral's staff aboard his flagship, *Petropavlovsk*. I was in constant and very close touch with him. He gave me much work to do, most of it of a confidential nature, and thus I obtained a good insight into what was going on.

Occasionally I had to rush off to one or the other of our shore batteries to stop them from firing at our destroyers at night. No lights were allowed and whenever our destroyers went out to sweep or lay mines or on patrol duty, there was nothing to distinguish them from the enemy. Our smaller ships were out nightly on various duties, as well as during the day time.

Meanwhile, the Admiral was preparing for a sortie with the whole of his squadron, to break through the blockade and to join his forces with the rest of the fleet at Vladivostok. Every night the Admiral had one of his ships anchored in the outer roads of the harbour between its entrance and our mine barrier. The idea was to prevent the enemy from taking us by surprise with a night attack and to watch out for any of his ships when they came to lay their mines. If any suspicious activity of any kind was observed, he would have the sea searched for enemy mines at daybreak.

The Admiral spent his nights on board the particular vessel whose turn it was to guard the harbour entrance. At the same time a careful watch was kept by our people in the forts.

On 12 April the sea was rough and visibility exceedingly poor owing to a violent blizzard. At 6 p.m., Admiral Togo dispatched some of his destroyers to lay mines outside Port Arthur at night.

At 11 p.m., these arrived at their destination and discharged their mines successfully. They had, however, been noticed by our forts, which shone their searchlights on the area of their activity, but owing to poor visibility were unable to retain them in the radius of their beams.

The cruiser *Diana* with the Admiral on board was on duty that night. I remember that I slept fully dressed on a sofa in the mess-room of this cruiser.

The observation post in one of the forts had warned us that suspicious objects had been spotted out at sea and thus we were fully aware of the situation. Makarov intended to have the sea searched for mines at daybreak, when an untoward incident diverted his attention elsewhere.

He had made it his principle that he would not allow himself to lose any of his ships before the day when the whole squadron would engage the enemy in a major battle.

During the night of 13 April he had dispatched a number of his destroyers to search for the whereabouts of the Japanese grand fleet, which he soon hoped to be able to attack.

During the blizzard that night two of our destroyers became detached from the rest. The destroyer *Strashnyi*[1] thought that it had found the other destroyers and joined their line. At daybreak its commander, Mallejev, saw to his horror that he had mistaken, owing to the poor visibility, the enemy destroyers for Russian ones and that he was following in their wake.

The Japanese engaged him at once. Mallejev kept them at bay until his ship was holed through and through, his

[1] The Terrible.

guns put out of action, and his engines destroyed. He defended his ship to the bitter end with a machine-gun and then the *Strashnyi* disappeared beneath the waves. Mallejev succeeded in jumping overboard, wounded as he was.

The other Russian destroyer, the *Smelyi*,[1] had found our ships during the night and had warned the Admiral of the danger in which the *Strashnyi* was.

Makarov, true to his principle, at once dispatched the cruiser *Bayan* to save the *Strashnyi*. The *Bayan* arrived just in time to pick up a few survivors from the sea, at the same time firing with her port guns at the enemy.

Makarov realizing the perilous situation of the *Bayan* decided to come to her rescue without delay.

I accompanied him to his flagship, the *Petropavlovsk*, as soon as she emerged from the inner harbour. If the *Bayan* was to be saved, no time could be lost, and for that reason the Admiral decided to meet the enemy with only a few ships, as the rest of his squadron were still getting up steam.

The *Petropavlovsk* led the *Poltava, Askold, Diana*, and *Novik*, which were flanked by destroyers. We proceeded full steam at the enemy.

Meanwhile the *Bayan*, having finished her rescue work and hitherto successfully warded off all enemy attacks, joined our line.

The sea by then had calmed down considerably and visibility was moderate, but it was bitterly cold.

Suddenly a number of large enemy vessels appeared on the horizon. The leading one was almost instantly recognized as the *Mikasa*. She, with the rest, was steaming full speed at us, scattering foam from her bows.

At first only the *Mikasa* and a number of other enemy ships had been clearly discerned, but a few moments later it became obvious that we had the whole of the grand

[1] The Daring.

fleet after us. Makarov was undismayed by our inequality and seemed at first willing to engage the enemy fleet with his five ships. I, and his flag captain, told him then and there that in our view it would be sheer folly to do so. Markarov then wheeled his line and took course for Port Arthur, where he was going to order the rest of the squadron to join him in engaging Togo's ships. While waiting for them to scramble out of the inner harbour, we were in the shelter of our shore batteries. Meanwhile Togo, who had been gaining on us considerably, was still coming on. His line included two of the most modern ships of the time, the *Nishin* and *Kasuga*. They had just joined his fleet, having recently arrived from Italy, where they had been built.

The *Pobieda* and the *Peresviet* had already joined us, while the rest of the squadron were coming out one by one.

I was standing on the starboard side of the bridge of the flagship talking to that famous painter and war correspondent, Vereshchiagin, who was sketching groups of enemy ships. Lieutenant Kube was with me.

The Admiral, Rear-Admiral Mollas and two signallers were standing on the port side of the bridge, signalling to our ships, while they were leaving the harbour, which stations in the line they were to take up.

Meanwhile we were manœuvring to adjust our position at the head of the fleet, when Vereshchiagin suddenly turned to me and said: "I have seen much fighting and have been in many a tight corner, but nothing ever seems to happen to me." Apparently he was looking forward to the scrap. 'You wait and see'—I thought to myself as he was still merrily sketching away.

It was about ten o'clock. Lieutenant Kube said to me: "I am going down below, sir, to have a cup of coffee while we are waiting for the rest to get into line." "Don't," I said. "You had better remain up here." But he went as he wanted to have a quick 'tuck in,' having had no breakfast that morning.

On the Admiral's side of the bridge they were still signalling, when suddenly there was a terrific bang, a fearful 'puff' 'as though a thousand giants simultaneously had said "Phoo."' It was as though a typhoon had suddenly released all the pent-up forces of its violence. This blast was followed by a dull concussion which made the large vessel shake from stem to stern as if a volcano had erupted immediately beneath it and a roaring wall of red fire rushed up within a foot from where I was standing.

Everything gave below my feet and I felt like one suspended by some uncanny force in mid air. I was badly burnt on my face and was bruised all over. Rear-Admiral Mollas was lying on the bridge with his skull crushed in among the signallers, who were either dead or badly wounded.

I rushed forward instinctively, clambered over the rail, dropped on the roof of the twelve-inch gun turret and thence on to a six-inch turret below. The *Petropavlovsk* was by then heeling over to port. For a moment, only for a flash of a moment, I stood reflecting what to do next. To port a gurgling and foaming sea was rising rapidly, churned up into ghastly whirlpools by the motion of the vessel, which was turning turtle with great speed.

I realized, as her hull was rolling over, that the only chance of escape lay to starboard, where the water was nearest, for otherwise I would be caught by the suction made by the capsizing vessel. I jumped into the fearsome 'maelstrom.' Something struck me a violent and stunning blow in my back. There was the sound of a hurricane around me. Then I was seized by the uncanny force of a swirling whirlpool. It gripped me and dragged me into the black depth of its funnel. Round and round I went with a mad, corkscrew-like motion, rushing round in ever-narrowing spirals until all around me became dark as night. All seemed lost now. It is the end! I thought. There was a short prayer and a last thought for the woman I loved. Meanwhile, I struggled violently against the force that held me in its fearful grip   At last, after what had seemed an eternity, its tension decreased. Light pierced the darkness feebly and grew stronger. I struggled madly and suddenly broke surface.

Something struck me. I gripped at it and held on for dear life. It was the roof of our steam launch that had got adrift. I pulled myself up and reaching out caught hold of its brass railings.

I had been more than lucky to have dived up at that distance from the flagship and at that moment, as otherwise I would have been caught and drawn under without a chance of escape by the suction created by the sinking vessel.

What had saved me were my clothes. I have already said that it was bitterly cold, and the water, incidentally, was just a few degrees above zero. I was dressed in a padded coat, underneath which I had a fur-lined jacket and an English woollen sweater. This very likely gave me some buoyancy, otherwise I would have gone to join the rest of the six hundred and thirty-one who perished.

The other ships of our squadron which were nearest the sinking flagship, which by now was taking her final plunge bows down, stern high in the air, and engines still working, had lowered their boats and were combing the sea for survivors.

One of our destroyers' whale-boats was quite near me. They noticed me and pulled in my direction. I shouted to them, I remember: "I am all right as I am, save the rest." They pulled me out and into their boat and in the effort, owing to the weight of my soaked clothes, nearly crushed my chest against the gunwale of their boat. It was filled to its utmost capacity with other survivors.

I was transferred to another boat, which took me to the destroyer *Bezstrashnyi*,[1] where they laid me on the bed in the captain's cabin. I caught sight of the captain, whom

[1] Fearless.

I knew. I saw him and the rest through a haze which was settling down over me. They gave me some brandy and vodka and then I broke down completely. I was asking them repeatedly: "When are we returning to harbour." Meanwhile the Japanese were shelling the squadron, making use of the temporary confusion.

Soon I came to. We had got alongside the quay of Port Arthur, and before I was helped off the destroyer I was asked whether I would like to see the captain of the *Petropavlovsk*. I was not anxious to see anyone in particular, and in any case he was lying like one dead without any sign of life stretched on the table of the mess room.

When I stepped on shore my brother Boris was there to meet me. We fell into each other's arms. It appeared that he had been watching the squadron from one of our forts when the disaster occurred, and this is what he says:

'At about 5 a.m. on 13 April we were woken up and told that the Japanese fleet had been sighted and that ours was preparing to leave the harbour to meet it.

'Prince Karageorgievitch and I went towards the port and on our arrival there ran into Admiral Makarov and Lieutenant Kube. Makarov, I remember, said: "Good morning—we are pushing out presently." They were in a great hurry and the activity on board was such that, although Cyril was searched for, the *Petropavlovsk* cast off without my having taken leave of him. Prince Karageorgievitch had suggested to me that we might go on board as it was a golden opportunity to witness a fight at sea. Fortunately we did nothing of the sort.

'From the port we rode to the top of the "Golden Hill," from which an excellent view could be had out to sea. We arrived in time to see some of the ships of our squadron crawling out of the narrow entrance of Port Arthur below. We watched them until they almost disappeared from view. Suddenly a great deal of smoke appeared on the horizon, but not from where our squadron was still faintly discernible. It was clear to us that an encounter with considerable Japanese forces was imminent, and almost at the same time the rolling thunder of big guns in action heralded the beginning of a battle. The ships of both forces became clearer as they drew nearer to Port Arthur. It was obvious that Admiral Makarov had met superior forces and was withdrawing his ships to Port Arthur, where he could await his reinforcements in the shelter of our batteries. Judging from what we could see of the enemy and the smoke from his ships, it was fairly clear that the Admiral must have come upon, if not the Japanese grand fleet, then at least some very considerable force.

'When at last our vessels anchored immediately below where we were, in the outer roads of Port Arthur, we were greatly relieved of our anxiety for their safety. They had had a race with the enemy, who had tried to catch them before they reached the shelter of our forts, and who had, in fact, gained on them considerably. It was one of the most stirring and exciting experiences imaginable to watch these momentous doings unfold themselves below one like on a stage, and yet this was a game of death.

'Prince Karageorgievitch, Serge Sheremetieff, and I went down to the signalling post below our batteries to find out what was being done on board our ships and what the Admiral intended to do next. We might get some indication of this from a signaller. We were told by the sailor, who was reading and answering signals from the flagship, that the Admiral had ordered munition to be removed from all guns and that officers and men of all ships were to be fed. Then I remembered that we, too, had not eaten anything that day. Serge Sheremetieff offered me some dry prunes. Suddenly there was a terrific detonation and the same signaller who had told us of the recent dispositions by the Admiral shouted: "Flagship blown up!" Where the *Petropavlovsk* had been but a few seconds before there was now nothing but a sinister pall of black smoke. Then there was another fearful explosion; and about a minute later, when some of the smoke had cleared away, we saw that the *Petropavlovsk* was disappearing into the sea bows first with her propellers turning in the air as her stern pointed skyward. It was a fearful impression, a ghastly nightmare. Cyril was on board—and from the momentary impression of this terrifying sight, one thing was clear to me, that no one could have possibly survived this wreck.

'We hurried down to the harbour, where no one knew anything about survivors. There was no news of any kind apart from the fact that the destroyers near the place of the disaster had put out their boats and were searching the sea. Great depression and pessimism expressed itself everywhere. I returned to my train in a fearful state of dejection, convinced that my brother Cyril had perished. Indeed, the very thought of the contrary, in view of what I had seen and heard, seemed idle. In about an hour and a half a naval officer rushed up to my train and announced that my brother had been saved, that he was on board the destroyer *Bezshumnyi*,[1] and that he wished to see me. This incredible news seemed to be too good to be true. I refused to believe him, but he gave me his work of honour that it was true. I hurried back to the port and on board the destroyer. All the time I found it hard to believe that he had really escaped from that colossal disaster, and yet it was true, and when I saw him I experienced that unique sensation of absolute relief after a great burden of fear has been removed from one. Considering what he had gone through, he looked in comparatively good condition. I took him to Harbin in my train.'

The *Petropavlovsk* had run on an enemy mine, one of those which Togo's destroyers had laid during the previous night. The explosion was followed by the detonation of all our magazines and torpedoes, which knocked part of the bottom out of her. At the time of the detonation's all her funnels, masts, and other parts had come hurtling down upon her decks and bridge. I do not know how I escaped all this. Of the 711 officers and men, only eighty were saved in all. Admiral Makarov perished with the rest, only his coat was found floating in the sea. With him perished all the plans of his intended operations as well as the whole of his staff except myself and a few others. His death sealed the fate of the whole squadron. Thereafter all further efforts to break through the blockade that were attempted did not succeed. The subsequent history of the squadron was to be nothing but a prolonged agony of a bottled-up fleet. The master-mind and its inspirer had gone. Gloom settled down over all things in Port

[1] Noiseless.

Arthur. The only man who could have done something was no more.

The Japanese as usual had had luck.

Kube, the friend and constant companion of my youth and of all my voyages, had perished, as did many of my other friends—they have no grave but the sea.

A few minutes after the disaster there was another fearful detonation. The battle-cruiser *Pobieda* had run on a mine. She was, however, hauled off into Port Arthur.

Even after this disaster our doomed squadron succeeded later in engaging the enemy and giving them a severe 'hammering.' It failed, however, to break the blockade and was scuttled when, after a heroic defence, Port Arthur fell to the enemy.

I boarded the Trans-Siberian express and left sinister Port Arthur behind me. I was in no fit state to be of any use for active service. Badly burnt, the muscles of my back strained, suffering from shell shock, and in a state of complete nervous collapse. I was for the time being an absolute wreck.

At Harbin I received a visit from General Kuropatkin, our Commander-in-Chief in the Far East, and also from Admiral Alexeeff.

The disaster which had befallen our fleet and the loss of Admiral Makarov had produced the worst effect on the Army, having serious repercussion on our troops. The Admiral could not be replaced by anyone.

Arrived at Moscow I was met by Uncle Sergey. It was the last time I saw him, for during the next year the Revolutionaries murdered him, because, while many of our administrators had lost their heads, he had kept his and had gone about his duty energetically. My brother Andrey had forwarded packets of letters and telegrams from Ducky, which reached me in Moscow as well as along the line.

I did not interrupt my journey there and continued

straight for St. Petersburg, where members of the Imperial Family gave me a very charming reception as my train drew into the station.

A few days later I had an interview with the Emperor. It struck me as odd that he did not inquire either about the *Petropavlovsk* disaster or about the Admiral, nor did he refer to the war or ask how it was progressing. The conversation was confined to an exchange of the usual politenesses which generally concern themselves with health and weather. He seemed tired and overwrought. He gave me permission to go abroad as soon as the doctors allowed me to do so.

I went off to Coburg and when I arrived at the station Ducky with her sister, the Princess Hohenhohe-Langenburg, was there to meet me. They were dressed in white for the occasion. I will never forget this reunion. I felt like one who was returning from the land of the dead to new life. It was a fine spring day—and there was spring in my heart too.

To those over whom the shadow of death has passed, life has a new meaning. It is like coming out of the darkness of a mine back to daylight. And I was now within visible reach of fulfilment of the dream of my life. Nothing would cheat me of it now. I had gone through much. Now, at last, the future lay radiant before me.

I will pass over this summer as it belongs to one of those very intimate and lovely episodes of one's life which are part of that secret recess in one's memory that cannot be shared with the world.

Suffice it then to say that this period was even gayer and more jolly than any of my previous stays at Rosenau. The good people of Coburg knew that I was courting their princess and treated me as one of their own wherever I went.

In the autumn I returned to Russia, where I joined the staff of the Admiralty.

My activity in the Admiralty was confined to some

advisory work on a new type of destroyer which was being planned, and was neither exacting nor interesting.

For some time past the Press had been proposing the entirely unpractical and absolutely quixotic scheme that we should send our Baltic fleet to the Far East to relieve the squadron at Port Arthur and establish naval supremacy there.

They made such a noise about it and were so insistent on proclaiming this 'brain wave' of theirs, that finally, and goodness only knows why, the Admiralty approached the Emperor with this 'brilliant' idea. The most that all these people could have done would have been to cover their madness with a cloak of secrecy. They did nothing of the sort. By the time the first steps were taken to materialize this scheme, the whole of the world, including, of course, the Japanese, knew every detail about the ships which were going to be sent on this 'Mad Cap' errand.

The most capable of our admirals was charged with the execution of this plan. I have already referred to Rojdestvenski. He duly informed the Emperor that, in his view, the plan was doomed to failure from the very beginning. Firstly, because we had no ships, barring a very few, with which we could oppose the Japanese Navy on equal terms, even if the whole fleet were overhauled and modernized, for which there was precious little time left. Secondly, because England, who had command of the sea, and who was an ally of Japan, would do her best to impede the Baltic squadron wherever and however she could, along the twenty thousand miles of the voyage. Thirdly, because such an armada, consisting largely of old 'crocks,' would be impeded in its progress by frequent breakdowns and would need a formidable retinue of auxiliary vessels and so forth. Then there was the essential question of coaling. Would the neutral powers and even those who, like France, were allied to us, dare to offend Britain by helping us? A fleet, once it is without a base, is at the mercy of chance. The whole scheme was beset by difficulties of the most formidable kind. It was a fantastic conception, the like of which had seen no precedent! The whole of this armada had in all about fifty ships. It would need provisions, coal, spare parts. Repairs would have to be done at sea. Some of the ships were entirely unseaworthy even in the Bay of Finland. They belonged to that scrap-heap which I have already described in connection with the gunnery school. And all this was to go to the Pacific through tropical seas!

The Admiralty seemed undismayed. Their attitude amounted to that kind of negligence which owing to its blatant disregard for natural consequences might be called 'criminal.'

They were intelligent beings, and must have foreseen that they were sending thousands of our best sailors to certain death. A fleet was being dispatched to add to the glory of the Japanese flag and to the humiliation of ours, because the Press insisted on it!

When the Admiral saw that his warnings remained unheeded, he set about his task at once. There was feverish activity in all our munition works in the land. Day and night the blast furnaces in the south were turning out the steel plates and guns as the great hammers knocked them into shape. Trains full of the necessary equipment arrived at Kronstadt and the old 'crocks' were being modernized.

Meanwhile the Press was busy in supplying the world with all the smallest details of the progress of the work and Togo was laying his plans accordingly.

At Kronstadt everything that could be got together was being assembled until the fleet was ready to leave for its destination. If it had not been for the Germans, who undertook to provide us with coal all along the twenty thousand miles of the voyage, the fleet would never have got beyond West Africa.

Shortly before Rojdestvenski set out from Libau on 17 October 1904 I accompanied the Emperor as his

A.D.C. to the Admiral's flagship, the *Souvoroff*, where a conference was held.

I was not present during this meeting, and, therefore, do not know what happened apart from its result, which sealed the doom of thousands of my compatriots. The Admiral had discharged his duty brilliantly, but the whole world ridiculed him. There were bets in all capitals that this fleet would never be able to reach its destination. We were made the laughing-stock of the world. All the naval experts laughed us to scorn. The 'Russians are no sailors,' so they said, and 'this armada of tubs will never get beyond the North Sea,' and when the Dogger Bank incident occurred there were hoots of sarcastic laughter. 'The Don Quixote had mistaken inoffensive North Sea trawlers for Japanese destroyers and had engaged them in earnest.' War with England was imminent!

Much has been written about this incident. I was not present, but, from my knowledge of the man, I can state that Rojdestvenski was a very capable officer. This he proved by taking the whole of a large fleet in the most difficult conditions possible to a battle at the other end of the world in perfect order, without losing one of his ships and—what kind of ships!

This epic feat was properly appreciated later.

When the whole of the Baltic squadron passed Singapore in perfect formation the *St. James' Gazette* wrote: 'We have underestimated the Admiral and greet him with that respect which valour deserves,' or words to that effect. Before the squadron left Libau he had been warned apparently that the Japanese had bought a number of destroyers in Britain, where they had been built for a certain South American country, and that they intended to provoke an incident in the North Sea which would either plunge us into a war with Britain or else force us to recall the squadron forthwith. If this was so, then it was a brilliant political move on their part. The Admiral set out fully prepared for any event of the kind. There is little doubt that there were a number of suspicious vessels resembling destroyers, and carrying no lights, among the trawlers, as independent evidence from our ships, as well as from the crews of some of the trawlers, showed during the investigation by the International Court which examined and tried this incident.

If these suspicious vessels—one of which remained for several hours at the place where the incident occurred when all our destroyers, without exception, were already nearing Dungeness—had attacked the squadron first, the Admiral would have been held responsible for the damage resulting to his ships, as well as for his negligence in allowing himself to be attacked. If, on the other hand, he attacked first, as, in fact, he did, then owing to the great number of trawlers that were about and owing to the absence of light on the suspicious vessel, damage was sure to result to neutral shipping and that would put us in a difficult position. If that be so, it was a Machiavellian plan![1]

And if this is what really happened, and there is much evidence in support of it, the Admiral acted properly in the dilemma in which he found himself, and no blame is attached to him or to our fleet.

Even though our ships were nearly all destroyed in an unequal contest on 27 May 1905 in the Straits of Tsushima, where our 'tin pots,' out-ranged and out-done in every conceivable way, put up a heroic struggle and battered the enemy considerably before they were sunk, this epic story of a doomed fleet sailing to certain death and fighting to the very last gasp, after a voyage of unprecedented length, stands alone of its kind among the naval annals of the world.

---

[1] An excellent account of the voyage of the Baltic squadron and of the battle of Tsushima can be found in Frank Thiess' *Tsushima*, 1937, Paul Zsolnay Verlag, Berlin, Wien, Leipzig.

THE AUTHOR'S WIFE, THE LATE GRAND DUCHESS
VICTORIA
Daughter of the Duke of Edinburgh and granddaughter of Queen Victoria.

THE GRAND DUCHESSES MARIA AND KIRA
Daughters of the Author.

The Admiral had been badly wounded during the battle and was a dying man, and when he was returning to Russia after his captivity in Japan, even the Revolutionaries cheered him and ran up to his train to see the man who had not spared himself.

But what did the authorities do with Rojdestvenski? They court-martialled him! For having taken a scrap-heap to order across the sea to Japan and for having lost it there. If this were not true, it would sound fantastic!—they condemned this man for having loyally carried out the Gilbertian plans of their own concoction. Two years later he died broken in body and in spirit.

In conclusion, I may add that the gunnery of our ships at the battle of Tsushima left nothing to be desired. They were most effective in finding their range and in hitting their objectives, if, from Japanese accounts, one is to judge by the hits they scored. Had our shells been of the same design as those of the Japanese, that battle might have had a very different result. The Japanese shells exploded at the slightest contact, even when they hit the surface of the sea, while ours were designed to burst only when hitting armour plate, and when they burst they split into clumsy fragments. The Japanese shells, on the other hand, produced a fearful effect on exploding, splitting into minute and glowing splinters which set everything combustible on fire. The force of their detonation was such that heavy armour plate was twisted like corkscrews by them and roofs of gun turrets were blown off as if made of wood. Further, they contained a chemical which was the precursor of poison gas. It is mainly due to their shells that our fleet was handicapped from the beginning in spite of its inequality in modern ships.

It was my intention all the time to rejoin the Navy on active service in the Far East as soon as my health permitted. The news from Rojdestvenski's fleet was good. Hitherto all had gone well with him, and he was approaching Japanese waters. In spite of the overwhelming odds against him he had, hitherto, overcome all obstacles on his way which human agency and wind and weather had put against him, and there was one slender chance which I knew might still come to his aid and enable him to escape from the clutches of his opponent Togo. The Sea of Japan, as well as the whole region between it and Vladivostok is, as I knew from my experience there, frequently given to fogs due to the meeting of warm and cold currents. With luck, the Admiral might pass through the narrow seas between the islands of Japan and Korea in a dense fog and thus break through to his goal without a battle. I intended to go to Vladivostok where we still had a few first class ships, and where I would await the arrival of the Baltic squadron and resume my duties with them.

The Admiral did, in fact, very nearly pass through the Straits of Tsushima and the Japanese fleet, unseen and unscathed. It was a matter of one day. Had he passed through them on 26 May, which was very foggy, instead of on the 27th, as he did, he would have broken through successfully as visibility was exceedingly poor. But on the 26th he had to crawl along with his fleet at a few knots owing to engine trouble in one of his ancient ships, which had joined him in Cochin China where, for a month, he had had to await their arrival.

When the news of the disaster reached us, my journey to the Far East lost its *raison d'être*. During my stay in the Capital, I had a consultation with Father Yanysheff, the Confessor of the Empress, concerning the degree of relationship between Ducky and myself, as I had now decided to bring this matter of our marriage to a head. I considered that it would be easier for the Emperor to make a decision if he were to be confronted with a *fait accompli*. Father Yanysheff assured me that from the point of view of Canon Law there was not the slightest obstacle. This encouraged me considerably. Accordingly I prepared the plans for our wedding, the date for which depended on the conclusion of hostilities between us and Japan. Practically the whole of that year I spent in Germany, mostly at Coburg, with some occasional visits to a sanatorium near Munich, where I was under treatment for my nerves which had been very badly shaken by the *Petropavlovsk* disaster. During that period I had my first impression of Bayreuth, where Ducky and I motored from Munich. We got into the very holy of holies of its musical *élite* and met 'Cosima' Wagner, the widow of the great composer. She was a daughter of Liszt. Then there was a very jolly visit to Schloss Langenburg in Württemberg, the family seat of the Hohenlohe-Langenburgs.

All our travelling in Germany was done by car. It was the autumn of the year 1905 when we decided to marry.

That autumn the Treaty of Portsmouth was signed, and we owe it in no small measure to Count Witte, who had been rehabilitated, that we lost so very little as the result of this war.

On 8 October Aunt Marie's spiritual adviser, Father Smirnoff, arrived at Count Adlerberg's house at Tegernsee near Munich, which we had chosen for the place of our wedding.

It was a very simple occasion. There were present Aunt Marie, Cousin Beatrice, Count Adlerberg, Herr Vinion, Aunt Marie's gentleman-in-waiting, her two ladies-in-waiting, and the Count's housekeeper.

My dear Uncle Alexey Alexandrovitch, who had stood by me in all my troubles, had told me on one occasion that if ever I stood in need of his help, I had only to let him know and he would do all in his power to help me. I will never forget his constancy in my cause throughout the dark period which now lay behind me.

He was in Munich at the time and I wired to him to come as soon as possible to Tegernsee, but did not tell him the reason.

We held up the wedding, as I wanted him to witness it for us. As he did not appear, we were married without him. Father Smirnoff was very scared, as he feared the wrath of the Holy Synod and the Emperor.

We were married in the Orthodox Chapel of the house on 8 October 1905.

And thus we were at last united as man and wife to go together along the path which lay before us and which was to lead us through much joy and great adversity.

There are few who in one person combine all that is best in soul, mind, and body. She had it all, and more. Few there are who are fortunate in having such a woman as the partner of their lives—I was one of these privileged.

The 'Wedding Feast' had been in progress for about half an hour. There was a blizzard raging outside, when Uncle Alexey arrived in the midst of it all. It was curious to see his amazement. This great giant of a man, so reminiscent of Uncle Sasha[1] in character and appearance, was at first dumbfounded, then he congratulated us warmly.

Apparently he had been chasing round Munich for a tarpaulin for his luggage, which he had piled up on the roof of the car, and had not succeeded in finding one. Tarpaulins, I presume, are more of a thing pertaining to the sea near which they abound rather than in a city like Munich. He complained that one of his new cases had been ruined by the blizzard.

He added to the gaiety of this occasion with his open, breezy personality and huge voice.

[1] Alexander III.

VII

Exile and Return

A FEW days after our wedding I left for St. Petersburg to acquaint my father with this fact. He was pleased that we had taken this step, and next day I intended to tell the Emperor. In the evening of the day of my arrival, after dinner, my father, I, and some others were playing bridge when Father's page announced that Count Fredricks, the Minister of the Court, had come to see him. I knew this late visit was ill-omened and also its meaning, but I did not anticipate the stringency of the measures which had been taken against me. They came as a great blow to all of us.

Count Fredricks's mission was to the effect that I was to leave Russia within forty-eight hours, that I was to be deprived of all my honours, that I was already struck off the Army and Navy list, and that I was henceforth to be 'outlawed.'

We were dumbfounded by the severity of this decision as the Emperor had at no time indicated or even vaguely hinted at such drastic steps, but had, quite on the contrary, whenever I had mentioned this matter to him, expressed his sincere hope that things could be straigthened out. However, all this was condoned later on, as I have already said, and both he and the Empress were always more than kind to Ducky and me after my return from the exile which now began.

The next day Father, who was most indignant about the attitude of his nephew, went to see him, and when he realized that he could not alter anything, handed in his resignation as Commander-in-Chief of the St. Petersburg garrison and military area.

My wife met me in Berlin, whence we went to Coburg. Owing to the draconic measures at St. Petersburg our marriage did not confer on her the title of Grand Duchess although she was an English Princess.

But the sudden vehemence of this storm did not mar our joy of being united at last, and life lay inviting and happy before us.

We spent a delightful winter at Cannes, where we went by car via Strasbourg, where my brother-in-law's father, Prince Hohenlohe-Langenburg, was Viceroy of Alsace-Lorraine. We stayed a night in his castle in that very beautiful and historical city which has witnessed so many dramas of history.

The three years of exile, and the first three years of our married life, belong to those very intimate and happiest experiences of my life, and in spite of the loss of everything, of my career, my position, and all the rest that the world can give, I had kept what was dearest to me. These years passed quickly as all joy does. We travelled much, generally by car, and saw a good deal of all that is interesting and beautiful.

About January of the year 1907 Ducky was received into the Orthodox Church, and on 2 February of that same year she gave birth to our first child, Marie,[1] at the 'Villa Edinburg,' in Coburg.

In the autumn of 1908 I was in Paris when I received a telegram announcing the death of my Uncle Alexey Alexandrovitch, and I received permission to return to Russia for his funeral. So, even in death, he had come to my aid as he had always done during his life. His memory

[1] Princess Marie Leiningen ; Grand Duchess Marie Kirillovna married Prince Frederick Charles Leiningen in 1925.

will always remain with me as that of one of the most exalted and noble figures which I have ever been fortunate enough to meet, for like his brother, Uncle Sasha, he was the embodiment of the type of our early heroes, a real 'Bogatyr,' both in appearance and character.

My brother Boris had obtained the Emperor's consent for me to wear uniform during the funeral.

Thus Uncle Alexey's death was the first step on the way to my complete rehabilitation and justification.

I spent two days with my parents and then rejoined Ducky and the baby 'Masha' at Cannes.

In the early part of 1909 my father became seriously ill. He died on 13 February of that year. Meanwhile Boris had been working hard for my complete rehabilitation in Russia. A few days before my father's death I received a short telegram from my mother which read: 'Ta femme est Grande Duchesse.' I have it still among the few things which I saved from the wreckage of the Revolution.

These few words meant that all had been restored to me and that I could now return. Thereafter the Emperor and Empress showed the greatest kindness and sympathy to both of us. I arrived in Russia for Father's funeral. His death was a great loss to me, for during his life, as I have mentioned previously, he had not only been a loving father but also a kind friend and a source of strength in times of trouble and sorrow; as in the case of Uncle Alexey, his death, too, proved an occasion which led to my restoration. Their last solicitude was for those for whom they cared. They embodied all that is best and noblest in man. Perhaps, had they lived, much of what was to come might have been avoided.

On 9 May 1909 my second daughter, Kyra,[1] was born at our Paris house in the avenue Henri Martin.

[1] Grand Duchess Kira Kirillovna of Russia, married, 1938, Prince Louis Ferdinand of Prussia, second son and heir of the Crown Prince.

Soon after her birth I was appointed to the light cruiser *Oleg* as her second-in-command.

We followed the usual routine of fleet exercises and gunnery in the Baltic until, as was our custom, the whole fleet returned to Kronstadt to be dismantled for its hibernation. The *Oleg*, however, was ordered to proceed to the Mediterranean, where, as I have said, we kept a few ships as part of the international squadron which guarded the Aegean. Its base was Suda Bay in the island of Crete.

I went overland to Cannes where my wife and the two babies were, and thence to Brindisi, where I joined the *Oleg*. After an uneventful service at Suda Bay, where we did very little apart from the usual routine, we went to the Piræus. Of Crete I may say that it is a most interesting island, containing much of that which has the greatest attractions for prehistorians. It is a place rich in the treasures of an extraordinary and unique civilization of pre-classical days. I regret not to have seen the palace of Knossus and the other remarkable remnants of the Aegean culture which seems to have been very much in advance of its time. When I visited Crete, archæologists had scarcely begun to investigate it thoroughly, but since then much has been brought to light which suggests that this island civilization had at one time an enormous influence on the whole of the Mediterranean basin, even on Egypt and distant Spain.

On 18 April 1910 I was promoted to the rank of Captain.

My wife was in Athens when the *Oleg* called at the Piræus, and I was given leave by the Emperor to take her to Toulon on board my ship. From Toulon she was to return to St. Petersburg with the babies, who had been in Cannes, while I continued with the *Oleg* on our homeward voyage.

Our arrivals in Russia were simultaneous—hers with the babies in the capital and mine at Kronstadt on the *Oleg*. It was our first meeting on Russian soil and the beginning of our married life there.

This was in May 1910. We were given the use of the 'Cavalier's House' (Kavalersky Dom) in Tsarskoe Selo. It was a splendid and very comfortable building with spacious rooms.

We settled down to a quiet family life. There were, of course, Court functions and social activities to attend, but they were, if I may use the expression, of a mild kind and nothing to compare with the brilliant occasions of Uncle Sasha's reign and those of the early years of the late Emperor's rule, except the Jubilee festivities held in 1913 in honour of the three hundredth anniversary of the accession of the first Romanoff Tsar to the throne of Russia. In the autumn of the same year I joined the Naval Academy, which was our nearest approach to Greenwich, where Naval officers received advanced instruction in various special subjects or else were prepared for Admiralty work. I was for two years a student at the Academy—from 1910 until 1912, when I finished my instruction there.

Car-owning members of the nobility of the Baltic provinces of Russia had organized an Automobile Club and had arranged annual motor rallies which were called the 'Victoria Fahrt' in honour of my wife. It was a very well organized affair and an enjoyable occasion, during which many of the famous castles of those three provinces were visited. We were semi-officially received by its members and were very hospitably entertained by the owners of the castles which lay on our route. I was especially struck by the great beauty of some parts of Livonia. One of the castles we visited was Cremon, the property of Pavel Pavlovitch Lieven, and I remember it particularly well as it stands amongst splendid surroundings overlooking the beautiful valley of the River Aa. The influence of the occupation of those countries by the Teutonic Order[1] and the Swedes from the thirteenth

---

[1] Teutonic Order (Deutscher Orden).
The Teutonic Order came to the coasts of Livonia in about the year 1225 and conquered what were later to become Courland,

century till 1721, when Peter the Great conquered them from Charles XII, gives them a half-German, half-Scandinavian aspect with their neat country houses, farms, and churches. Riga, which was the capital of Livonia, has a striking resemblance to a North German seaport, and was at that time one of our major ports and factory towns. The harbour was teeming with shipping, and great Russian trade flowed to it along the railways and thence by sea to the West. Its old quarter contains very picturesque corners with houses from the sixteenth and seventeenth centuries, and three fine churches built in Hanseatic style.

From Riga, Ducky and I continued our journey by car to Germany and Coburg.

In the early spring of 1912 I finished my work in the Naval Academy and received the command of the *Oleg*. When I joined her at Libau she was still icebound with the other ships of our fleet. To us all this ice and snow which is now so exalted through the modern craze for winter sports was a veritable curse. It interfered with everything. We waited for the ice to break and when that happened put out to sea. This, in a way, was my first command, although I had had a ship of my own when we lost our captain on the *Nahimov*. However, this was at last a command in my own right. I had laboured up the ladder with the rest. I had faced with them the perils and hardships of the sea and had tasted of the favours and the sudden responsibilities which the sea brings to those who are hers, and of the terrors of death too, and now I had

Livonia, and Estonia, where the Order established itself until the end of the sixteenth century. In about the year 1585 the Order was secularized, Livonia becoming a Polish province; Courland a vassal duchy of Poland, whilst Estonia submitted to the Swedes. In 1621 the then Polish province of Livonia was conquered by King Gustavus Adolphus of Sweden. Later, on the signature of the Treaty of Nystad, Sweden ceded Estonia and Livonia to Russia.

reached the fulfilment of an ambition—I had a ship of my own. Yet my experiences at Port Arthur had impressed themselves with rather unfortunate results upon me. I had a dread of the sea for many years after. It was a very natural psychological reaction, and it was unfortunate because it constantly interfered with my career.

The vision of that gurgling maelstrom, the dark depth of the swirling whirlpools and the roaring blast of air issuing from the sinking ship as it pulled hundreds down with her while they were swarming about on the capsizing hull, was often with me in my dreams, and whenever I was on water I was haunted by the spectre of the disaster. It was many years before it left me.

During the early summer of that year we joined in the exercises of our Baltic fleet under the command of Admiral Essen, who had completely reorganized our Navy on the most modern lines. Our fleet had been put on a completely new footing and was very efficient in every detail. We had learnt our lesson from the Japanese War and owed it to the Admiral's energy and thoroughness that our fleet was at that time, for its size, one of the best in the world.

In July of 1912 the Olympic Games, which had been held for the first time after an interval of two thousand years at Athens—in 1910, I think—were to be held in Stockholm. The idea apparently was the same as among the ancients, it was to remind Europe that in spite of territorial differences the various nations were yet members of the same family and civilization.

I was appointed by the Emperor to be the delegate of the Russian Empire.

I went to Stockholm on board the *Oleg*. King Gustavus paid us an official visit on board. He wore the uniform of a Russian Admiral, and as such I received him. As captain of the cruiser I reported to him in Russian; the King smiled and said that my words did not convey anything to him, but that he was sure that my report was correct.

Ducky was on our Admiralty yacht at the time and we enjoyed ourselves splendidly in that beautiful island city.

My cousin, the Grand Duchess Marie Pavlovna, was married to Prince William of Sweden and was Duchess of Söedermanland. We joined with them in the many social activities and yachted among the skerries in the lovely surroundings of the capital with their myriads of pine-clad granite islands.

When this thoroughly gay and delightful visit came to an end I took the *Oleg* back to our side of the Baltic, where we continued our exercises and gunnery practice.

In the late autumn of that year I was ordered with my ship to the Mediterranean, but before reaching Reval the 'evil' which pursued me in the shape of that ghastly and haunting awe of the sea came upon me once again with all its force. I had to leave my ship. It was a sad experience for me thus to be forced to abandon my first command; however, it had to be done.

Ducky joined me at Reval and we spent two very happy weeks at the country place of the Orloff-Davidoffs near that interesting medieval town. From their house there was a magnificent view of the bay of Reval.

The property belonged to the family of the Countess, who before her marriage had been Baroness Thekla Stael. Their son, Serge, married the Hon. Elizabeth Scott-Ellis, one of the charming daughters of Lord and Lady Howard de Walden, in 1935.

I was to rejoin my ship in the Mediterranean, and left for the south of France in the company of my wife. When I was about to board a German steamer at Marseilles, which was to take me to Port Said where the *Oleg* was at the time, a 'holy terror' of the sea again overtook me, and I must admit that it was absolutely impossible for me to set foot on board.

I had a motor yacht building for me in Southampton at the time, where Messrs. Thornycrofts had just begun work on it, and I was very keen on going to England to see how it was progressing.

Accordingly I went to Paris to catch the boat train there, but when I entered the train the very thought of having to cross the channel so overwhelmed me that I had to abandon the journey. The haunting spectre of the sea chased me mercilessly and brought my career afloat to a conclusion. I could do nothing whatever against it. I have faced death and much danger, but against this malady I could summon nothing to come to my aid.

A strange individual had entered into the close surroundings of the Imperial Family, it was Rasputin.[1] About him a great deal of untruth has been written. The Emperor and Empress have been unjustly criticized with regard to this man.

Although I personally have never come into contact with him, yet I am in a position to say that his presence in the intimate 'entourage' of the Imperial couple had its perfectly reasonable explanation. The heir to the throne, the Czarevitch, was an only son. His parents were naturally greatly attached to him. Unfortunately he was an hæmophilic and whenever he cut or hurt himself in any way which caused loss of blood, it was impossible to stop the bleeding. All the celebrities of the medical world had been consulted, but in vain. The Emperor and Empress were desperate in the presence of this incurable ill and realized that science was unable to save the child. The heir to the throne was doomed.

Precisely how Rasputin came to the capital I do not know. The fact is that he was introduced to the Emperor and Empress by someone who was on intimate terms with them.

A native of a township of no great importance in Siberia, he had lost his parents early in childhood, and was brought up by some monks together with other orphans. When he

[1] Born in 1871 in a village near Tobolsk, Siberia.

was old enough to earn his living he followed many professions, and seems to have led a vagrant existence.

He is supposed to have attracted attention to himself by various cures which he effected among the peasantry of the region of his origin, and this, in the popular mind, was associated with sanctity.

He was neither a saint nor a monk, nor, indeed, mad. He was quite simply a very healthy and canny Russian peasant with an unusual gift for which science has hitherto found no explanation, but which is more frequently to be found among primitive peoples than among those who have been touched by civilization.

The fact remains that when Rasputin was called to the bedside of my ailing nephew, he was able to stop the internal bleeding and the terrible pains that accompanied it. What methods he used I know not. The fact remains that he alone succeeded where all others failed, and because he was indispensable he was used by many of the satellites of the Court for their own purposes. He had risen straight from the people to an important position in the capital. This went to his head. Such a rapid rise to fame and power was bound to produce this effect. He was spoilt by the good things of life to which he was not used. He knew the credulity of people and played the saint. In his private life he was immoral, but at Court his good conduct left nothing to be desired. In his dealings with the Emperor and Empress he was perfectly natural and well-behaved.

It may be said to his credit that he had the common sense of a peasant to remain to his end a son of the people to whose cause he was always greatly attached. He was often approached by various people for honours and advancements. The whole Rasputin episode has been greatly exaggerated. Those who consulted him and sought his company were seeking to curry favour, and the flattery and admiration thoroughly demoralized this peasant, as was only natural for a man of his extraction. Meanwhile the Czarevitch lived, and that was the most essential thing to the Imperial couple. They have not deserved the calumny which has been poured over them because of Rasputin.

In 1913 the three hundredth year of the accession of Michael, the first Russian Czar of our dynasty, was celebrated.

During the rule of the Romanoffs, Russia emerged from an almost unknown entity in the north-east of Europe to become a great world power.

Russia's rise to a position of world power was not only due to the dynamic genius of a Peter the Great, but to the constancy also with which his ancestors and successors untiringly applied themselves to the historical mission which was theirs, to make and to keep Russia great and strong among the peoples of the world.

Russia and they are inseparable. They are linked together in one destiny, even though for the time being this work has been interrupted—and twenty-one years in our history is but a brief spell. Countries, like individuals, are bred through certain experiences which are part of the moulding process of history, and although it is hard to discern the real meaning of great sorrows with which nations and individuals are afflicted, yet when time has passed, the whole pattern of the scheme, only the details of which are now visible, will unfold itself clearly before one and show why this path of Calvary was necessary.

The Jubilee festivities had attracted to the capital the representatives of all the Russian provinces. There were the delegates from our Asiatic possessions in their picturesque national dress, and hundreds of others from this vast country which counted about fifty various peoples among its population. Once again the great beacon of our country's glory flared up before it was to be extinguished for a time, and before sorrow and dismal darkness were to replace its light, and the fine structure of our glorious Empire was to be made into a heap of ruins and ashes; yet among these ashes the spark still smoulders, and one day, like the phœnix, out of them the new Russia will rise to an even greater glory and strength, to continue on the path of her destiny and to fulfil among the peoples of the world the task which Heaven assigned to her.

During the same year I was sent by the Emperor to unveil the memorial to the Russian and Allied soldiers who fell fighting at the battle of Leipzig, called the Battle of the Nations, which was the beginning of the deliverance of Europe and Napoleon's downfall.

Towards the end of July 1914 my motor yacht arrived from Southampton with an English engineer and crew of our Naval Guards. Ducky and I did a little cruising on it in the Bay of Finland and then went to take part in the annual motor rally in the Baltic provinces. That year it was even a greater affair than usual. We went from castle to castle and finished up at Riga, where a gala banquet was given for us in the fashionable Strandt Restaurant of that hospitable city. We were to go to Coburg the next day and had made all the necessary preparations for going to Germany, when suddenly during the banquet the Governor-General, M. Zvegintzov, made his appearance and read a telegram to the effect that Germany had declared war on us.

This news produced the effect of a bomb on the gay gathering.

I must admit that it came most unexpectedly, even more so than the Japanese war. It appears that the Emperor, who was always solicitous for peace and goodwill among the nations, had fought to the last for peace, but that his ministers, and these were often his misfortune and in the end the cause of his tragedy, presented the international situation in a way that suited their purposes best, but which was neither to the interest of the Emperor and his policy nor that of the Russian people.

Our army was still in the process of reorganization and was by no means ready to engage Germany's military machine with much hope of success. We had just emerged less than ten years before from the disastrous war with

Japan and from a revolution which, though it shook the structure of the Empire badly, had not led to its collapse, but it gave some indication of the kind of thing that lay in store for us in case of another unsuccessful war.

We left Riga for Tsarskoe in Count Sergey Schouvalov's car. He was an excellent driver but apt to be reckless at times. Fearful commotion and chaos reigned on the roads, which were teeming with people, cattle, and horses. Reservists were moving to the various rallying points, and mobilization was in full swing.

Either at Luga or Pskov we managed to get onto a train, as it was impossible to make any headway by road. They were blocked with traffic which became worse the nearer we came to Pskov. The railways, too, were in a chaotic state and we deemed ourselves fortunate to be able to complete the rest of the journey in a third-class carriage.

VIII

War and Revolution

During the first few days of the War all private motor cars were requisitioned for ambulance purposes. My wife was one of those who undertook the organization of this service.[1] It saved the lives of thousands. The task which she undertook required hard work and great thoroughness to make it function smoothly in the changing and difficult circumstances of the War. She helped in making her motorized ambulance work one of the best run auxiliary services in Russia. It worked with great regularity and was absolutely reliable, at a time when these characteristics, owing to our total unpreparedness, were, alas, conspicuously lacking in many of the various branches of our armies.

I was appointed to the Naval Department of Admiral Russin on the staff of Grand Duke Nicholas, who was our Commander-in-Chief at the beginning of the War.

His headquarters were at Baranovichi in Poland. It was a desolate and God-forsaken place not far from the famous primæval forests of Bieloveshch, where the last European bisons led a State-protected existence. These forests were an Imperial preserve and are now, I believe, a National

---

[1] Russian Imperial organizations, such as Red Cross, schools, hospitals, etc., were either financed by members of the Imperial Family, or associations such as the Association of Nobility, Provincial Councils, Towns, or Merchants.

Park of Poland. At the end of the War only a very few of the bison remained; they have, however, been saved from total extinction.

The first few weeks of the War we slept in railway cars, and worked in barracks which had previously been occupied by some railway battalions and had then been turned into offices.

The place was very lonely and distant from civilization and even war—we were about sixty-five miles from the front—and there was little I could do in making myself useful in my capacity of naval officer, so I was more than pleased when after about a year of this inactivity I was transferred to our new headquarters at Mogilev.

In the very first weeks of the outbreak of hostilities we had lost the flower of our armies at Tannenberg. It was more than a defeat, it was a calamity of the very worst kind.

The men who fell at Tannenberg could not be replaced, they were of the best in the land. Tannenberg!—a curious coincidence, perhaps, and possibly more. In 1431, I believe, the Teutonic order was annihilated near that very place by an allied Lithuanian and Polish army, and, so I am told, for the first time in history Germans and Russians faced each other in battle on that occasion, as the Principality of Pskov had dispatched some auxiliary forces to help the Lithuanian cause. Four hundred and eighty-three years later Slavs and Germans met again at the very same place and this time with exactly opposite results.

Why, it may be asked, did we send our armies, unprepared as they were and at break-neck speed across the sandy wastes of Lithuania into East Prussia?—It was to save the hard-pressed French on the Marne, and at their urgent request. This caused the Germans to detach two army corps from their armies in France and rush them through Germany to their eastern boundaries. Our sudden advance into Germany saved our Allies in the West. Our movement had been so rapid that when the armies engaged the enemy most of the supplies were miles behind, as they could not keep up with the troops. All the death-defying courage for which the Russian soldier is famous did not suffice in the absence of thorough organization and leadership for which the other side was well known. Hindenburg knew every inch of that region.

Great gloom settled over us. Things became worse when this disaster was followed by the one of the Mazurian lakes. Thereafter a desperate struggle began as the War shifted onto Russian ground.

We had more men than we needed and little enough in arms and munition. The supplies system worked badly. Train loads of food, arms, and other equipment were sent off, and disappeared completely, others arrived with stuff that no one wanted. There was much disorder in the rear and lack of cohesion. Yet on our front the men fought desperately and well, and scored great successes on the Austrian section. They had set their faces against adversity with the baffling endurance of hardship that is typical of our soldiers. In mud and swamps and among the forests and mountains they did their duty loyally and admirably in circumstances which would have made many others throw up the game. Some had no rifles, others no shells, and in the rear among the idle reservists and the factories, among the many little and hidden places, coming more and more to the fore out of its hiding, first cautiously, later ever bolder, the lurking hydra of revolution began to raise its head. It whispered, inspired, and suggested, it burrowed its way into the machinery of the State.

Late in 1914 and during 1915 I paid a number of visits to the front near Warsaw, when I met Ducky, whose work was progressing well. Unlike many others who were playing at Red Cross nurses, she had chosen hard and practical work, and on several occasions had carried out her duties under the enemy's fire.

There were desperate battles in progress in the region of Grodno, where we forced the Germans to raise the siege of Ossovetz. On another occasion—at Lodz—we had almost completely surrounded one of their armies, but had left a gap in our ring which was rapidly closing around them. In the last moment they succeeded in withdrawing through this gap. There was a fearful muddle on that occasion. Germans and Russians were so completely mixed with one another that at times it was impossible to tell which side was fighting the other. During this appalling slaughter the fleet of ambulance cars was plying to and fro from the front to the rear full of wounded.

Apart from Ducky's activity on our western front, she paid a number of official visits to Roumania with medical supplies to their army. Things were going badly with our allies.

In 1916 I was promoted to the rank of Rear-Admiral and received the command of a naval detachment which did some useful work on our lakes and rivers as sappers.

While we were working among the lakes and swamps in the neighbourhood of Pinsk, a Polish gentleman provided a welcome diversion from the duties of war by inviting me to shoot elk on his estates. It was an endless trip among a primeval wilderness, and, although no elk were shot, it was an interesting experience, because it gave me an impression of the untouched wilderness of unknown Europe.

Later on during that year I went to Lake Peipus, a huge inland expanse of water between Esthonia and Russia, and if the War had shifted as far inland as this lake it would have provided a very vulnerable spot. For that reason we mined it carefully.

Here I wish to say a few words about the work of our navy during the World War. Little is known abroad of our activity at sea. There were no spectacular major engagements between our large ships and those of the enemy, they were kept at their base at Helsingfors and rarely went to sea. Their crews were forced into demoralizing inactivity, and having nothing to do, like our reserve troops of the army became contaminated with revolutionary propaganda. The Baltic Fleet later played an important part in the drama of the Revolution, and it was mainly due to the sailors that the Bolshevik Party was able to seize power on the fall of the Democratic Provisional Government of Kerensky.

Not so our destroyers, light cruisers, submarines, and smaller vessels. They were constantly active in enemy waters, where they laid their mines very successfully and caused great damage to German shipping. Germany imported all its iron ore from Sweden. Our ships greatly impeded this traffic.

In the tactics of mine-laying we had become experts, and a considerable number of ships of the German Navy were lost that way, both in their own waters as well as in ours.

We had the very welcome and efficient collaboration of a number of British submarines, which succeeded in destroying some large enemy men-of-war.

Being constantly busy, except in the winter when ice prevented any activity, the crews of our destroyer, submarine, and trawler flotillas remained loyal to the end.

Although we had first-class modern battleships, some of which were among the first to carry triple gun turrets, the superiority of the German Navy was such that it would have been extremely unwise to have met them in a major encounter.

Meanwhile the fighting on our fronts had become one of trench warfare.

Pessimism could be felt and seen everywhere. The country, too, was getting tired of the effort and strain of war. The machine of State was beginning to show the first signs of a break-down. Trains were late, theft and criminal violence increased. There were strikes in the industrial areas, discontent among all classes of the population, and the revolutionary forces were hard at work to make the best of their opportunities, for which they had prepared themselves ever since the failure of the Revolution of 1905. The Emperor, meanwhile, had taken the supreme command of his armies. This concentration of all command in one person made a considerable difference to our fortunes of war.

The demoralizing and constant retreat from one fortified position to another was checked. Hitherto we had been in need of equipment and munitions. All this, however, was now arriving in plenty by way of Archangel from America and our allies, and when Archangel became icebound in the winter navigation was deflected to the port of Murmansk. It is quite near the frontier of Norway, and remains open during the winter months in spite of its northerly position beyond the Polar Circle. A railway linking it to the rest of Russia was in the last stages of completion.

Our armies now had all they needed, even hope of final victory for the first time since the beginning of the War. At various places of the German front we began to take the initiative, as we had done throughout the War on the other sectors of our far-stretched battle line. There had been a complete reorganization, re-equipment, and a re-grouping of troops in every part of our armed forces. There was optimism now and self-reliance. The enemy was hard pressed. An offensive along the whole front had been decreed for April of 1917, and had not the Revolution intervened our armies might have broken through the German lines as, in fact, they were beginning to do in places, and nothing would have stopped their progress. There was great enthusiasm now among them and certainty of winning. This sudden change of the situation in our favour was not felt in the rear, where things were going from bad to worse with our administration. Among the soldiers the assumption of the supreme command by the Emperor was a welcome move. At the front there was renewed hope—behind it increasing disorder.

I often had occasion to meet the Emperor at his headquarters at Mogilev during this time, as I was attached to his staff. He rarely spoke of the War to me and was visibly tired and overworked.

Those who were appointed to responsible positions by him were, with few exceptions, alas, badly selected for their tasks. He felt that he could trust very few of those who were around him. Ministers changed every five minutes, so to speak, and this led to lack of stability, certainty, and cohesion.

The whole situation gave one the feeling of being poised on the brink of a precipice or of standing on the uncertain surface of a swamp. The country was like a gradually sinking ship with a mutinous crew.

The Emperor gave orders which were at times not carried out promptly or even at all by the civil authorities, or else they were interrupted before they reached their destination. The tragedy of it all was that while our soldiers were giving of their best, the men in the arm-chairs in the rear seemed to be doing little to check the growing disorder and to prevent a collapse, while the agents of the Revolution increased their efforts in spreading discontent by all means.

Meanwhile our Roumanian allies had suffered a very serious reverse which had left a gap in that part of the front. We dispatched a number of army corps to their aid, which succeeded in stemming the enemy advance and in saving that country from being completely overrun. Late in 1916 my wife went to Roumania for the last time with provisions and medical supplies for their armies. She remained there until early in 1917.

I had much opportunity of judging the situation at the fronts as the Emperor used to send me to distribute decorations among the troops. Among the soldiers on active service I found nothing but stoical and fatalistic courage, great loyalty in the cause of their country and Imperial master, and confidence in victory. Not so, alas, among the reserves; they were contaminated with revolutionary ideas, which these simple sons of the peasantry did not even understand.

The whole country was exhausted and in that state was like an ailing body at the mercy of any germ. It was a relief to be occasionally at the front.

Early in 1917 I went to Murmansk where three men-of-war, which we had bought from the Japanese Government, had just arrived. They had belonged to us and had been captured by the Japanese when they captured Port Arthur. They had been modernized, and when I arrived I found them in excellent condition.

When I went to 'Romanovsk' the new railway had just been completed. The workmen employed on its construction were German and Austrian prisoners of war. I found that they were well looked after, but owing to the rigorous climatic conditions of these wild northern regions the mortality among them had been great.

My train took me through seemingly endless virgin forests until it reached the 'tundra.' These vast bogs of Northern Europe, almost uninhabited swampy regions of a peculiarly savage and desolate aspect, in spite of the utter loneliness have yet their fascination of a kind which the vastness and grandeur of nature bestows upon some desert regions of the earth. The endlessness and the sadness of these sub-polar regions have their peculiar charm, and as my train drew nearer to the frontiers of Norway the savage beauty of the scenery increased. What struck me most was the grimness of this wild scenery which unfolded itself around me the nearer we drew to Norway and the sea. Murmansk was in a pioneering stage at that time. The coast is rocky and wild and the sea, which stretches from there to the utmost North, storm-ridden and gloomy.

The inhabitants of these northern wilds are the Laps, Europe's most primitive people who live by their reindeer herds, which are their only wealth. Further to the east there are a whole collection of primitive races which live the life of nomad trappers, and are about the nearest kin to Eskimos and Red Indians, with whom they have much in common.

The Port of Murmansk is splendidly situated, as are several places along that coast which provides excellent natural harbours.

At that time Ducky was still at Yassy in Roumania. She returned to St. Petersburg via Kiev and early in February 1917 we met in the capital.

I had received the command of the Naval Guards from the Emperor, and as these were quartered in the capital my duties held me there.

Meanwhile the disorder in the rear of the front increased. There was a noticeable shortage of food in the capital, especially of bread, but the situation was not yet critical in that particular respect. The railway system was disorganized owing to the war. Crime and violence increased daily and the police were frequently attacked by gangs of hooligans. The Government did little to check the growing disorder in St. Petersburg.

There were strikes in the industrial areas and in the factory towns and demonstrations of workers. Among the million surplus soldiers discipline was badly shaken. There were reports of mutinies in barracks and of violence against officers.

One could not help feeling that the whole edifice of the exhausted Empire had begun to totter badly and that the collapse was imminent. If energetic measures had been taken to check the growing storm at that time all might yet have been saved. Nothing was done and everything, as if on purpose, was left to chance.

In the end, during the later part of February, the mob got out of hand and a mass murder of the police began. In the barracks reserve contingents of soldiers either arrested or massacred their officers. There was shooting in the streets by rival gangs. Gangsterdom and hooliganism took the upper hand.

My Naval Guards had hitherto remained loyal to me, my officers, and our armies at the front, and had not been infected by the happenings in the rear. Nor, indeed, could it be said that even the mob and the revolutionary soldiers in the capital were particularly antagonistic to the Emperor. From their talk and manifestations it could be gathered that they wanted bread, peace, and distribution of land and wealth. Much of what they shouted and of what was told them by the agents of the revolution they did not even understand. They had picked up slogans and repeated them like parrots. The people as such were not disloyal to the Emperor, as were those in the Ministries and in his entourage. As for the troops in the capital, they had enough of everything and far too little to do.

The Emperor who was at Mogilev gave orders, but sometimes they never reached their destination. He wanted, for example, a regiment of the Guards to be dispatched to the capital to re-establish order there. The message which he sent to the commander of the Cavalry Guards, for example, was intercepted on the way and never reached him.

The ones who paved the way to the revolution were those who owed their high positions to the Emperor. No blame attaches to the Russian people. These were deceived. It has been rightly said that 'Revolutions are hatched under top hats,' by the educated classes, by the 'intelligentsia' of professors and social theorists.

No one save these desired the revolution. Theirs is the guilt for the death of their Imperial Master and for the twenty-one years of Russia's martyrdom.

Those who were in command of the troops in the capital had lost their heads completely.

Next the report of the mutiny of the Baltic Fleet at Helsingfors was received. Things went from bad to worse and people lived in fear of their lives.

Some suggested to the Emperor that the only thing to do to save Russia now was to conclude a separate peace with

Germany. The Germans made tentative offers to that effect. Constantinople, our historic ambition, and the Dardanelles would be ours. The Emperor's reply to this was that he would remain loyal to the cause of the War and his Allies to the end, and this he did until his death.

Later, when the news of the Revolution was received by the countries for whom we had sacrificed so much and who were our Allies, the 'glorious Russian Revolution' was hailed by liberal opinion with joy. After all it was a war to make Democracy safe in the world! If that was the reason for which millions had fought and died in the greatest massacre that the world has ever known, and which will ever remain a stain on Western civilization, then this war was fought in vain.

One of my Naval Guard battalions was protecting the Imperial Family at Tsarskoe Selo, but the situation had become so dangerous in the capital that I ordered them to rejoin the rest of the Guards because these were almost the only loyal troops still left which could be relied on to keep order if things became still worse. The Empress agreed to this measure of emergency and other troops who carried out their duties well were dispatched to Tsarskoe.

The military authorities in the capital gave contradictory orders. One day they were to the effect that certain streets were to be occupied, on other occasions some equally useless measures were to be taken, when the only really effective step would have been to hand over all power to the military. This alone would have saved the situation. One or two regiments from the front would have sufficed to re-establish order within a few hours.

Mob rule, hooliganism, and chaos ruled supreme. There was continuous shooting at night and during the daytime, and it was hard to tell who waged war against whom. St. Petersburg was in the hands of rival gangs, which went about looting shops and stores. At night they encamped round bonfires at street corners where they had planted their machine-guns, and passed their time yelling and singing and shooting at anyone who ventured abroad along the deserted streets of the doomed city. Having plundered the wine cellars of private houses and hotels, anything could be expected from these armed gangs. Seeing that no measures were taken against the mutineers they became even bolder, as they realized that the real power was in their hands.

One day an armed rabble broke into the courtyard of my house. Their leaders demanded to see me. I went out to them expecting the worst, and was not a little surprised when I was asked fairly politely to lend them my car as they wanted to go to the Douma. I told them that they could take it provided they did not smash it, whereupon they all burst into cheers and shouted to me to lead them.

I think there was something in that demand which the masses felt very strongly. They felt the absence of leadership, they wanted guidance of some kind and were then still harmless enough.

No one knew at the time what had become of the Emperor, or where he was. The absence of stability, of someone at the helm, of at least some semblance of direction was felt by all. If leadership could have been found at that moment, and if this drifting ship of State could have been steered on some definite course, even the mutinous soldiers and the rabble would have followed, no matter where. They were more like sheep without a shepherd than a pack of dangerous wolves.

It is precisely this lack of guidance which was used by the Bolshevik Party later. They provided leadership and a course, although both led the country to a tyranny and bloodshed without historical precedent.

One day an officer of the Naval Guards came to me in a sad state of alarm. Apparently my sailors had locked up their officers and trouble of a serious kind was brewing in their barracks. I hurried off at once and spoke to my men. They were in an ugly temper. I succeeded in re-establishing order, but it was an unpleasant experience. I found, however, that in spite of revolution and anarchy my men were still very loyal to me. They had volunteered to provide me and my family with a guard, and in spite of the chaotic state of affairs we were not molested. Every night friends would drop in to inquire how we were and to discuss the situation. They did so risking their lives, for anyone who went into the streets of the city at night was shot at indiscriminately.

It was a time of extravagant rumours and there was a complete lack of reliable news.

During the last days of February the anarchy in the metropolis had become such that the Government issued an appeal to all troops and their commanders to show their allegiance to the Government by marching to the Douma and declaring their loyalty.

This measure had been decreed to re-establish some kind of order amid this intolerable chaos. The Government hoped that if the troops could be got to carry out its emergency measures in the capital, normal conditions might yet be established and the rule of gangsterdom checked for good and all.

Meanwhile there was no news from Mogilev, only wild rumours. No one knew of the actual whereabouts of the Emperor beyond that he was trying to come to Tsarskoe backed by loyal troops which would help the Imperial train to break through the cordons of disloyal revolutionary contingents.

I was put in a very awkward position by the decree of the Government. I was the Commander of the Naval Guards, which constituted one of the military contingents of the capital. The order of the Government, which was the last vestige, even though a sorry one, of authority in St. Petersburg, applied to my men as it did to all other troops, and, further, it applied to me as their commander.

I had to decide, therefore, whether I should obey that

PRINCE LOUIS FERDINAND OF PRUSSIA AND THE
GRAND DUCHESS KIRA OF RUSSIA
Taken at the time of their wedding.

BREAKFAST AT KER ARGONID
A repast in the English tradition.

order and take my men to the Douma, or else whether to leave my men leaderless in this dangerous situation by resigning, and thus to let them drift on to the rocks of revolution with the rest. Hitherto I had succeeded in preserving loyalty and good discipline among them. They were the only loyal and reliable troops left in the capital. It had not been an easy task to preserve them from the contamination of the revolutionary disease. To deprive them of leadership at this time would simply have added to the disaster. My main concern was to do my utmost to re-establish order in the capital by every means available, even with the sacrifice of my personal pride, so that the Emperor might safely return.

The Government was not yet a manifestly or officially revolutionary one, although it was tending that way. It was, however, as I have said, the last certain thing among the wreckage, and if the Emperor only returned backed by loyal troops and order could be re-established then all might yet be saved. There was some hope left.

Accordingly I went to the barracks of the Naval Guards, still hoping that it would not be necessary to drink this bitter cup. When I arrived, however, I saw that I had no course left to me other than take them to the Douma. They wanted to be led.

Accordingly, I marched to the Douma at the head of a battalion of Naval Guards. On the way there we were shot at by some infantry soldiers. I continued by car.

Arrived at the Douma I found the place in absolute pandemonium. It was like a bear-garden. Soldiers with unbuttoned tunics and their caps pushed to the back of their heads were shouting themselves hoarse. Deputies were yelling at the top of their voices. The place was in a state of chaos and confusion. Cigarette smoke filled the air, the place was in a filthy mess, and torn paper littered the floor. Meanwhile officers were driven up the stairs by their soldiers with the butts of rifles. They were being insulted and bullied mercilessly. Among them were many whom I knew well. That was what I found in the seat of the Liberal Government. Liberalism and Socialism expressed themselves in complete anarchy.

I spent the whole of the afternoon and evening in this painful atmosphere guarded by my men. In the end a mining student came to my room and said that a car was waiting to take me away.

On the way back we were held up by an armed gang which demanded to know who we were. The student shouted at them: "Students, comrades!" Whereupon they let us pass. There were buildings on fire which lit up the night with their ghastly glare. An armed and shouting rabble went through the streets. Machine-gun and rifle firing could be heard quite near.

The trouble and disorder, because it had not been checked in time, had spread meanwhile to Moscow and other towns. Russia was collapsing and sinking before our eyes.

When I reached home I found my wife in a state of great anxiety owing to my long absence. She thought that all was over with me.

Soon after this tragical day order was re-established and normal life resumed its course. The capital woke up from this fearful nightmare.

After this sad and dangerous farce in which I had witnessed the triumph of the forces of disorder and of ill-placed Utopian idealism, I realized that it was the end and that the time for strong action had been missed, and that henceforth the country was being plunged headlong into anarchy, bloodshed, and complete dilapidation in the name of all the various human virtues.

On 3 March 1917, old style, the consummation of this ghastly tragedy came with all the crushing weight of an overwhelming and sudden catastrophe. It was the end.

On the night of 2 March the Emperor had abdicated

for himself and his son the Czarevitch Alexis.[1] Grand Duke Michael had refused to assume leadership. All power and authority had been handed over to the Government.

It was the saddest moment in my life. Thereafter all seemed futile and hopeless. Hitherto there had been hope. Now the whole reality had revealed itself mercilessly and like a lifeless vacuum before one. It was as though the very ground had given way beneath one's feet. All that one had worked, fought, and suffered for had been in vain.

When the troops at the front heard of the disaster, they at first refused to believe it. They had been confident of victory. The offensive had been fixed for April, and that might have led them to the long-expected triumph for which they had suffered much during these dismal years of war.

They suspected treason. Many hardened fighters wept. They bore no ill will to the Emperor. They knew that he had been betrayed and abandoned. The regiments awaited the order to march on the capital to make short work of the traitors. They waited in vain. The order never came.

As soon as I heard what had happened I handed in my resignation, and with a heavy heart went to address my men.

I told them that in my position I could not continue to lead them. I exhorted them to remain loyal to their country, to keep good discipline, and to obey their superiors; that for twenty years I had been with them and that this was the hardest day in my life.

Like many of the seasoned fighters at the front, when they heard the news that the Emperor had abdicated there were tears in their eyes. Then they rushed up to

[1] Czar Nicholas II abdicated the throne of Russia in his own name and in that of his son and heir, the Czarevitch Alexis, and appointed his brother, the Grand Duke Michael Alexandrovitch, as his successor.

me, seized me in their arms, and lifted me up on their shoulders shouting: "Where you are, sir, we will be."

Darkness and bitter sorrow settled over all things. The curtain had fallen. Henceforth there was nothing left but to face the game of life to the end, in the hope of a resurrection after this bitter calvary which had now begun.

Some came to look me up, they continued guarding me until I and my family left the capital. One of my sailors used to come to us when we were in exile in Finland, bringing us provisions, wine, cakes, and delicacies of all kinds. He looked upon this revolution with the common sense of a man of the people. It was a farce, he said, which would end sadly.

These were some of the fruits of the doctrine of progress and enlightenment, of liberty and 'understanding,' but they were at most innocently farcical when compared with some others—for example, that the 'Social Experiment' of the Revolution cost Russia the lives of about fifty million human beings. If this sacrifice had at least produced a Marxian paradise on earth and happiness for all, it might have been a dear price to pay, but it produced nothing but continuous starvation for more than twenty years, tyranny of the worst kind, and an absolute negation of all natural rights of the individual. This Utopian doctrine has expressed itself in more suffering, bloodshed, and privation than the most merciless campaign of extinction by the world's cruellest conquerors.

On Easter Saturday a delegation of my sailors came to my house and insisted on my coming with them to our chapel in the barracks to attend the Liturgy of Easter night with them. I was rushed away by them. They showed me where to stand in the Church.

That was my last Easter on Russian soil.

We did not leave our house until May 1917. Meanwhile some kind of order had been re-established; it was merely an uncanny calm before the great storm which was gathering over the country.

It is an interesting fact worth mentioning that during the troubles of March, the electric light, gas, and the water supply had never failed in the capital.

Quiet had settled down. I did not trust this calm any more than I would have trusted one in Asiatic seas when the sky is ominously threatening before a typhoon. It was not a natural calm.

After considerable difficulties I obtained permission from the 'Government' to leave for Finland with my family. Our departure was very well and quietly arranged by a commissionaire.

In June of the year 1917 I left St. Petersburg by train with my two daughters; Ducky followed me alone.

Crossing the Finnish frontier I left Russia behind me for an exile that has now lasted for twenty-one years.

Before me lay the unknown, behind me the gathering shadows of the night. But amid the utter darkness there was the light of hope, but that hope is with me still, and it will never leave me.

My Father (an Epilogue) by H.I.H. the Grand Duke Vladimir

The Author's decease prevented him from writing of his exile. This phase in his life has been ably described below by his only son, H.I.H. the Grand Duke Vladimir, now Head of the Romanov Dynasty, and does not form part of the original work.

My late father, the Grand Duke Cyril, began writing his memoirs when his health was already failing. The last chapter written by him is Chapter VIII, which he concluded on 22 September, the day when he had to be taken to Paris to the American Hospital. On 12 October he passed away. God has not willed it that he should have completed his memoirs, and accordingly I, his son, consider it my duty to write a concluding chapter comprising the period from 1917 to the year of his death—1938. This task has been made all the more easy for me as Father was in the habit of making notes day by day, recording all facts of interest.

· · · · ·

In the spring of 1917, when Father, after the abdication of the Emperor Nicholas II, did not consider it possible to remain in the Service any longer, he decided to take up residence in Finland, hoping that conditions there would be easier and provide more safety. This was all the more important at that time, as Mother was expecting my birth. In order to undertake this journey a special permit from the Provisional Government was required, and Father had to apply to A. F. Kerensky, then Minister of War and Marine, with whom he met full sympathy, and the necessary documents were immediately issued to him.

My mother and father decided to settle in Borgo, a small Finnish town not far from Helsingfors. Their choice fell on this little town because not far from it was the Haiko estate which belonged to the family Etter, our close friends.

My parents had visited Haiko several times before. They were there with my two sisters, Marie and Kira, in July 1914. Father and Mother left the two girls with the Etters when they had to come to St. Petersburg for the receptions organized in honour of M. Raymond Poincaré, President of the French Republic, who was then visiting Russia. When the War was declared Marie and Kira were still at Haiko, and my parents had some trouble in getting them safely back in St. Petersburg, as the trains were full of troops. In summer 1916 Mother again visited Haiko with the girls, and they were later joined there by the Grand Duchess Marie Pavlovna. My sisters spent all their time out of doors and bathed. Mother did a lot of painting, and often visited the small military hospital for the wounded which had been organized on the estate.

When my parents arrived at Borgo in the beginning of June 1917 they proceeded straightway to Haiko, accompanied by two Englishwomen, Miss Burgess and Miss Gregory, and by some of the servants. The rest of the servants were placed in a house which Father had rented at Borgo, and Father's equerry, K. N. Hartong, also took up his quarters in the house. After spending a fortnight at Haiko, our family moved to Borgo, where they lived till the end of August. On 30 August I was born, but in September, as soon as Mother was well, my parents accepted the invitation of the good Etter family and returned to Haiko, hoping that it would be a safer place.

My christening took place at Haiko on 18 September. The Very Rev. Protopresbyter Alexander Dernoff, Head of the Court Clergy and Dean of the Cathedrals of the Winter Palace in Petrograd and of the Annunciation in the Kremlin of Moscow, came to conduct the ceremony, and was assisted by V. I. Ilyinsky, Psalmist of the Cathedral of SS. Peter and Paul in Petrograd. My godparents by proxy were the Grand Duchess Marie and the Grand Duke Boris. The christening was attended by a few Russian exiles and some of our Finnish friends.

Even at Haiko my parents could not feel secure. Revolution was in full swing. In Helsingfors was stationed the whole of our Baltic fleet, and though the command was still in the hands of the officers, their authority had suffered considerably from revolutionary disintegration in which the Sailors' Revolutionary Committee played a great part. Finland herself was on the eve of seceding from Russia, and the discontent of national elements against Communist influence assumed growing proportions. In other words, the 'White' movement against the 'Reds' had already started, and this unavoidably led to civil war.

One day a group of sailors appeared unexpectedly on the estate and declared that they had orders to search the house. One has to know what a 'search' by sailors meant at that time in order to appreciate the anxiety which overcame Father and Mother. They had already heard that the majority of the members of the Imperial Family had been arrested, and were prepared for the worst. They moved with us children to the second floor and went through some trying moments. Yet no arrest nor search followed. It later appeared that when the sailors were told that the house was inhabited by my father and his family they decided not to proceed with the search and left. One of them had served on the cruiser *Olej*, which had been under Father's command. Father had been very popular with the crew, and in remembrance of that love the man persuaded the others not to disturb him.

In December civil war between the Finnish Reds and Whites broke out. The first hostilities took place in our district; a battle was fought not far from Haiko, and we could hear the firing of big guns. Our family was in a very difficult position, and the question of obtaining food was highly complicated. It was not easy to get the most essential products, such as milk, meat, butter, and bread. The winter was a very severe one, which did not prevent my sisters from enjoying their winter sports with the young Kleinmichels, Serge Melikoff, and Vladimir Etter, who were all staying at Haiko at the time. The Grand Duke George came for Christmas.

The position grew worse in January and February. The Reds took to shooting the squires, and one squire by the name of Björkenheim was taken away to the forest and shot only two miles away from Haiko. Seven Finnish Whites took refuge on the estate and some of them spent three weeks in the house. Their whereabouts then became known to the Reds and they left. On 9 February a band of fifteen Finnish Reds appeared near our house. They asked if there were any arms hidden in any of the rooms, and three of them made a brief search of the ground floor. We were all on the second, but no one went up there. They behaved very politely, and the way in which they put their questions suggested that they had orders not to touch anybody in Haiko and to be particularly polite towards us.

The civil war raged on. We were practically cut off from the rest of the world, and only heard rumours which were often fantastic and contradictory. On 27 February Father received news from Helsingfors that the French Government were making inquiries as to whether our family was safe and if it was necessary to take official steps for our evacuation. Father hesitated as to what reply he should make. It was, of course, very painful to go on living as we were, but Father protested that Russia would soon be freed from the Reds, and to go abroad seemed to him too much like desertion.

A few days later the news arrived that King Gustavus of Sweden had inquired through the Swedish Legation if he could help us and the other members of the Imperial Family. Father thanked the King for his consideration, admitted that he did not look upon the position of his family as safe, but replied that the moment had not yet come for an intervention. He gave such a reply because at that time it was expected that the Bolsheviks would fall at any moment.

March and April were marked by the arrival in Hango, and later in Helsingfors, of a German squadron; by a German ultimatum demanding the withdrawal of the Russian Baltic fleet to Kronstadt; the entry into Hango of the German Iron Division under the command of General von der Goltz; and by the final victory of General Mannerheim's Finnish White Army over the Reds. Civil war thus came to an end and life became considerably easier.

General Mannerheim, and later also General von der Goltz with his suite, called on Father.

In the autumn of 1919 we went to Borgo once again. Life was now becoming normal, supplies became plentiful, and order was re-established. In 1920, however, an epidemic of Spanish influenza broke out and resulted in many deaths. One of the victims was our English governess, and her death was a severe blow to all the members of our family.

At long last the Great War came to an end, and we now had the opportunity of going to Zurich through Germany to meet my maternal grandmother, the Grand Duchess Marie Alexandrovna, Duchess of Edinburgh. Our endeavours were successful, and in May we were able to leave hospitable Finland. We were all very glad of the change, as we were naturally tired of living in the modest provincial town of Borgo, especially in conditions so primitive and trying.

We did not stay in Germany. We only remained two days in Berlin with my aunt, the Princess Alexandra Hohenlohe-Langenburg. We met my grandmother in Munich and went to Zurich together. In the course of that same year my paternal grandmother, the Grand Duchess Marie Pavlovna, succeeded in escaping from Russia and settled in the South of France. In the beginning of August we got news that she was ill and Father and Mother went to see her. On 24 August she died and was buried in Contrexeville. The health of my grandmother, Marie Alexandrovna, was also failing, and she was often indisposed. On 22 October she died suddenly in Coburg. Thus my parents lost their mothers almost simultaneously.

In 1921 my family moved to the South of France. At long last we could begin our life in normal surroundings. My parents, however, were ever mindful of that duty to their country which fell to their lot as a result of the tragic death of the Emperor Nicholas II, his family, and the Grand Duke Michael Alexandrovitch, whereby my father became the senior surviving member of the Imperial Family.

That year marked the end of the civil war in our country. The Reds came out victorious, and the Russian White Army, led by General Baron Wrangel, was compelled to leave Russian territory. Its remnants settled in foreign countries, mainly in the Balkans and France. The real struggle between the White Russians and the Red Russians thus came to an end. True enough, a hope of renewing the struggle again still existed in the ranks of Baron Wrangel's heroic army, but my father considered that the international political situation was such as to preclude the realization of any such hope.

The only form of government which Russia had known

from the earliest times of her historical existence up to the year 1917 was the monarchical one. It was a form of government which, under all its aspects, fully corresponded to the requirements of all the peoples that inhabited Russia. The Revolution—with the Republic that lasted a few months and finally led to Communism—brought only suffering to the Russian people.

For this reason—with a clear conscience, without any regard for his personal feelings, and prompted solely by a desire to save his country from suffering and misfortune—my father decided to raise the monarchist standard and to assume the leadership of the struggle for the restoration of a rightful monarchy in Russia.

The prevailing political tendencies of that time were not at all favourable to the monarchist principle. The downfall of a number of the world's greatest monarchies led many people to the belief that the time of the monarchies had passed. Among the Russian *émigrés* even convinced monarchists did not venture to voice their views aloud.

My father, however, did not allow himself to be led away by such tendencies. Being deeply convinced that only a monarchy could save Russia, he decided that it was his duty to come into the open there and then, to maintain his rights to the Russian Throne, and to assume the leadership of the divided efforts which were being made by Russian monarchist groups. Before coming out into the open, however, he deemed it necessary to prepare the ground among the Russian *émigrés*.

On 8 August 1924 my father issued his first Manifesto, in which he declared himself Guardian of the Throne. At that time we lived at S. Briac. My father's declaration, however, did not receive the support of the Grand Duke Nicholas, who, as former Commander-in-Chief of the Russian Armies during the Great War, had by that time already assumed the leadership of all those groups of exiled Russians which had been formed from the evacuated units of General Baron Wrangel's army. Nor was it supported by Baron Wrangel himself. My father was also opposed—and this was the strangest thing of all—by the Supreme Monarchist Council, which claimed the leadership of all monarchist organizations in exile. The reason for this opposition lay in the fact that the wide circles of the Russian *émigrés* still believed in the possibility of a new intervention, and they thought that the Grand Duke Nicholas, in his capacity of former Commander-in-Chief, had sufficient authority to bring about such an intervention in practice. This was, of course, an illusion, and my father, knowing it as such, firmly believed that, in the long run, the majority would come round to his point of view, and that the patriotic cause which he had initiated would grow and develop. In this he was right.

The immediate result was a split in the monarchist ranks. In spite of this, my father was supported by a very large number of Russian monarchists, who shared his belief in the triumph of the legitimist principle. The Legitimist Movement was thus inaugurated, and in every country where Russian exiles had settled groups were formed which acted in close contact with my father. They endured considerable opposition, but the movement began to grow and gain strength.

Two years rolled by. By that time the legend which was widely believed by many Russians, namely, that the Emperor Nicholas II and his family had not been massacred and that the life of the Grand Duke Michael had been saved, was finally disproved. M. Sokoloff, the examining magistrate who had been charged by Admiral Koltchak, the Head of the White Government of Russia, to investigate the murder of the Imperial Family, had returned from the Far East and brought with him all his findings, as well as material proof of the disaster.

Sokoloff paid a number of visits to my parents, and acquainted them with his findings in every detail. They never really doubted the fact that the Imperial Family had been murdered. Now, with the findings and proofs before them, they were convinced that there could be no longer any hope that the Imperial Family had been saved. From Bolshevik sources came the confirmation that the Grand Duke Michael, too, had perished. There could, accordingly, be no longer any doubt that my father had become, beyond dispute and by right of primogeniture, the senior member of the Imperial House of Russia, and, consequently, the Head of the Dynasty, nearest to the Throne and the Succession.

At the same time his position was very unstable. Attacks were constantly made against him—attempts to prove that he and his brothers had no right to the Throne as they were born before their mother had embraced the Orthodox Faith, rumours that he had abdicated his right while he was still in Russia, and so on and so forth. Some wanted the Grand Duke Nicholas to advance his rights. Impostors appeared within Russia and outside. Insistent reports from Russia stated that nobody was clear as to who was the rightful claimant to the Throne, as the title 'Guardian of the Throne' was too vague.

For this reason—in order to consolidate his position and determine once and for all his own right and the right of his descendants to the Russian Throne, and to remove any doubts which the world at large might have on the subject—my father decided to assume the Imperial Title which belonged to him by right of primogeniture and in accordance with the Fundamental Laws of the Russian Empire regulating the Succession.

On 13 September 1924 my father signed the Manifesto in which he assumed the Imperial Title. It was very hard indeed for him to resolve on this step. Outward pomp did not attract him in the least, and vanity was not one of his failings. As he himself put it in a letter to the Grand Duchess Xenia: 'Nothing can be compared with what I shall now have to endure on this account, and I know full well that I can expect no mercy from all the malicious attacks and accusations of vanity.' He was quite right. He took on his shoulders a heavy cross, which he carried to his very grave.

The assumption of the Imperial Title by my father was appraised in all its seriousness by the Press of the whole world, and was considered to be an important new factor in the struggle against what was being done in Russia.

Among the Russian *émigrés* this step created a very strong impression, and gave a fresh impetus to the further development of the movement headed by my father.

Apart from his indisputable right to the Throne, the success of the cause which he had inaugurated depended to a very great extent on the line of policy which he would choose. If his choice was a happy one, success was bound to follow sooner or later. If it was faulty, no efforts in the world would aid its realization.

To get a clear picture of the task which confronted him, we must try and recapture the atmosphere of 1924–1925. At that time the Russian *émigrés* were still under the spell of the 'White idea'—that is to say, they were still convinced that Russia could be delivered from Communism only by action from without. As, however, the forces of the *émigrés* were wholly inadequate to effect such a task unaided, the 'White idea' implied the necessity of enlisting foreign aid, that is to say, the necessity of a foreign intervention. With regard to the future social structure of Russia, the monarchist circles advocated a complete restoration of the old order.

Such views were quite natural and even logical at that time, when the horrors of the Revolution and the civil war were still fresh in everybody's mind. It made my father's choice of policy, however, all the more difficult. To go against the prevailing sentiments of the *émigrés* was bound to result in driving their majority into opposition. To follow the path of restoration meant crippling his chances of success within Russia itself.

My father was accustomed to be guided by his common sense and personal experience, and he considered that the sentiments that prevailed in Russia were far more important than the sentiments of the *émigrés*.

He rejected the idea of an 'intervention,' for he considered that a Russian Emperor could not seek to recover with the aid of foreign bayonets a Throne which belonged to him by right. As for social restoration, he regarded it as a chimera.

My parents repeatedly asserted that our first and foremost problem was to convince the whole world that a restoration of Russia's rightful monarchy would not mean reaction, and that monarchy was the most enlightened, the most flexible, and the most perfect form of government imaginable. My father was often vexed at the opinions expressed by a number of enlightened foreigners, who suggested that a restoration of monarchy in Russia would inevitably lead to an archaic form of despotism—a form of government which has never in fact existed in Imperial Russia.

In view of this my father issued a number of pronouncements in which he expressed his views on the future structure of Russia, and not long before his death—on 24 March 1938—he published an Act in which he expressed his views in their final form.

I look upon this Act as a document of immense political significance, for not only does it illustrate my father's views, but it also gives a profoundly correct analysis of the present position in Russia. The purport of this Act I shall now reproduce.

My father considered that from the very beginning of the Revolution the discontent of the masses against the dictatorship which had been thrust upon the country expressed itself in various forms. One might have thought, nevertheless, that those persons who had attained high rank under the dictatorship were loyal to it. The events of recent years, however, and especially the events of the past year, have shown that there is an ever-growing ferment even among such persons as have attained power, honour, and material prosperity. In the entourage of the dictator conspiracies constantly arise, and such attempts as have so far been made to overthrow the tyrannical Government—and which have up till now proved abortive—have all proceeded from circles closely connected with that Government. My father considered that there could be no better proof of the general hatred which surrounds the existing regime. If the dictator himself sees treason everywhere and has no one on whom he can rely, then his dictatorship will inevitably come to an end. His real and imaginary enemies he destroys mercilessly. In its life and death struggles against an opposition which reveals itself in every sphere of the political and economic life of the country, the dictatorship is ruining the whole structure of the State, it undermines Russia's military might and poisons the nation's life-blood. By pursuing such a policy the dictator has proved to the whole world that he is prompted solely by a lust for power, that his objects are purely personal, and that he has no care for the good of the people.

At this moment of grave crisis my father deemed it his duty, as heir of the Czars and Emperors who created Russia's might, to remind the Russian people of those foundations on which our country must be built anew.

After the inevitable downfall of the present dictatorship, the absence of a new Government capable of assuming immediate control of the administration would be fraught with untold calamities for Russia. The greatest danger of all would be another civil war which might lead to the disintegration of the State and the loss of lands which have for centuries formed an inalienable part of Russia. Russia's boundless territories would again be steeped in Russian blood, and all that the nation's effort had succeeded in reconstructing during the arduous years of oppression would again be razed to the ground. In order to overcome that prolonged crisis which has been dislocating Russian life for wellnigh a quarter of a century it is essential that a stable national government should come to power without delay. This can only be assured by a legitimate monarchy, whose policy would combine a continuity of traditional administration with the new demands and spirit of the times. It would be a monarchy founded on the unity of the nation, on the elimination of factious politics and class antagonism, on religious toleration and freedom of conscience, on equal rights for all the nationalities of the Empire, on the wide participation of the people in the political and economic administration of the country, and on the heredity of the sovereign power of the Crown—a constant, impartial, and natural arbiter. My father firmly believed that such a monarchy would save Russia from internal weakness and external dangers, and would lead her out on to the path of progress and prosperity.

Furthermore, he pointed out that personal and social liberty is a mere mirage without a monarchical sovereign power which can guarantee the continuity and stability of the established order. It is this continuity of power which makes a monarchy capable of embarking on radical and decisive reforms, such reforms as are often necessary for the salutary progress of a people.

A question which my father regarded as being of quite exceptional importance for Russia was the question of the Church, for Russia has always been a champion of the Christian spirit among nations. The Orthodox Church, as the guardian of this sacred and precious heritage, now hallowed with the crown of martyrdom and strengthened by the struggle and suffering borne in the long years of persecution, must preserve her canonical administration. Her position of priority among the other churches must be maintained, but at the same time no one should be prevented from glorifying the One God in another confession of faith.

The question of nationalities is of immense importance in a country like Russia, which is inhabited by a large number of different peoples, who have preserved their peculiar national cultures. Accordingly, my father considered that the new Empire should be grounded on a close alliance of all the nations and tribes which constitute its population. Any oppression of the other nationalities by the Russian majority cannot be tolerated. The Cossacks, too, must have their rights safeguarded—rights which they have well deserved throughout the history of our country.

My father always declared that the monarchy will not bring vengeance and retribution. It must and will give full recognition to all labours achieved for the good of the country by Russians within Russia and abroad during the years of trial and hardship.

One of the most serious questions for Russia's future development is the agrarian question. My father held the opinion that the present regime has pauperized our agricultural population: its policy of 'collectivization' has become an instrument of oppression directed at every section of the peasantry. The resuscitation of the prosperity of the country-side should be the first and foremost care of the new Government, a problem which should be tackled in a spirit of fair play and adjusted to the general demands of the good of the community. The agricultural population of the Empire must occupy a place which corresponds to its actual position in the State and in the economic life of the country. It must enjoy the benefits of a law which accords equality to all classes, safeguards the liberty of labour, and recognizes the stability and integrity of landed property. The right of private ownership of land must be extended to all the workers of the country. The new system of civil law must allow the acquisition, alienation, and inheritance of landed property. Every worker on the soil must be given complete freedom in the distribution of the fruits of his labour.

My father recognized the fact that the Government

which has been created by the Revolution has expended much energy on the development of industry. The development of the country's industrialization and the creation of new industrial bases called in their turn for an increase in the number of working hands. The Government has tried to exploit for political aims the great masses of labourers employed in the factories. In order to win the support of the workers, whose champion it pretends to be, the dictatorship claims the merit of having achieved the social emancipation of the working class. In actual fact, however, it has not only failed to achieve any improvement of labour conditions or to raise the minimum wage of the Russian worker, but it has actually brought about the enslavement of the entire mass of the labourers. Socialist society has in practice turned out to be a new form of serfdom in the hands of an impersonal State. In Russia to-day there is not a trace of that social progress which has been achieved in other advanced countries.

The entire concentration of the country's trade and industry in the hands of the State was a thing in which my father never believed. The countless sacrifices which have been borne by the Russian people have not, in any way, been justified by the results achieved. Freedom of trade and of personal initiative in industry must be safeguarded within the limits allowed by the general interests of the whole community. The solution of economic problems must be governed by considerations of expediency and remain uninfluenced by political passions. The economic structure of the Empire must not be weakened by class divisions which undermine national unity, but it must be cemented by the constructive collaboration and creative solidarity of all the constituent elements of every branch of production. All who take part in the economic life of the country should have a share in its administration through corporate and professional organs, and the measure of responsibility borne by each individual for his share in production should be balanced by a corresponding measure of personal interest. The regulation of wages and working hours, the health and personal safety of the workers, especially women and minors, and the insurance and maintenance of the aged and invalids will be the subject of special legislation.

National defence was, of course, a question in which my father was specially interested. The first-class naval and military training which he had received in Imperial Russia, and his own practical experience—for he had held responsible posts in the Navy—made him a competent judge in such matters. His interest did not wane in exile, and he kept in touch with every new development in military technique. He considered that Russia should not lag behind in the feverish international race for rearmament, and never failed to give due recognition to those Russian soldiers and military specialists through whose efforts the Army and Air Force have been brought to such a high level of perfection. And yet those very same generals, who deserved so well of their country, have now been shot down by the present insane Government!

Such was the political outlook of my father. The most striking feature of his character was that, though he had the best part of his life behind, he always remained alive to everything that happened in the world, and took a keen interest in that evolution of statecraft which, in the post-War period, has manifested itself in varying forms in all the great countries of the world. He was an advanced man in every sense of that word, and all his political views, as can be seen from my summary, were prompted by the demands of modern life.

. . . . .

In 1924 my family settled in Coburg, where we lived in the Villa Edimbourg. This villa belonged to my parents— it was given to them by my grandmother, the Grand Duchess Marie Alexandrovna Duchess of Edinburgh, and it was here that they lived after their marriage, before they could return to Russia. Everything here reminded them of the best part of their lives—the first few years after their marriage, all the more so as the interior decoration of the villa had not been changed at all. Every piece of furniture was exactly in the same place where it had been twenty years before.

Coburg itself is a small town, situated in very fine surroundings. Like every other 'Residenz-Stadt' in Germany, it is equipped with all the amenities of a big city, only in a miniature form—a theatre, an opera house, good restaurants, hotels, shops, and so on and so forth. It is neat and tidy and rather dull, as every small provincial town should be. Father found it quite pleasant in small doses, but boring to stay for any length of time. We led a very cloistered life in Coburg, for we had no friends except the family of Duke Karl of Saxe-Coburg and Gotha and King Ferdinand of Bulgaria.

Father was very fond of motor cars ever since they first appeared. He was, in a way, one of the oldest and most experienced motorists of our time, for he had toured practically the whole of Western Europe with Mother, especially Germany and France. He fell back on this favourite pastime of his during our Coburg years, and there was hardly a day when we did not drive out into the beautiful environs of the town.

Every morning Father was busy at work with his political assistants, and Sunday mornings were often included in this routine. All kinds of political workers came to visit him from every corner of the world. They came with reports on the internal situation in Russia, on the life of the Russian exiles in the countries in which they lived and worked, and on their own efforts to bring about a united front. I was a small boy at the time, but the visitors were always presented to me and I had to talk to them. The whole of our family, indeed, from the moment that Father began his political activity, lived in the world of political events and our conversations usually gravitated towards politics. I often saw troubled looks on the faces of my parents, and I knew what those looks meant. They were always caused by some new events which had taken place in Russia, or some fresh developments of the Russian question in general.

In November 1924 Mother received an invitation to visit the United States, and was away for a month. She was very well received in America, where a number of big receptions were organized in her honour. The moral success of her visit was very considerable, which was only natural, as she was an exceptional woman in every sense. Her brilliant intellect, her profound knowledge of life, and her great presence never failed to win the hearts of all with whom she came in contact.

In accepting this invitation my mother had one end in view—to further my father's cause in America, and in this she undoubtedly succeeded. It was rumoured at the time that her object was to collect funds, but this was untrue. Mother had no such object in mind, and considered it far more important to establish connections with prominent Americans who were interested in the Russian question.

Mother's journey was a cause of great anxiety to Father, and he eagerly awaited news from her all the time.

On 25 November 1925 my elder sister, Marie, was married in Coburg to Karl, the Hereditary Prince of Leiningen. The first ceremony was celebrated according to Orthodox rites in our private chapel in the Villa Edimbourg. The vestments and decorations of this chapel were presented to my grandmother by her father, the Emperor Alexander II, and originally belonged to the movable military chapel attached to his headquarters during the Russo-Turkish War of 1878. After the Orthodox ceremony a Lutheran marriage was celebrated in the local church. All our relatives came to the wedding, and a number of merry festivities followed. My parents were very pleased with the match.

The following summer we spent, as usual, at Saint-Briac, a place for which we had all developed a great fondness. This time my parents bought a villa there, and Mother got busy with alterations in the new house, its furnishing, and the lay-out of its garden. She had a passionate love for flowers, and was an expert gardener. She also loved painting them, and her flower studies were the works of an accomplished artist.

The house itself was an ordinary Breton stone building. Its interior was planned by Mother, and the furniture was brought from our flat in Paris, which had been kept on by my parents right through the War. This, of course, increased its sentimental value.

It was only in the winter of 1927–1928 that we finally succeeded in settling in our new house, and from that time onwards we made Saint-Briac our permanent home. We led a country life there, but it was far more lively than at Coburg, as before the World Crisis came on a number of English families lived permanently at Saint-Briac and Dinard, and we kept up the friendliest relations with them. An added attraction for Father was the golf course. He was a keen golfer, and could now play right through the year, which gave him great pleasure and was very good for his health.

On 13 October 1928 the Dowager Empress Marie Feodorovna died, and Father went to Copenhagen for her funeral. He had a great love and respect for the deceased Empress, and wanted to pay her his last act of devotion. While in Copenhagen he was the guest of the King of Denmark, and was received with all the honours due to the Head of the Imperial House of Russia. Most of the members of the Russian Imperial Family gathered at the funeral, and some of them Father met for the first time since his departure from Russia.

As a crowned Empress, Marie Feodorovna was considered by many Russians to be the highest authority in the Imperial Family, and her death made Father's position still more prominent. A few months later, on 5 January 1929, the Grand Duke Nicholas died at Antibes, on the Côte d'Azur—an event of great significance for the Russian *émigrés*, as the majority of the military organizations looked upon him as their leader. At the time of his death his authority was on the wane, as his prolonged illness had prevented him from taking part in public affairs for some time.

Father never really had any relations with him. In exile they had never even seen each other. Father fully recognized his authority as the oldest member of the Family and did not belittle the services which he had rendered Russia as a soldier, but as it was Father who, by virtue of the Fundamental Laws, was Head of the Dynasty, he considered that the Grand Duke should have supported his endeavours, while the Grand Duke only showed a marked hostility. This was the cause of considerable vexation for Father, who tried on several occasions to establish friendly relations with the Grand Duke, but always without success.

With the Grand Duke's death the military organizations were deprived of their natural leadership, and it seemed as though the obvious course for them to take would be to recognize the authority of my father. This, however, they did not do. Not that the Legitimist Cause was any the worse for it—on the contrary, it grew and gained strength from year to year. Legitimist groups were organized in every country where Russians had settled. My father's General Secretariat was thus in touch with every country in the world, and was well informed about everything that happened among the Russian *émigrés*. The importance of the movement increased with every year that passed, all the more so as the main protagonists of the 'White Movement,' one by one, left the political arena, and the chances of a foreign intervention diminished. The soundness of my father's forecasts was continually being confirmed by the trend of political events, which assured the success of his cause.

In the spring of 1929 Father transferred his General Secretariat to Saint-Briac, and resumed his Coburg habit of hearing reports from the Secretary-General every morning.

On 3 October 1930 my parents celebrated their Silver Wedding. It was a great event, both for them and for us, their children. In his memoirs Father has dwelt at some length on his marriage to Mother and on the events which followed it. It was a marriage which was based entirely on the mutual love of my parents, and which took place in spite of the circumstances in which they found themselves. For twenty-five years they lived together with one heart and mind, and our family could well be an example to all. We adored our parents, and their love for us was infinite. All the hardships and bitterness we had to endure in the years of exile were fully covered by our mutual love. We were proud of our parents, and the celebration of their Silver Wedding had a special significance for all of us.

My aunt Alexandra—Princess Hohenlohe-Langenburg—came to join in our festivities, and my parents received greetings from all parts of the world and many presents. On the evening of the 8th there was a big dinner, to which members of Father's entourage as well as all our friends in Saint-Briac and Dinard were invited. After dinner *tableaux* were produced, and they were a great success.

On the following Sunday, which was on 12 October, representatives of monarchist organizations arrived from Paris to present their loyal greetings. Their visit was made an occasion for a luncheon party, and in the evening there was a reception at Dinard in the house of an American friend of ours.

In the following year Father made a tour round Italy, and then went on a cruise in the Mediterranean, visiting Lebanon, Palestine, Egypt, Greece, and Dubrovnik.

Everywhere the scattered Russian colonies gave him a warm reception. The greatest impression that remained in his memory from this cruise was his pilgrimage to the holy places in Jerusalem.

On 30 August 1933 my majority was celebrated. I had reached the age of sixteen, and this gave me, according to the Fundamental Laws of the Russian Empire, the right of exercising all the prerogatives which belonged to me by virtue of my birth. Father issued a special Manifesto addressed to the Russian people, and a circular letter to all the Royal Houses, informing them that I had reached my majority. My Uncles Andrew and Dimitri, and a number of representatives of monarchist organizations, came from Paris to attend the ceremony, in the course of which I took my oath. The ceremony was followed by a banquet given in my honour by my uncle, the Grand Duke Dimitri.

The next important event in our lives took place a year later when, on 26 November 1934, my parents, my sister Kira, and I were invited by the King and Queen of England to attend the wedding of my cousin, Princess Marina of Greece, to the Duke of Kent. It was Father's first visit to England since the War and the Revolution, though Mother had been paying frequent visits to London, which she thoroughly enjoyed. A British princess by birth and a near relative of the King, she had many friends in England.

My parents stayed at Buckingham Palace, where a vast concourse of relatives had gathered for the wedding. Father and Mother knew them all, of course, but it was the first time in my life that I was present at such a gathering of the clans, and there were many whom I did not know at all. On the eve of the wedding there was a big reception at the palace, to which all the relatives, the Diplomatic Corps, and a number of others were invited. Among the diplomats was M. Maisky, the Soviet Ambassador. It was the first occasion on which Father found himself in such close proximity to a representative of Soviet Russia. No conversations passed between them.

I had never before attended a Court function on so vast a scale, and the impression it made on me was very great. Before the reception I was presented by my parents to King George V, for whom I conceived an immense liking. There was something exceptionally attractive about the old king's manner.

The reception itself I found very tiring, for I had to stand all the time, but I went round the rooms of the palace with great interest and watched the invited guests. I was introduced to so many friends and relatives that I found it quite impossible to remember them all. Apart from the reception there were several family dinners, but the number of relatives that gathered at those 'family' dinners was so great that they did not look like family affairs at all. One dinner was attended by no fewer than seventy-four. We had a good many jokes about this abundance of kin.

I looked over the wedding presents, and I remember being struck by the vast number which came from quite ordinary people. It was a remarkable testimony to the popularity which the Royal Family enjoys in England. A great surprise was in store for Father when we went to look at the presents. We found a number of elderly ladies there, and they turned out to be the nurses of some of the Royal guests. Imagine my father's astonishment when he met his own nurse, Miss Crofts, among them. The old lady—she was eighty then—was overjoyed at the meeting, and Father found great pleasure in remembering his childhood days with her.

The actual wedding took place on 29 November. There is no need for me to say anything about the ceremony in Westminster Abbey, with which my British readers are well acquainted, except that my sister Kira was Princess Marina's bridesmaid, and that I was groomsman at the Greek Orthodox ceremony which took place in the palace chapel.

On the day after the wedding we went to stay for a few days with the family of Lord Howard de Walden, an invitation which gave great pleasure to my parents, who were very fond of the Howard de Waldens. An amusing incident occurred with my mother at a party given a few days after our arrival. She had put on her evening dress and come downstairs when the party was already in full swing. While she was engaged in a long conversation with one of the guests she suddenly looked at her feet and found she was wearing bedroom slippers.

After thoroughly enjoying the hospitality of the Howard de Waldens we went to stay with the Astors. Lord Astor very kindly took it on himself to initiate Father and me in everything that was to be seen in London, and in the course of the six-day plan which he had worked out for us we visited the Tower, the Battersea Electrical Power Station, *The Times* printing works, Hanworth Aerodrome, where I went up in an autogyro, Biggin Hill Aerodrome, the British Museum, the Zoo and the Aquarium, and Westminster Abbey. It was while we were staying at the Astors that a luncheon was given in our honour at the German Embassy.

On 18 December our family left London. We left with very pleasant memories of the hospitable reception which was given us both by the Royal Family and by London Society in general.

In the winter of 1935 Father and I went to Paris, where I was to be coached for matriculation. We arrived on 8 December, and our visit was not a success, for I very soon became ill, causing great anxiety to Father. On 19 December Mother came to Paris, and on the following day she had to proceed to Germany to my elder sister, the Princess of Leiningen. It was only eleven days since I had left Mother, and I got quite a shock to see how ill she looked. She felt very nervous, too, and hated the idea of leaving me while I was still unwell. I was out of all danger, however, for I only had whooping cough, and all that had to be done was to send me home. Mother went to my sister Marie, who was seriously ill and was expecting a child. She left Paris, and as we parted I little thought that I would only see her again on her deathbed.

Soon after her arrival in Würzburg, where my sister was ill in bed, Mother got a chill, but she insisted on visiting Marie. The childbirth was not attended by any complications, and in the middle of January they all returned to Amorbach Castle. Here Mother again became ill, and the doctors found her condition serious, as she was steadily getting weaker. On the day of the baby's christening, however, Mother did not want to spoil the festive atmosphere. She summoned up all her will and attended the ceremony, but the effort taxed her strength very greatly. Her condition did not improve, and on 5 February my sister Kira went to Amorbach.

Father and I were in terrible suspense. Bad news followed good news, but we were far from the thought that the end was so near. On 18 February, however, we got a message to say that Mother's condition had taken a distinct turn for the worse, and on the following day we both set out for Amorbach. It was a terrible journey which I shall never forget.

We found Mother in a semi-conscious state. She was so weak that she could hardly move or speak, and only occasionally muttered words which could be understood with difficulty. She recognized us, however.

The days that followed were one long nightmare for all of us. Mother was getting weaker and weaker, the doctors could do nothing, and we were expecting the end at any moment. In the evening of 1 March the doctors noticed a rapid weakening of the pulse. Mother's sisters—the Infanta Beatrice of Spain and Princess Hohenlohe-Langenburg—had joined us, and we all gathered at her bedside. At fifteen minutes past midnight her pulse stopped beating. Mother had passed away. We all had such an infinite love for her that our grief knew no bounds. It was painful to look at Father.

On 5 March Mother's coffin was brought to Coburg and placed in the family vault of the Dukes of Saxe-Coburg and Gotha. A great many relatives came to the funeral, but there were no official representatives of the Royal Houses related to us, as Mother disliked pomp and ceremony, and it was decided to make the funeral—which took place on 6 March—a purely family affair. As we followed the coffin to the mausoleum we found the streets of Coburg lined with many of the local inhabitants, who had a great regard for Mother's family and came to pay her their last tribute.

The funeral was attended by my aunt, Queen Marie of Roumania, with her daughter Queen Elizabeth of Greece, the Grand Duke of Mecklenburg, the Duke of Saxe-Coburg and his family, King Ferdinand with his daughter Eudoxia, my Uncles Andrew and Dimitri, my aunt, the Infanta Beatrice of Spain, the family of my aunt, Alexandra of Hohenlohe-Langenburg, and the family of the Prince of Leiningen. There were many representatives of Russian organizations.

After spending ten days in Coburg and about the same length of time with my sister at Amorbach we returned to our orphaned home at Saint-Briac. My sister Kira had returned earlier and was awaiting us. It was terrible to enter the house for the first time after Mother's death —that house where her spirit seemed always to be present. Every object reminded us of her. Every flower in the garden had been planted by her.

Mother's death was a severe shock to Father, and for a long time he could not reconcile himself to the thought that she was dead. In every conversation he would always return to the one topic that interested him: reminiscences of Mother. He spent hours reading over her old letters and looking at her photographs. After her death he concentrated his affection on us, his children, and especially on me. He tried to be inseparable from us and was sick at heart when we were away.

Throughout the spring and summer of that sad year I was busy at my work, preparing for the matriculation which was to take place on 22 October. On 30 September Father and I came to Paris, and every moment I could spare from my work we spent together. The examination took place in the Russian School in Paris and lasted about a week. I got through it quite successfully and Father was very pleased. He came with me every morning, and often called for me at the school when my day's ordeal was over.

For Christmas I went with Father and Kira to London, where we thoroughly enjoyed our holidays with friends and relatives. In the middle of January we passed through Paris on our way to Switzerland for the winter sports, where we spent four months, and then went on to Munich so as to arrive at Coburg in time for the anniversary of Mother's death. In Munich Father became very ill. He recovered slightly, and was well enough to go to Coburg, but when he got there his condition became worse, and we could only return to Saint-Briac on 5 April. This illness was an indication of the general weakening of his organism. He had developed arterio-sclerosis, which affected his blood circulation, impaired his eyesight, and partly paralysed his left leg and the fingers of his right hand.

We spent the whole of the summer of 1937 at Saint-Briac, where I was preparing for my entrance examination to London University. In the autumn I came to London with Father and Kira, and I started my life as an undergraduate. We lived in the house of my aunt, the Infanta Beatrice, at Kew. Father was often alone in the house, as I was attending lectures for the greater part of the day. He was bored and complained that he was not feeling well. He underwent medical treatment, but it did not seem to do him much good. He blamed the state of his health on to the London climate, and was eager to return to Saint-Briac, where we were going to spend Christmas. Shortly before the day fixed for our departure, however, my sister and I received an invitation from the Crown Prince of Germany to spend Christmas with his family at Potsdam. We were sorry to leave Father alone at Saint-Briac for the holidays, but he considered that we ought to accept the invitation, and we parted in Paris. Father went to Saint-Briac, while I went to Potsdam with Kira.

On 23 December my sister became engaged to Prince Louis Ferdinand of Prussia. A telegram was immediately dispatched to Father, who gave his blessing. We were most keen to get back to Saint-Briac, but had to go to Doorn first, as the Emperor Wilhelm was also very eager to bless the engaged couple.

At last, on 5 January 1938, my sister, the Prince, and I returned to Saint-Briac. Father's joy knew no bounds. He very much approved of Kira's engagement, and said that his mind was now at peace.

On 18 January I had to return to London to resume my studies at the University, and on the 25th my sister went to Doorn. Father remained alone with Captain Graf, who had been his Secretary-General for many years. His attacks of illness became more frequent, and he constantly complained of his failing eyesight and of the empty feeling in his head. On 15 February Kira returned to Saint-Briac, and on 9 March my elder sister, Marie, also arrived. This cheered Father up considerably, though he was still very lonely without me. Throughout March the state of his health was very poor, but by the time I returned on the 29th he became much better, so much so that he could come with us to Paris for the big reception which the Russian colony was organizing in Kira's honour on 3 April to celebrate her engagement. Afraid of taxing his strength with too much excitement, Father did not go to the reception, but remained in the hotel where we were staying. He was anxiously awaiting our return and was very keen to know how everything went off. The reception proved a great success, and we were all in excellent spirits that evening.

On 8 April we returned to Saint-Briac, and in the same night Father suddenly felt a terrible pain in his right leg. From that day the frightful pains in his leg never ceased till his death.

Kira's wedding was fixed for 2 May, and Father and I had, of course, to attend it. Right through April, however, Father was so bad that it seemed quite impossible for him to go. Still, he was very keen to go to the wedding, and his doctor considered that it would do him a lot of good, as it would cheer him up. Up till the very last day we could not make up our minds, but finally on 27 April we went to Paris, and decided that we would there see if Father could go any further. His pains continued, and it was not without considerable misgiving that on 30 April we decided to go. Though he found all the ceremonies at Potsdam and Doorn a severe strain, Father was still very happy to have attended Kira's wedding, and returned home in a much more cheerful frame of mind.

We spent the summer in Saint-Briac. Father's state of health improved now and again, but a relapse invariably followed. His pains did not cease and he was continually suffering, especially at night. The summer passed, and on 4 September I again had to return to London for my studies. On the 10th my sister Marie also had to leave Saint-Briac to join her family in Germany. Our doctor considered that Father's condition was not critical, and that there was nothing to fear.

On 12 September, however, were detected the first signs of the gangrene which had set in. My sister and uncles were immediately informed, and a specialist was summoned from Paris, who advised that Father should be transferred to one of the hospitals in Paris without delay. On 21 September my sister and Father's two brothers—Boris and Andrew—arrived at Saint-Briac, bringing a doctor with them. On the following day, on the insistent advice of the physicians, Father was taken to Paris by car and placed in the American Hospital. I had by that time finished with my examinations, and left London for Paris immediately.

In the hospital Father was examined by a number of prominent specialists, and it then appeared that his position was far from hopeless, and that it might even be possible to avoid an operation. We were all filled with the hope that he would recover. On 7 and 8 October, however, the pains in his right leg became unexpectedly worse. Father was in terrible distress and no soothing remedies were of any avail. In the morning of 9 October, while bandaging his legs, the doctor found fresh symptoms of gangrene, and considered that the position was very serious. He immediately held a consultation which came to the decision that the position of the patient was hopeless and that in view of the general weakening of the organism an operation was impossible. When I was told this, I could hardly believe that all hope was at an end. Father was fully conscious and, as his pains had ceased, he thought that his condition had taken a turn for the better. He spent a comparatively quiet night, but it was obvious that his strength was giving way, and he could hardly move. He slept for the greater part of the day, waking at intervals and talking to the people who surrounded him. But he was all the time getting weaker and weaker, and on the 11th he was so weak that he remained motionless the whole day and was in a state of coma. On that day he confessed and received the Sacrament.

At 7.30 a.m. on 12 October my sister and I, Father's brothers, and his sister, Princess Nicholas of Greece, were summoned to the hospital, as the doctor was expecting Father to die at any moment. We all gathered at his bedside. There was still a lingering flame of life in him, and only at 1.15 p.m. his pulse ceased to beat. He passed away in his sleep. The expression of his face was so calm that it seemed as though he realized that he had at last found peace and quiet after six months of uninterrupted suffering.

Father's death came as a great shock to the Russian exiles in all countries. It was a Russian national sorrow. Requiem services were held, and everywhere churches were filled with mourners. His coffin was a mass of flowers. On the morning of the 17th it was conveyed by a special car to Coburg, and I followed in my own car. The funeral took place on 19 October, and Father's coffin was placed in the family vault of the Dukes of Saxe-Coburg and Gotha, next to the coffin of my mother.

He was only sixty-two when he died. God did not suffer him to return to his country, which he had loved so passionately all his life.

I have no doubt that history will give due recognition to his life's work. It will recognize my father's high sense of duty as a member of the Imperial House and a true patriot.

Years will pass. Russia will be delivered from the terrors which she is now enduring. I am confident that she will return to her historical form of government as the logical end of the experiments which have been carried out on her by the usurpers of power. Then will the Russian people appraise the great merit of my father, who, in a spirit of self-sacrifice and with a deep understanding of surrounding conditions, launched the struggle for Russia's salvation along the only true channel.

He raised aloft the standard of the monarchy, which for Russia is also her national standard. The emblem of peaceful life, progress, and prosperity. The pledge of the peace of all Europe.

Appendix

Manifestoes of the late Grand Duke Cyril of Russia, the head of the Imperial Dynasty

THERE are no limits to the sufferings of the Russian people.

Our great nation, enslaved, tortured, offended in its faith, is dying out as a result of increasing illnesses and epidemics. Now an even greater evil has befallen Russia—a dreadful famine. Human words are unable to express the sufferings of mothers who are the helpless witnesses of their children's death from starvation.

Three years ago many millions of our compatriots perished from hunger in that very Russia which formerly had a surplus of bread and was the granary of Europe. But then the sympathetic and generous America and various organizations came to the assistance of those that were perishing, and many were saved.

At present the hopes of foreign help are in vain, because the immoral Communistic Government, having ruined Russia, robbed her of her wealth and riches, has obtained for itself in the last years gold by exporting bread from our starving land. The Communists need gold for their own enrichment, for extending trouble in other countries throughout the world and to attain the aim of world revolution.

Notwithstanding the clearly undeniable failure of the harvest in a broad belt of the most fertile part of Russia, the Communists continue to export bread this year.

It is quite clear that America, knowing that her help would only serve to strengthen the destructive activity of the third international, is unwilling to give further help, realizing its futility.

I have received the same answer to all my requests for help for the Russian people, namely, that during the continuance in Russia of the present political conditions and an ascendancy over her of the enemy of Christian civilization, the third international, no help can be given until a law-supporting Government is established in our Fatherland, and that only upon the establishment of legal government can the measures and methods of widest help be introduced in Russia.

Let the Russian Army, although named Red, but in whose ranks the majority are forcibly enrolled faithful sons of Russia, say the decisive word, rise in defence of the rights of the Russian people and, having re-established the historic motto for the Faith, the Czar, and the Fatherland, re-erect the former law and order in Russia.

Let the mass of the people rise together with the Army and recall its lawful national Czar, who will be a loving, forgiving, caring Father, the Sovereign Ruler of the great Russian land, feared only by our enemies and by conscious destroyers of the people.

The Czar will re-erect the churches, forgive those who erred, and will lawfully give the land to the farmers. And then Russia will receive wide help during the famine and will be saved from destruction, and later she will rebuild her destroyed trade and industry and will obtain peace and prosperity.

The duties of the Czar will be heavy and difficult in Russia, ruined and deprived of her foundations. It is not for personal glory, not for honours, and not because of a greed for power that the Czar will return to the Throne of His forefathers, but to do His duty before God, His conscience, and His Fatherland.

When calling for the sacred effort of the liberation of the Fatherland from a disgraceful and destructive yoke, I am the first who is obliged to carry out the law and My duty, while setting aside all hesitation and notwithstanding the fact that at present I must live outside the Fatherland.

In making the sign of the Cross, I proclaim to the whole Russian Nation:

Our hope that the most valued life of the Lord Emperor Nicholas Alexandrovitch or of the Heir and Czarevitch Alexis Nicolaevitch or of the Grand Duke Michael Alexandrovitch had been spared, has not been fulfilled.

It is now time to announce for all to know:

On the 4th/17th July, 1918, in the town of Ekaterinburg, on the instructions of the international group that has seized power in Russia, the Lord Emperor Nicholas Alexandrovitch, the Lady Empress Alexandra Feodorovna, Their Son and Heir and Czarevitch Alexis Nicolaevitch, and Their Daughters the Grand Duchesses Olga, Tatiana, Marie, and Anastasia were brutally murdered.

In the same year, 1918, near the town of Perm, the Brother of the Lord Emperor, the Grand Duke Michael Alexandrovitch was killed. May the sacred memory of these crowned Martyrs be a guiding star to us in the holy work of the restoration of the former well-being of our Fatherland, and may the day of the 4th/17th July be for all time a day of sorrow, contrition, and prayer in Russia.

The Russian laws of Succession to the Throne do not permit the Imperial Throne to remain vacant after the death of the previous Emperor and His nearest Heirs has been established.

Also in accordance with our laws the new Emperor becomes such on the strength of the Law of Succession.

The terrible hunger and the cries for help which again

are heard from Russia strongly demand that the work of the rescue of Russia should be headed by a legal supreme authority which is above classes and parties.

And in accordance with this I, the senior member of the Czarist House and sole legal Heir of the Russian Imperial Throne, take the title of Emperor of all the Russias which without possible doubt is mine.

I proclaim My Son, Prince Vladimir Kirillovitch, as Heir to the Throne with the title of Grand Duke Heir and Czarevitch.

I promise and swear sacredly to observe the Orthodox Faith and the Russian Fundamental Laws of Succession to the Throne, and engage to protect at all times the rights of other faiths.

The Russian people are great and have many gifts of mind and heart, but have fallen into terrible misfortune and disaster. May the great tests which have been sent them by God purify them and bring them to a bright future, having renewed and strengthened before the Almighty the sacred union between the Czar and the People.

Kirill.

Given on the 31st August/13th September, 1924.

TO ALL LOYAL RUSSIAN PEOPLE

Among Russian people there have lately again been rumours of preparations of an armed incursion into Russia of the remainders of the military volunteer organizations, with the help of some foreign powers.

Hereby I declare to all those who are loyal to me that, while leaving it to everyone to act according to his conscience in the lawful wish to re-establish in the Fatherland the disrupted law and order, I cannot in any circumstances share the views of those leaders who might give way to the temptation of going to war against their compatriots with the support of foreign troops, however much the national masses of Russia might still be misled at the present time.

Under the banner of liberation from Bolshevism these leaders will bring our Fatherland the enslavement of its character, the looting of its natural riches, and, perhaps, the further loss of territories and the closing of the outlets to the seas.

The hour of God's Judgment is not far off and the structure of the usurpers' power, built on sand, will collapse under the pressure of the awakening national consciousness.

Any ill-timed interference in the work of the salvation of Russia and the establishment there of the historic legal state will only hinder Me in the execution of My duty to the Fatherland, will postpone the long expected hour of its liberation and will bring it more blood and sacrifice, sorrows, and dangerous disappointment, and will also deepen mutual hate.

1/14th January, 1925.   KIRILL.

The hour of liberation of the Russian people from the power of the enemies of the Orthodox Faith and of Holy Russia is nearing.

Having proved before the whole world its inability to rebuild Russia from the ruins to which the blood and troubles have reduced the thousand-year-old Czardom, those who have seized power have completely exhausted the national treasure. Only the very generous monetary help from the outside could have lengthened the sufferings of the Russian nation under the Communist yoke.

But, however much the enemies of Russia would like to come to the assistance of her executioners, the Merciful God will not allow this; the nations themselves need money in order to rebuild their national economy after the War. As a result the Soviet Government must rely on its own resources in its struggle with the Russian people; it must rely on the Communist Party, split by internal differences, and on armed hirelings who have lost the last vestige of conscience.

During this year, when the fate of our Fatherland is being decided and a new and brighter page of her history is opened, I, the Bearer of the title of Emperor of all the Russias, which belongs to me by virtue of the right of succession, in accordance with My manifesto of the 31st August, 1924, have thought fit to announce to the Russian nation the foundations on which, according to the best of my understanding, the Russian Empire should be rebuilt.

I repeat that, as before, I discountenance any attempt by self-appointed saviours of Russia to seek the support of foreign military intervention in the fate of our Fatherland.

However high the rank of any leaders of the *émigrés* might be and however great their services in the past to the Throne and Fatherland, all their present activities abroad are treason to Me and Russia, a breach of duty and the oath of allegiance.

May they be repudiated by the Russian people, who hope for the pacification of the Fatherland under the rule of the lawful and hereditary Czar.

Only the lawful Czar by the Grace of God, responsible only before God, independent of the caprice of people and supported by the broad masses of the Nation, can really be the protector of the just interests of the whole people in equal measure and will put an end to the destructive manifestations of class struggle, having given everyone his proper place and weight in the Russian State.

I know that the group of adventurers who have seized power by deception, and support it by immoral falsehoods, intimidate you with the idea of the return of the Sovereign Ruler of the Land of Russia. They tell you that the Czar will bring Russia executions and punishments for the disorder, the confiscation of the farmers' land, the re-establishment of class privileges and the enforcement of a yoke on the workers.

All these are lies of the Communists and their assistants, who assume that the real truth concerning my intentions

H.I.H. THE GRAND DUKE VLADIMIR OF RUSSIA
The Author's only son and now Head of the Imperial House.

THE AUTHOR AT WORK IN HIS STUDY AT SAINT-BRIAC
With the Grand Duke is seen his private secretary, Rear-Admiral Graf.

will not reach the heart of the people under the circumstances of terrible suppression of every free word.

I have many times spoken against punishments and revenge for those crimes into which the Russian people have been driven by the rule of the Communists. The sins of those who had been tempted we will leave to God's judgment. Let only those be held responsible who destroyed the sacred foundations of Russia while fully conscious of their deeds.

Equally I do not intend to destroy those national institutions which have been called forth by the necessities of life and to begin a new breaking up of the system and method of working life which has developed. It will be necessary to abandon only those institutions which soil the soul of man by encouraging a lack of faith, destroying family and moral foundations, and substitute the Communist international for the national state.

I have put the following guiding foundations at the base of My reforms, which must bring order to life in Russia:

The whole population of Russia will be guaranteed a real participation in the life of the State.

The definite and continuous participation of the representatives of the people in the legislation and administration on the Empire should be, I believe, the keystone of the new Monarchical Russia.

Therefore, without wishing to abolish the Soviet (council) system of national representation, I will assure the free election to the Soviets of the representatives of all the trading and productive classes of the population, as well as the members of professional organizations and of specialists who have distinguished themselves in the affairs of the State by their knowledge and experience.

Village, district, county and national soviets, with sometimes a periodically called All-Russian assembly of soviets—that is what would be able to bring together the Russian Czar and people and make impossible any wall between them in the form of an all-powerful bureaucracy or of any other class having special privileges.

The Russian Empire will be built on a basis of the widest local self-government, and there must be no place for the oppression of national minorities by the Russian majority. Local functionaries of the administration and law-courts should be natives of the district or well acquainted with its conditions by virtue of their previous activities.

Privately owned land which had been taken by the farmers during the revolution will remain theirs. They will not be obliged to pay compensation. But the new owners will be burdened with the sacred responsibility to work the land they have received in the best possible way, so that the interests of the State may not suffer from this fundamental change in relations on the land. The local administrations will have to take measures in relation to the land, with the help of the representatives of the population, to establish the sizes of the plots of each farmer and to furnish him with legalizing documents.

Landed property may be freely sold in accordance with the law, but the preferential right of purchase at its real price will belong to the State and communities.

I will give my fullest support to the representatives of other branches of society; those of town dwellers, the military, office employees, and workers, who might wish to give all their energies and talents towards increasing the productivity of our agriculture, so that they might purchase on easy terms such unused areas of land which are suitable for cultivation.

The Imperial Government will evolve a series of effective measures to encourage the increased use by farmers of machines, to supply them with cattle and good seeds and generally to improve agriculture. In view of the fundamental destruction of our agriculture, the realization of these measures will have to be gradual.

The eight-hour working day should be that standard

which would protect the worker from undue exploitation. At the same time no one should be forbidden to increase his well-being by personal work in addition to this.

The Imperial Government will take all measures which will be necessary in order that the new rising small trading and industrial capitalism should not injure the interests of the workers. The special care of the Imperial Government will be the protection of working men and children.

I will encourage by every means the healthy growth of professional associations, the creation of health protection, and insurance schemes for all workers, and the avoidance of differences between employers and workers through the establishment of State referees courts. But at the same time all measures will be taken to protect the workers from the self-appointed leaders of the workers who might attempt to enforce their will on them in the determination of their working conditions. The workers will realize themselves that in co-operation with the Government they will reach far more than when opposing it while led by party bosses that have, in all countries, enforced their will on them to a far greater extent than governments.

The Imperial Government will employ all means to encourage the building of houses in towns and the improvement of living conditions throughout the whole Empire, with the help of industry and house-owners.

Industrial and trading enterprises will become private property in all those cases where this would not be in conflict with the interests of the State of the co-operative movement, organized on a healthy foundation.

Wide freedom of private trading and initiative will also be restored.

I retain the supreme right of the State to the ownership of the wealth beneath the soil and of large forests throughout the Empire. Equally will the oil fields remain in the possession of the State. These measures will help to relieve the population of excessive taxation.

All those who have suffered loss by such measures will

be gradually compensated, as well as those who have lost the ability to work during soviet rule, this being at the expense of the State and only in such measure as the resources of the State conveniently permit.

The Orthodox Church—that rock of Faith upon which the Russian State is founded—will be given its canonical form in the Empire. At the same time everyone will be free to glorify the God of all in another faith.

The other basis of our State should be the family built on the foundations of a religious morality. The protection of motherhood will be a special care of the State, as well as that of the young, of the homeless and of orphans—the innocent victims of the communist experiment.

I promise that all capable and efficient persons, irrespective of their origin, will have an equal opportunity to occupy State offices in the resurrected Empire. I will restore to the Russian Nation a quick, just and merciful administration of justice, on the basis of the legal reforms of My great and famous Grandfather, the Emperor Alexander II.

The further measures I consider necessary for the peaceful development of the Empire and the healing of the wounds left by the present troubles are:

Wide national education of the people and the encouragement of professional specialization.

Merciless extermination of hooliganism and laziness.

The reduction of indirect taxation and the taxation of small industries and workshops.

A reasonable freedom of the Press and of social life.

Cheap railway and postal charges.

The widest possible medical help for all those suffering from serious illnesses which have spread so much during the years of communist rule.

This is the path along which I intend to lead the Russian Nation to peaceful work, to sufficiency and order so as to restore our Fatherland to the position of the protector of the peace among other nations.

I call upon all Russian people to realize the firmness of My intentions to see the whole population of the Empire of all the Russias free, pacified and happy. All must remember that only the self-sacrificing work and united effort of the whole Russian Nation can help Me in the quickest possible realization of My intentions.

The Almighty God is with us. He will support us in the struggle with those who mock His Name. I believe in His ever-present mercy and My near return to the execution of My Imperial duty.

KIRILL.

Saint-Briac, 13/26 January 1928.

In the Manifesto of 31 August 1924 I declared for all to know that I had taken the Imperial Title in exact accordance with the Fundamental Laws and My conscience.

I did this so that the Russian people should know that the Russian Imperial Dynasty is prepared to come to their assistance, while strengthening the cause of the re-establishment of the lawful Monarchy, which alone can give Russia her proper place among the other great powers and give her peace and happiness.

By this act I made the union of the true sons of the Fatherland easier and gave them a legal leadership for the work of saving the country from final destruction. Not all Russian people living abroad, however, wished to realize the meaning and the sacrifice underlying My impulses.

In the Fatherland My call was differently understood. There the true sons of Russia, under the dreadful yoke and terror of the enslavers of the people, do their unselfish work with heroism and sacrifice, knowing that the only hope of her salvation lies in the establishment of the legal monarchical form of government.

The foundations of the NEW RUSSIAN PEOPLES' MONARCHY are well known to all, having been often proclaimed, but not so many know that I made known these foundations after a careful study from all points of view of the opinions within Russia, in accordance with the hopes and wishes of the people and in tune with the actual demands of the present.

At present, when a fusion of Russian monarchists abroad is taking place, and in answer to repeated requests from the Fatherland, I again turn to Russians with the urgent request that all those who are prepared to give their energies to the re-establishment of the Great National Russia should forget their quarrels, their party narrowness, and their ideological and personal differences, and should gather round the Imperial Standard with the one aim of all working in harmony in the struggle with the executioners of the Russian people and against those who wish to plunge Russia from the present slavery into still worse catastrophes by depriving her of lands, robbing her of her riches, and imposing their new yoke on her people.

Russians abroad, let us be worthy of our brothers who are, in the Fatherland, self-sacrificingly bearing deprivation, suffering, and mortal danger.

They demand union and help and it is our duty to obey their call.

Let us unite on the basis of the common, only, and sacred motto—the salvation of our beloved and suffering Russia.

Saint-Briac, 2/15 May 1929. KIRILL.

In order that the memory of the Martyr's death of the Lord Emperor Nicholas Alexandrovitch and all His Family may be observed, I declare the 4/17 July a day of general mourning of the Russian people.

I hope that in all places the Russian Orthodox Church will, on this day, offer prayers before the Throne of the Almighty for the souls of those killed, for Russia and her people, and for the Imperial Martyrs.

KIRILL.
THE METROPOLITAN ANTHONY.[1]

Saint-Briac, 28 June/11 July 1929.

[1] The late Metropolitan Anthony was head of the Russian Orthodox Church abroad.

The generous admiration and remembrance of the living for the deeds which glorify the Fatherland, and the care to preserve their everlasting memory for the generations to come, has ever been the quality of all great nations, as a manifestation of the healthy creative spirit of the Nation.

The Great Russia, too, knew how to mark the glorious deeds of her sons.

The Holy Orthodox Church of Russia decreed for all times the remembrance in prayer of heroes on the anniversaries of great events.

By the will of the Monarchs of Russia many monuments were erected to speak to generations to come of the glory of the past.

The efforts of the people created throughout Russia churches in memory of great events of the past, and historical museums and buildings preserved, fully and true to life, the pictures of the great past.

Following the example of our ancestors and fathers, it is our sacred duty worthily to mark the difficult and self-sacrificing effort of the Russian people during the terrible years of the great World War which began in 1914.

But a terrible disaster has overcome the lands of Russia. A dishonourable and foreign power which has enslaved our Fatherland has made, for more than ten years, the greatest efforts to efface from the hearts and minds of our silent people even the remotest remembrance of the former greatness of the Russian Empire, as this is a threat to that power.

Together with all Russian people, I firmly believe that the Almighty Lord, in His mysterious ways, testing the hearts of the people, will lead Russia, cleansed by suffering, to a new life, inspired by a faith in a glorious future remembering the example of a glorious past.

Now, however, while the years of trouble still continue, I consider it essential and timely, in the name of the coming Russia and the memory, sacred to us all, of the Supreme Chief of the Imperial Armies and Navy, the late Lord

Emperor Nicholas Alexandrovitch, to dedicate gratefully to the Russian national fortitude, military courage, and civil sacrifice during the years of suffering in the struggle of the nations—the Order of Saint Nicholas the Miracle Doer in memory of the great World War.

In accordance with this I have approved the design of this order, which had been approved by the late Emperor Nicholas Alexandrovitch, and have ordered that the description and statute of the order should be made known to all.

May this visible sign be an uninterrupted connection between us and the glorious past, an offering of our admiration for the great memories of the titanic struggle of the Russian nation and for the sacred memory for the best sons of Russia who received the crowns of blood and glory in the unparalleled battles.

KIRILL.

Saint-Briac, 19 July/1 August 1929.

I note with satisfaction that among Russian people abroad the realization of the necessity for union is growing, this being essential for the fight against the enslavers of the Fatherland, and now the impending terrible events force Me to call for a speedy consummation of this union, as only then will we be able to give real help to those who are fighting in our Fatherland.

Our union is built on the motto: 'For the Faith, the Czar, and the Fatherland,' as this is the motto that is desired and understood by the Russian people and can therefore be the strong link that will bind our ranks together and will give them strength in the struggle.

Officers, soldiers, and sailors of the Russian Armies and Navy and the old Imperial Guards, remember that on your colours this motto was always emblazoned, remember that to your ancestors it was sacred for many centuries, and that you yourselves fought for it on the battle-fields of the Great War.

The Civil War proved to you that it is impossible to reach anything with empty banners and that mottoes, which are strange to the Russian people, bring harm.

I remind the young generation, too, that you should quickly fill your ranks and take up the principles of your forefathers. Take up firmly our old banners and bear them proudly back to Russia. All her future is in you; you will have to build her and to create the happy future of the people of Russia, and for that reason you should be the first to unite and to come to us.

May there be no Russians who should refuse to be under the banners on which the motto 'For the Faith, the Czar, and the Fatherland' is inscribed, as these are the symbols which have created our great Fatherland and saved her in times of danger and only they can now rescue the Russian people.

Saint-Briac, 3/16 October 1930.   KIRILL.

To the Russian People

My best wishes for the new year to all Russian people who believe in the speedy resurrection of their country on the foundations of her great past, in harmony with the new requirements of life.

A difficult year has passed which has brought the collapse of ideas and hopes to which humanity had clung when trying to emerge from the economic crisis which developed after the world war and the accompanying convulsions. A new year begins. Inevitably this year will lead the peoples to a change of former ideas and the choice of new social methods.

We are standing on the threshold of a new epoch. Capitalism has degenerated into a form of exploitation of the mass of the people by a small minority. The nations are beginning to awaken and a struggle against the enslavers is commencing. Does this mean that capitalism will be saved by police dictatorships or replaced by Communism?

Of course not; we are experiencing an intermediate period and all the state forms which have at present appeared are of a temporary kind, and only with the passing of time will permanent forms develop, which will lead humanity to a new organization and will give it real freedom.

Russia was the first to be drawn into the terrible maelstrom which shook the centuries-old foundations of her State. Having gone through this difficult period, she will rise again and begin the work of her world-wide mission—the creation of a new culture. Russia is on the path to a great future. She will create the foundation of the coming life of nations.

The power of the Communists is doomed. It will disappear, leaving the memory of a terrible destroyer and oppressor. Now the creative period begins. In Russia a new man has matured steeled by struggles and misfortune, and has begun to forge the happiness of his native people.

Long years the forces of destruction have ruled over the huge expanses of Russia. But the Russian Commonwealth, built up during centuries, has resisted the pressure of the destructive forces. Now she is recovering. The Government tried to hide her under the label U.S.S.R., but in the hearts of the Russian people the sacred name of RUSSIA is again alive.

Does not all that is happening in Russia prove this? Is not the work of building up the effort of the Russian people themselves—a genuine desire to rebuild their Fatherland?

In this rebuilding effort no credit can be given to the Communist Government. On the contrary, by the negative results of their inefficient leadership and muddle, by attempting to carry out unworkable ideas, the Communists have nearly brought the effort to failure. They realize that just in the possible success of the rebuilding efforts lies their own end, and yet they must support these efforts as they fear the wrath of the people.

I wish, with all my heart, success to the creative efforts

of the Russian people who have been strengthened and learnt the love of country. I regret deeply that the present Government has created unbearable conditions of slavery and forces hunger and want on the people. But still a few efforts, a little firmness and patience, and the Russian nation will throw the rotting garments from its wide shoulders.

I welcome the beginning of the new life as a dawn of the greatness of My Fatherland and the future happiness of mankind. Every success in the rebuilding is a victory of the Russian nation. Is it possible to prevent its full triumph? Every Russian should help with all his might to bring about the resurrection of the power of his country.

It is particularly important that we, who are forced to live outside Russia, should realize this. Only by helping in the re-establishment of the power of Russia will we again become one with the Russian people and return to our native land.

My eyes are turned only to the future. I feel the feverish efforts of the Russian people to attain the rebirth. I am proud of their powers of resistance and their creative will, and I suffer deeply when I see the terrible pains they must bear in the struggle for a better future. But the hour of triumph is nearing and the day is not far off when the whole world will recognize the greatness of a free Russia.

Saint-Briac, 10/23 December, 1931.   KIRILL.

Russia, steeled by a difficult experience, is rising. Her immemorial powers are awakening in all classes of the population of Russia and are defeating the lifeless Communism.

I have pointed out that the Soviet Government, taking advantage of the creative efforts of the Russian nation, only hinders that rebuilding with the Socialist five-year plan, inefficient leadership and in the perseverance in holding to lifeless ideas.

Now that one year has passed, it is possible to judge to what a great extent this Government has increased the deplorable position of the Russian nation. There is no hope for it in the future while the power in the State is held by an alien and incompetent Government.

National consciousness is growing in Russia and is the sign of near liberation. The Army and Navy are filled with this consciousness, though still bearing the name of red. They are becoming that Russian force which will be capable of saving Russia from foreign attack, internal disintegration and Communist misrule.

Russian warriors, I address you. Your power is the guarantee of the wholeness and safety of the Russian State. Having become the armed forces of Russia, being an integral part of her people, you have taken on yourselves the glory of many centuries of the Russian Army and Navy, who have always been prepared to defend the Fatherland and served as a support of international peace. Nothing of a passing and superficial nature can change the essence of your military service. You already realize that you are the defenders of your native land. The time will come when this realization will decide the fate of Russia. During the present you must prepare yourselves for the future. Russia needs a strong Army and Navy. She needs them for the defence of her borders and to rid herself of the yoke of Communism.

It is your duty to strengthen the power of the Army and Navy, to fire their spirit, to support discipline and to work hard at the technical improvement of the equipment.

When, with God's help, you will, together with the people, put an end to Communism, then the era of the re-creation of a real Russian State will begin, during which the chief duty of the Army and Navy will be to prevent their own disintegration and to protect the unity of the Empire, to ensure the free development of the peoples which inhabit it. You must remember the lessons of the past.

I, the Heir of the Czars and Emperors who had built the Russian State with the heroic help of the Russian Army and Navy, and who have established it upon a sixth part of the globe, having spent many years in the closest contact with the Russian fighting forces, tell you that only by faithful service to the Fatherland will you again earn the right to our thousand-year-old history.

I firmly believe that you, the warriors of the Russia that is being reborn, will be worthy of your Fatherland and a reliable support of the peoples' Empire. Our common duty is to serve the Fatherland and we will carry it out to the end. I declare, as once upon a time my ancestor the Emperor Peter the Great declared, that you should know that I do not value My life if only RUSSIA will live in glory and contentment, for your well-being.

KIRILL.

SAINT-BRIAC, 12/25th November, 1932.

I, the Head of the Imperial Dynasty, firmly bound to the Russian people by bonds of the glorious past of our Fatherland, accuse, in their name, the present rulers of Russia of having, during fifteen years of their rule, brought nothing but terrible harm to the Russian nation.

During these years of national suffering the population has been brought to utter poverty, and the whole country is flooded with blood: all measures, whether rebuilding, the arrangement of the life of the farmers and workers, or other legislation, which, in the words of the Communist Government, should have brought benefits to the population, bring, in their hands, only further suffering and ruin.

In the fateful years of Communist rule, their power has brought forth only hate and curses. For its own crude mistakes it punishes and executes thousands of innocent people, and, fearing a catastrophe, it tortures its victims in prisons and exile. The Government is not based on the support of the nation, but on the G.P.U., which bullies and cows the people; the country is ruled by force and terror.

The leaders of Communism in Russia try to convince the people that they are opening up new paths to a happy life and are bringing them to a leading place among other nations. Instead they indulge in experiments on them which are doomed to failure and do not permit the people to go along the historic path towards development and civilization.

The nation has been deprived of the right to proclaim its faith in God, and by this it has been deprived of a faith in life. Its soul is being debauched and spiritual development is being put back many centuries.

Dumb dissatisfaction, which is even noticeable among orthodox Communists, risings which take place from time to time all over the country, differences among those in power—all go to show that the hour of reckoning is near.

The dawn of a new epoch, which is now rising over the whole of humanity, has also lit our suffering Russia. There a healthy nationalism is emerging and this indicates the nearness of the end of Communism.

The time has come to accuse you, the rulers of Russia, before the whole world.

You alone are responsible for all the sufferings of the Russian nation. You have sacrificed Russia to the third international. In putting into practice the ideas of Communism and in acting under the influence of the enemies of the Russian State, who hate and despise the Russian people, you bring her terrible harm.

At present even those foreigners who had watched your progress with sympathy, and hoped to find a revelation in your deeds, have come to the conclusion that these are but feeble attempts to change the laws of human existence.

I and all Russian people on both sides of the border are unanimous in our accusations and in the wish to assist the national forces in Russia to destroy the Communist yoke, and to prevent the appearance of anarchy in the Fatherland.

A terrible fate awaits you and your destruction is inevitable, as the destruction of all that is incapable of life is inevitable, of all that goes against the laws of nature. There have been enough tortures and ridicule of the Russian nation. The time of the triumph of all truly national forces of the Russia that is being reborn is at hand.

KIRILL.

Saint-Briac, 26 April 1933.

On the 17/30 day of August of this year 1933, in accordance with the Fundamental Laws, Our First-born Son, the Heir and Czarevitch and Grand Duke Vladimir Kirillovitch, became of age.

This happy event is the first in Our House since the time when great troubles engulfed Russia and, in the mysterious ways of God, fifteen years ago, the valued life of Our Cousin, the Lord Emperor Nicholas Alexandrovitch, His Son, the Heir and Czarevitch and Grand Duke Alexis Nicolaevitch, and His Brother, the Grand Duke Michael Alexandrovitch, was ended.

Having assured Ourselves with the deepest sorrow of Their untimely Martyr's death, We, being fully conscious of the sacred duty imposed on Us, hereditarily took upon Ourselves, in accordance with the hereditary supreme right of Head of the Russian Imperial House, all the rights and duties belonging to Us in accordance with the Fundamental State Laws of the Russian Empire and the rules of the Imperial Family.

On this day, solemn to Us, of the coming of age of Our Heir, We turn Our thoughts to the great family of the Russian people.

The sufferings imposed on the Russian Land are unlimited. Russia is governed by iron and blood, hunger and cold, slavery and universal ruination. Sacred things and churches have been desecrated, mocked, and destroyed, the family, faith, all the foundations of social life, even the name of Russia, are being annihilated with merciless hate and cruelty.

To-day We confirm that We, while the Almighty is pleased to continue Our days, will continue without cessation to work for the salvation and happiness of the suffering Russia. In these efforts We derive great happiness from Our well-beloved Son, the Heir and Grand Duke Vladimir Kirillovitch, and we call upon all Russian people who are true to the deepest Russian traditions, to offer prayers to the Almighty God for the health and well-being of Our Heir.

May the Wisdom of God send Him untiring strength for self-sacrificing work for the great Land of Russia and all the peoples that inhabit it, following the example of Our crowned ancestors, under whose sovereign rule the great State of Russia grew, strengthened, and developed.

Saint-Briac. KIRILL.

In recent times new proofs of the disintegration of Communism have appeared in our Fatherland. The Communist Government has been forced to tread the path of retreat from the basis of Communism, and to adjust itself to the new moods which are so strongly affecting the Russian people.

Every day may bring victory to the national forces and the defeat of Communism, thus bringing the triumph of Russia nearer, she being cleansed and steeled by the sufferings experienced.

Full of hope, I watch these tendencies. The Communists have underestimated the power of the Russian spirit. They celebrated their victory too soon. In the struggle with the destructive power of Communism our, people has realized its national character and possibilities.

They are beginning to understand the meaning of the liberty of the individual, of a healthy family, of free work. The creative efforts during these difficult years of test have awakened the spirit of co-operation and national pride. The love of country is becoming stronger and unites the sons of Russia, independently of their racial origin and social position.

Communism is disappearing. It is falling a victim to its struggle against the everlasting foundations of life, which are appearing with renewed strength during our changing times. One after another, the Communist fantasies are crumbling and every retreat of the Government indicates an increased pressure of the nation. The realization of the necessity of new methods will give Russia victory.

It is the duty of all Russians firmly to take the path of national regeneration in the struggle about to begin and which will end in the victory of national consciousness against the deceptions of Communism, together with all the fighters for the power, independence, and well-being of our native land. Fear and doubt must be banished, old quarrels must be forgotten, and personal considerations must be sacrificed. Russia has no need of cowards, people who sell their principles and such as would be willing to face defeat.

I welcome the approaching rebirth of my Fatherland, whose sacred name is again spoken on her immense territories. I welcome those strong spirits that have overcome temptations, discredited deceptions, and who conquer the ground of the enemy step by step. I remember with admiration those who have fallen in the struggle of the nation for its great future.

With all my heart do I share with the Russian people its heavy suffering, with all my heart do I share the joys of achievement. I believe in God's help in our struggle for liberation.

The Russian national victory will give the answer to

decades of tortuous searching, and the difficult struggle will unite all Russians in one creative effort.

KIRILL.

Saint-Briac, 28 July 1934.

Ten years ago I issued a manifesto in which I confirmed My right to the Throne of all the Russias belonging to me, and in accordance with the fundamental laws of the succession to the Throne, I took the Imperial title.

Then, on the threshold of the post-War period, political ideas were such that not only in non-Monarchist, but even in Monarchist countries, the majority of political leaders did not believe in the future of the Monarchy. Even those forces which should have been the support of the Monarchy and had lived by it became influenced by these mistaken ideas. Throughout the whole world the faith in liberal dogmas was supreme. Freedom seemed assured in politics as in trade. Democratic parliamentarianism had reached its prime.

Although Communism in Russia was recognized as an undesirable state of affairs, yet after it only a democratic republic seemed possible.

My manifesto was published in the Press of the world and given serious attention in all countries, but nevertheless with concealed doubt of the possibility of re-establishing the Monarchy in Russia. In opposition to the general opinion, I recognized that the key to the solution of the fundamental problems of our time lay in a return to personal hereditary rule.

Years passed. During this time changes of historic scope became evident. The parliamentary democratic system, based on a party elective basis, was seen to be incapable of dealing with the new demands of our time. Deep reconsiderations of customary ideas were forced on all. In Italy Fascism was born, finding support in the hereditary Monarchy. It has become strengthened and proved its chance of survival, becoming a model for many countries. In Germany a system similar to Fascism has appeared. In Russia Communism has left its unnatural bases and the Government has been obliged to compromise with nationalism.

Everywhere a desire to find new paths is evident, in order to find a way out of the crisis which was the beginning of the end of a whole system of State, social, and economic relations. All attempts at preserving this doomed system were unsuccessful. It became obvious that the world was experiencing an intermediate stage during which a strong personal power was essential.

But the search for new paths continues, and in this connection, in many countries, the demands for a return to Monarchical principles are becoming stronger. The nations are realizing that the loss of a Monarchical leadership, which had been imposed on them in the name of supposedly great ideals, was most unfortunate.

It is for this reason that, ten years ago, I declared the necessity of Monarchy in Russia, and that now again I raise my voice. The time is drawing nearer and humanity expects the inevitable.

The future belongs to Monarchy founded on the union of the nation, on the abolition of party differences, on the widest participation of the people in the government and economics of the land, on religious tolerance, on the equality of the rights of all the peoples inhabiting the State and on the hereditary power of the Monarch—the permanent and impartial referee of the administration of the whole life of the State.

The freedom of the person and of Society are illusions without the supreme authority of the Monarch which guarantees the continuity and stability of the law and administration of the land. It is just this continuity which gives the hereditary Monarchy its peculiar power for deep and definite reforms which prevent the nations from falling back. The hereditary Monarchy gives a living link between the State and the nation. This connection gives rise to the interest of the hereditary Monarch in the final solution of the pressing problems of national importance, with the postponement of which he cannot be satisfied. The Monarchy is not only concerned with the maintenance of outward order in the life of the people, the Monarchy is not only interested in the problems of the day, but also in the problems of the whole life of the nation. At the foundation of the idea of Monarchy lie the conceptions of truth and justice, which make the Monarchy realize in practice the highest ideals of the nation.

The conscience and the hereditary responsibility of the Monarch are guarantees of a sane and humane rule of the fate of the people. The destructive action of inevitable historical catastrophes is softened by a Monarchical supreme power, which, more than any other, is capable of overcoming big difficulties. The hereditary continuity of authority increases its advantages and decreases its shortcomings.

Peace and prosperity—those are the internal and external aims of the Monarchy, which is called upon to bring a calming and reconciliation into the cruel and tumultuous life of the world to-day. Only hereditary Monarchy is capable of not being extreme and yet firm and able to bring peace to international life. The Monarchy, more than any other power, is interested in the creation of sound balances.

The reasons which have led to the downfall of a number of Monarchies in the past do not take anything from the advantages of the Monarchical supreme power which are so necessary in our times. The fall of the Russian Monarchy was due to a loss of Monarchist consciousness which broke the union between the Czar and the people. The rise of the national spirit leads to national union. The consummation of this union will be the work of the Monarchical supreme power, which expresses it in the fullest way.

I deeply believe that God's wisdom will give the final victory to the principles which I have proclaimed. Their triumph is inevitable and the future belongs to them.

KIRILL.

In my manifestoes and addresses I have many times already declared the fundamental principles which guide Me in My work of establishing Monarchist supreme power in Russia. Nevertheless, from time to time rumours are current that I intend to depart from the principles which I have proclaimed.

I announce once more that no one can presuade Me to change the direction upon which I have decided. I will remain true to this direction until the end, as My faith in Russia is unshakable and the truth of My policy is continually confirmed by events.

I am the enemy of Communism and the teaching which gave it birth. I strive for the liberation of the Russian people from the Government which has been forced on them and which is responsible for numberless sorrows and destruction. I strive with perseverance and continuity for the re-establishment of the Russian State through the lawful Monarchy, which alone can guarantee the nation contentment and satisfy its demands in accordance with the conditions of modern life.

I consider the interference of a foreign armed force in the question of the change of the form of government in Russia absolutely undesirable. This question must be decided by the forces of the Russian nation. I am opposed to the interference of foreign powers in internal Russian affairs, as such interference would bring harm to Russian national interests.

I see clearly that the Russian people are gradually freeing themselves from Communistic Utopias, that the Government is forced to make concessions under pressure of the leading sections of the nation, and that the regime does not survive the contact with real life. The Russian nation, having survived trials which cannot be compared with anything similar, is gathering new strength before which those forces which are opposed to the Russian national renaissance will not be able to survive.

In the work which I lead I always hold to My fundamental principles, which must be shared by all My collaborators. Any departure from My path always leads to their removal from any participation in the leadership of the work. It is only possible to bring final success nearer by full unanimity in the understanding of the problems which confront us.

If I permit My collaborators to express their opinions freely in speech and in the Press on all political questions, I do not permit these opinions to contradict the fundamental postulates which I have laid down. Therefore, no opinions can be considered as Mine which are expressed in the Press by persons or organizations which are My subordinates, if there is no special indication that this or that opinion has been approved by Me.

In My work I demand the strictest subordination and discipline. I alone can judge My nearest collaborators for their actions, and I cannot permit that some of My collaborators should oppose others in their expressed ideas. In my addresses I have often criticized differences, defamatory informers, petty quibbling and unneccessary polemics, which are harmful for all good efforts. I will be even firmer in preventing such things. By these energies are only wasted on a useless struggle with each other while the main object is ignored. Much harm is also done by the lack of mutual understanding and co-operation between old political workers who have again entered this field. The old ones must understand and take into consideration the enthusiasm and impatience of the new ones. The new ones must respect the experience and judgment of the old ones. In such responsible times there must be no differences among us Russians, who all strive for one sacred aim.

I take all opinions into consideration, even if they contradict My principles. I stand above all classes, parties, and organizations. One must understand that on the Throne of Russia there can be only the supreme leader of the whole nation, but not the head of any particular party.

Russian people abroad, while experiencing all difficulties and troubles, do not forget that you are Russians, that you are only by chance and temporarily forced to be outside your Fatherland. May the faith in the resurrection of Russia never fail you.

Saint-Briac, 16 July 1935.　　　　　　　　KIRILL.

The Almighty God has thought fit in His mysterious ways to cut short the valued life of my dearly beloved wife, the Lady Empress Victoria Feodorovna, who departed to God on the 18 February/2 March.

Boundless and inexpressible is My grief. All these years of exile the Departed was an irreplaceable companion and helper to Me, who burned with a self-sacrificing love for our much suffering Fatherland, who did not spare either efforts or health in working for it, and who believed to the last day unshakably in the great future of Russia.

In the heavy trial which has been sent to Me, I have found a sincere sympathy in the hearts of all Russian people who were able to express their feelings to Me. Numberless declarations of their sympathy speak of their grief, and these help Me to bear the weight of this great sadness.

In expressing My thanks for this sincere sympathy, I believe that the true sons of the Fatherland, preserving in their memories with deep respect the great example of the Empress who has been called to God, will unite still more strongly in the struggle for the rebirth of the land of Russia on the natural paths of her historic development.

Saint-Briac, 26 March 1936.　　　　　　　　KIRILL.

Many years already I continue the struggle for the re-establishment in the Fatherland of the historic form of government, under which it has grown and increased in power during centuries. It is not personal motives that force me to fight for the Russian lawful Monarchy, but the conviction that this alone is able to neutralize all the evil which has been done to Russia and her peoples.

The dissatisfaction of the masses with the dictatorship that has been imposed on the country has been manifested from the beginning of the Revolution in different ways. But it might have seemed that at least the persons that have risen under the dictatorship would be devoted to it. But the events of the past years, and especially the past year, have shown that amongst these people who have received power, honours, and material gains, dissatisfaction is continually growing.

In the entourage of the dictator himself conspiracies continually take place. The attempts—as yet unsuccessful—of overthrowing the tyrannical power, which are made by the spheres most closely connected with it, are the most convincing proof of the universal hate of the existing regime.

The dictator sees treason everywhere. He cannot rely on anyone. He destroys mercilessly his real or imagined opponents. In the bloody battle with the opposition, which is seen in all spheres of the country's political and economic life, the dictatorship destroys the machine of government, weakens the military power of Russia, and undermines her forces of life. By this the dictator proves to all the world that he is only interested in retaining power, that he is moved by personal motives, and that he is not concerned with the welfare of the people.

However, he labels as 'enemies of the people' all those whom he suspects of disloyalty to himself. But the first genuine enemy of the people is he himself.

I, the Heir of the Czars and Emperors that have created the power of the Russian State, now, at the time of great crisis for Russia, once more remind the Russian people of the foundations upon which our Empire must be rebuilt.

On the inevitable collapse of the present dictatorship, the absence of a new government that could immediately take the power into its hands, would threaten Russia with many dangers. The chief danger would be a new civil war, which would lead to a threat of the disintegration of the State and the loss of ancient Russian territories. The huge expanses of our Fatherland would again be covered with Russian blood, and all that would be destroyed which has been re-created by the efforts of the people during the years of oppression.

May the Lord protect our country from these new sorrows.

In order to overcome the trouble and turmoil which are disintegrating Russian life during nearly a quarter of a century, the speedy establishment of a strong national government is essential. This can be guaranteed only by a lawful Monarchy, the synthesis of which combines the continuity of government with the demands of modern times.

The Monarchy, founded on the union of the nation, on the destruction of party and class differences, on religious tolerance and freedom of conscience, on the equality of rights of all the peoples of the Empire, on the widest participation of the people in the administration of the land and of its economics, on the hereditary power of the Monarch, the permanent, impartial, and natural judge—will save Russia from internal weakness and external dangers and will lead her along the path to well-being and happiness.

The freedom of the person and of Society is a deception without the Monarchical supreme power, which maintains the continuity and stability of the State. It is just this continuity which gives the hereditary Monarchy its capacity for fundamental and decisive reforms which permit the peoples not to be left behind.

Russia was always the bearer of the Christian Spirit. The Orthodox Church, as the container of this sacred and valuable inheritance, crowned with the martyr's wreath after many years of struggle, suffering, and persecution, must retain her canonical form. Her leading position among other churches must be maintained. But it will not be denied to anyone to glorify the One God in another faith.

The Empire, which is inhabited by many different peoples which have retained their characteristics, must be built on the principle of the close union of all the peoples and tribes which compose it. Within it there can be no suppression of other nationalities by the Russian majority. The rights to their own customs must be guaranteed to the Cossacks who have earned them throughout our history.

As I have declared many times, the Monarchy does not bring retribution and revenge. It will value highly the services to the Fatherland during the times of trouble of Russian people in Russia and outside, and will know how to reward them.

I know to what an extent the present regime has ruined the agricultural population, having made its policy of the 'collectivization' of agriculture into a weapon for the oppression of all classes of farmers. For that reason I consider of especial importance the manifestation of particular care of its well-being and success. A just, workable, and lawful solution of this most important subject in accordance with the demands of broad national interest, I consider a problem of the greatest importance.

The agricultural population of the Empire must occupy a place which corresponds to its real political and economic importance. It must be guided by a law impartial to all, which protects the freedom to work, the safety and fullness of land tenure. The right of private ownership of land must be extended to all who work on the land. The ownership of land must be subject to purchase and sale and inheritance by all citizens. Each worker on the land must have full freedom of disposal of the fruits of his labour.

The Government created by the Revolution has made big efforts to develop industry. The carrying out of the programme of industrialization of the country and the creation of new industrial bases demanded the progressive increase of the number of workers. The Government tried to use the great masses of the workers employed by the factories for political purposes. In speaking in the name of the working classes and looking to them for support, the dictatorship attempted to ascribe to itself the merit of having socially freed the workers.

Nevertheless, it has not only not succeeded in bringing about the slightest improvement in the conditions of work, it has not only not raised the standard of living of the Russian workman, but it has brought about the enslavement of the whole mass of the labouring citizens. The Socialistic society has proved, in practice, to be a new form of serfdom in the hands of an impersonal government. In contemporary Russia there is no trace of the social progress of the leading countries.

The complete control of all trade and industry by the State seems to Me unsatisfactory. The colossal sacrifices made by the Russian people are not justified in the slightest measure by the results obtained. The freedom to trade and of personal initiative in industry must be guaranteed within the limits set by the general interests of the State. Economic questions must be solved in accordance with the practical necessities and not under the pressure of political passions.

At the foundation of the economic structure of the Empire must lie not class distinctions, which disintegrate the national unity, but constructive co-operation and creative unity of all the component parts of each branch of production. All participants in the economic life of the country must be given a share in its administration through corporative and professional organs, and the part of the responsibility of each for the whole productive process must be balanced by a corresponding amount of personal material participation.

At the same time carefully considered laws will protect the amounts of the earnings, the conditions and length of work, the protection of the health and safety of the workers, especially those of women and young people, and the insurance and pensioning of the aged and infirm.

At the present time, when the whole world is in the throes of feverish rearmament, one of the chief problems will be the strengthening of the military power of Russia. I must praise the efforts of the Russian officers and men, thanks to whose work the armed might of Russia on the land, the sea, and particularly the air, has been created. The resurrection of the military spirit and the mastery of modern technique will remain the merits of those military leaders who have fallen victims of the criminal hand of the insane Government.

The military might of modern Russia was the guarantee of the wholeness of our land. The military forces of Russia, still subjected to the doomed dictatorship, have been created on the old military foundations. They compose a section of the population in whom I see the heirs of the former military strength of Russia. International theories, programmes, and slogans, were unable to weaken the love of country and national pride among these people. They are an integral and the best part of the Russian nation, the heirs of the centuries of glory of the Russian Army and Navy, which had always stood at the defence of their country and were a guarantee of peace in the world. The fate of our Fatherland is in the hands of the military.

My eyes, as always, are turned to the future. I feel more strongly still the irresistible urge of the nation to free itself from the yoke of the bloodthirsty dictatorship. I am proud of its capacity to live, its heroism, and its creativeness. It is with great sorrow that I see the tortures which our people undergo in its struggle for a better future. I am always prepared to come to its help and to tie again the fate of the Imperial Dynasty to that of our people.

I know that our country needs a government which could again give it the place which belongs to it among the great powers. The first task of the continuer of the Imperial inheritance must be the re-establishment and affirmation throughout the world of the honour and glory of the name of Russia. The hour of our national triumph is nearing. Under the Imperial Sceptre Russia will again live in quiet and peace.

KIRILL.

Saint-Briac, 24 March 1938.

GENEALOGICAL TABLE

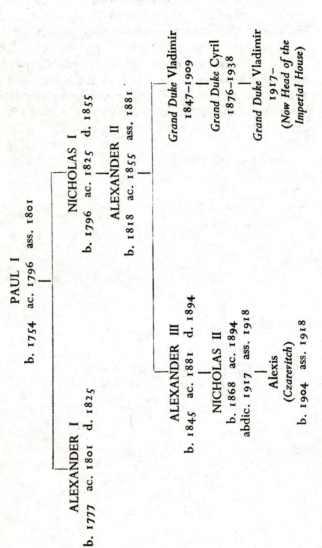

INDEX

A

Albers, Captain, 100
Alexander II, H.M., 11
Alexander III, H.M., 19, 53, 54, 182
Alexander III, H.I.M.S., 147
Alexandra Fedorovna, H.M., Empress, 28
Alexandra of Hesse, 57
Alexandrine of Mecklenburg-Schwerin, H.H., Grand Duchess, 28
Alexeeff, Admiral, 161, 173
Alfonso XIII, H.M., 31
Alfred, Duke of Edinburgh, 69
Anastasia, H.H., Grand Duchess of Mecklenburg, 18, 122
Anichkov Palace, the, 20, 56
Arisugawa, H.R.H. Prince, 139
Askold, H.I.M.S., 166
Astasheff, General, 32

B

Battenberg, H.R.H. Prince Louis, 25
Battenberg, H.R.H. Princess, 69, 105
Bell, Mr., 98
Bezshumnyi, H.I.M.S., 172
Bezstrashnyi, H.I.M.S., 169
Boyarin, H.I.M.S., 154
Brevern de la Gardie, Countess, 26
Bridge, Admiral Sir Cyprian, 146
Britannia, H.M.S., 101
Boukhvostov, Captain, 147
Buckingham Palace, 72

C

Cantakouzene Count Speranski, Prince, 35, 67
Carlos I, H.M., King of Portugal, 149, 150
Catherine the Great, 12
Cecilia of Prussia, H.R.H. Crown Princess, 18
Chabarovsk, 88
Chernavin, Vsevolod, 24, 25
Chernavin, Vyacheslav, 25
Christine of Spain, H.M. Queen, 31, 32

[281]

Connaught, Duke of, 65
Crofts, Miss Millicent, 13, 14
Czarevitch, the, 191, 192, 211

D

Daller, General Alexander, 23, 24, 42
Delerskaya, Mlle, 23
Denmark, H.M. the Queen of, 18
Diana, H.I.M.S., 165, 166
Diernoff, Father Alexander, 24
Dimitrieff, Gunnery Officer, 115
Dimitry, H.H. Grand Duke, 32
d'Orliac, M. Fabien, 25
Dournovo, Navigation Officer, 115
Dubasov, Admiral, 83

E

Edward VII, H.M. King, 72
Ekaterinburg, 112
Elizabeth, Empress, 12
Elizabeth, Grand Duchess, 71
Ermitage Palace, the, 106
Essen, Admiral, 189

F

Feodorovna, H.M. Empress Maria, 17, 19, 55, 63
Feodorovna of Baden, H.R.H. Princess Olga, 18
Ferdinand of Prussia, H.R.H. Prince Louis, 18
Flotov, Mme, 19
Francis II of Mecklenburg-Schwerin, H.R.H. Grand Duke Frederick, 11, 29
Francis III of Mecklenburg-Schwerin, H.R.H. Grand Duke Frederick, 18, 29
Frederick William III of Prussia, H.M. King, 28
Frederick William IV of Prussia, H.M. King, 28
Fredericks, Count, 183

G

General Admiral, H.I.M.S., 103
Greville, Sydney, 101
Grodekov, General, 88, 91
Groziashchi, H.I.M.S., 59
Gunzberg, Baron, 86
Gustav of Sweden, H.M. King, 189

H

Hapsal, 26, 27
Hindenburg, 198

Hodura, 22
Hohenlohe - Langenburg, H.R.H. Prince, 184
Hohenlohe - Langenburg, H.R.H. Princess, 105, 174
Hunius, Doctor, 27

I

Iosifovna, H.R.H. Grand Duchess Alexandra, 17
Ivan IV, 66
Ivanov, 160

K

Kaiser, the, 60, 116
Kanin, Prince, 93
Kasuga, the, 167
Kerber, Lieutenant, 96
Ketzerau, Herr, 25
King, Baldwin, 66
Kirollovna of Russia, H.R.H. Grand Duchess Kyra, 185
Knark, Frau, 22, 23
Korjeetz, H.I.M.S., 154
Krasnoe, Selo, 21, 28, 67
Kreml, H.I.M.S., 102
Kremlin, the, 45, 62, 102
Kube, Lieutenant, 41, 74, 80, 98, 101, 115, 148, 151, 160, 170, 173
Kündiger, Herr, 25, 26
Kuropatkin, General, 173

L

Leiningen, H.R.H. Princess Marie, 184
Lieven, Pavel Pavlovitch, 187
Lindholm, 87
London, 71

M

Madenokosi, Baron, 94, 140
Makarov, Admiral, 148, 158, 161, 162, 165, 167, 170, 172, 173
Mallejev, Commander, 165
Melita of Hesse, H.R.H. Grand Duchess Victoria, 104, 112
Michael, H.R.H. Grand Duke, 19, 26, 54
Michaelovitch, H.R.H. Grand Duke Alexander, 31, 112
Michaelovitch, H.R.H. Grand Duke Nicholas, 109
Mikasa, the, 166
Minin, 66
Mollas, Rear-Admiral, 168
Moriak, H.I.M.S., 38, 41, 46
Moscow, 45, 46, 62, 63, 64, 65, 67
Mumm, Herr von, 134
Mutso Hito, H.M., Emperor of Japan, 83, 94, 134

N

Nahimov, H.I.M.S., 138, 139, 141, 142, 145, 146, 147, 149, 150, 151, 158

Nicholas, H.R.H. Grand Duke, 196
Nicholas I, H.M., 17, 18, 28, 117
Nijniy Novgorod, 66, 67
Nikolaevitch, H.R.H., Grand Duke Alexey, 52
Nikolaevitch, H.R.H., Grand Duke Constantine, 16, 17
Nikolaevitch, H.R.H., Grand Duke Michael, 16
Nikolaevitch, H.R.H., Grand Duke Nicholas, 16, 52
Nikolaevsky Palace, the, 62
Nishin, the, 167
Novik, H.I.M.S., 166

O

Oleg, H.I.M.S., 186, 189, 190
Olga of Greece, H.M. Queen, 78, 79
Osborne, H.M.Y., 150

P

Pallada, H.I.M.S., 154
Paris, 31
Paul I, H.M., 17
Pavlosk, 17
Pavlovna, H.H. Grand Duchess Marie, 190
Peresviet, H.I.M.S., 112, 113, 114, 118, 120, 124, 125, 137, 167

Peter the Great, 188, 193
Peter and Paul, Cathedral of St., 15, 17
Peterhof, 21, 22, 27, 29
Petropavlosk, H.I.M.S., 41, 137, 164, 166, 168, 170, 171, 172
Petrovsky Palace, the, 62
Pobieda, H.I.M.S., 114, 167, 173
Poklevski-Koziell, M., 95
Poliarnaya Zvesda, H.I.M.S., 113
Poliashenko, 36, 37, 39
Poltava, H.I.M.S., 166
Port Arthur, 81, 82, 83, 96, 103, 112, 114, 129, 130, 137, 140, 142, 157, 161, 162, 167, 170, 171, 173, 203
Powerful, H.M.S., 70
Prince Pojarsky, the Training Ship, 46, 49, 51
Pskov, Province of, 21
Pusanoff, Paymaster, 98

R

Rasputin, 191, 192
Retvisan, H.I.M.S., 154
Reuss, H.H. Princess Charlotte, 102
Reuss, H.H. Princess Maria, 11
Rojdestvenski, Rear-Admiral, 103, 175, 176, 177, 178, 179, 180

Rosen, Baron, 92, 94, 154, 156, 157
Rossya, H.I.M.S., 69, 70, 74, 78, 80, 83, 88, 93, 96, 97, 98, 114
Rostislav, H.I.M.S., 106, 107, 111
Royal Sovereign, H.M.S., 75
Rurik, H.I.M.S., 59
Russin, Admiral, 96
Ryolva, Mme, 77

S

Savell, Miss, 14
Schlippenbach, Baron, 99
Schouvaloff, Count 'Pavel,' 108
Schouvalov, Count Sergey, 195
Schwerin, 28, 29, 30
Shaeck, Chevalier de, 36, 37, 52, 60, 124
Shokalsky, Youri Michaelovich, 44
Sheremetieff, 61
Shouvaloff, Count, 52
Shulgin, M., 53
Singapore, 80
Skrydlov, Admiral, 59, 124, 137, 138, 141
Smelyi, H.I.M.S., 166
Smirnoff, Father, 181
Stemann, Captain, 138, 143, 144
St. Petersburg, 26, 33, 37, 44, 45, 52, 62, 105, 148, 206, 208

Strashnyi, H.I.M.S., 165, 166
Strutton, Miss, 13
St. Sebastian, 31
Souvaroff, H.I.M.S., 177

T

Tatishchev, Ilia, 112, 115
Tchoudov Monastery, the, 66
Terrible, H.M.S., 70
Tolstoi, Alexey, 16
Togo, Admiral, 158, 167, 172, 176, 180
Tsarievna, H.I.M.S., 54
Tsarkoe Selo, 11, 12, 13, 14, 17, 19, 21, 26, 33, 44, 51, 52, 57, 67, 152, 187, 206
Tzarevitch, H.I.M.S., 154
T'Sin, H.R.H. Prince, 135

U

Ushakoff, 67
Uspenski Cathedral, the, 64

V

Variag, H.I.M.S., 154
Vereshchiagin, 167
Vernyi, H.I.M.S., 58, 60
Victoria, H.R.H. the Dowager Empress, 116
Victoria, H.R.H. Princess, 150

Victoria, H.R.H. Queen, 69, 72, 73, 122
Vladimir, H.H. Grand Duke, 11
Vladimir Palace, the, 14, 16, 52, 58, 106, 159
Vladivostok, 82, 86, 87, 88, 89, 91, 93, 137
Voyin, H.I.M.S., 53

W

Wagner, 'Cosima,' 181
Wales, H.H. the Prince of, 101
William I, H.R.H. Emperor, 28
William II, H.R.H. Emperor, 59

Winter Palace, the, 15, 57

X

Xenia, H.H. Grand Duchess, 106

Y

Yanysheff, Father, 180
Yenissei, H.I.M.S., 154

Z

Zvegintzov, M., 194